AF522619

# CORPORATE DEPRECIATION ACCOUNTING

# CORPORATE DEPRECIATION ACCOUNTING
## *A Critical Study*

by

Subrata Kar

2008

SBS Publishers & Distributors Pvt. Ltd.
New Delhi

ISBN10: 81-89741-66-7
ISBN13: 978-81-89741-66-2

Indian Price - Rs 695
Foreign Price - USD 34.95

First Published in India in 2008



Published by:
SBS PUBLISHERS & DISTRIBUTORS PVT. LTD.
2/9, Ground Floor, Ansari Road, Darya Ganj,
New Delhi - 110002, INDIA
Tel: 23289119, 41563911
Email: mail@sbspublishers.com

Printed in India by SALASAR IMAGING SYSTEMS, New Delhi.

# Preface

Depreciation accounting has always been a controversial issue in corporate financial accounting and reporting. The leading accounting standard setters of the world have spent considerable time and energy in developing effective solutions to depreciation accounting problems but problems persist. Depreciation affects both the profit and loss account and the balance sheet. It affects the way in which net profit is computed and also the way in which the carrying values of depreciable assets are determined in the balance sheet. Depreciation accounting also suffers from the problems of determination of actual costs, estimation of useful service lives, and estimation of residual selling values. They involve a great deal of uncertainty and subjectivity. The problems of depreciation accounting are complicated further when depreciable assets are subjected to a process of revaluation. There also exists a controversy as to the treatment of costs of funds tied up in the fixed assets. Under the traditional system, the costs of funds tied up in fixed assets are not included in periodic depreciation. Being unable to resolve the controversies which centre around depreciation accounting, the rule makers have been rather forced to keep depreciation-related rules as flexible as possible. As a result, there is a wide diversity in depreciation accounting practices among the companies.

The objective of this book is to examine how companies in India account for depreciation in their published annual accounts. In order to do this, we first examine the regulatory requirements. The existing regulatory requirements are not very rigid ones; they permit companies to choose between procedures. To understand of how companies in India use the flexibility contained in prevailing depreciation accounting rules to compute their financial result, we have taken a sample of 100 Indian companies which covers all major segments or divisions of Indian industries. In this book, a comparative analysis relating to depreciation accounting prevailing in some selected developed countries, has been made to judge the effectiveness of the rule relating to depreciation accounting prevailing in India. This book, will assist the rule makers in India in developing a more realistic approach in framing the depreciation related rules.

I am extremely happy to express my gratitude to Dr. Uttam Kumar Dutta, Reader and Head, Department of Commerce, the University of Burdwan for guiding and encouraging me. In spite of his very busy schedule each day, I must admit that he gave me all his attention that my present work deserved.

I am heavily indebted to Professor A.K. Basu, Department of Commerce, University of Calcutta who has been my constant source of inspiration and encouragement. Without his help, it would not be possible to complete the work.

I record my deep respect and sincere gratitude to Dr. J.B. Sarker, Reader (Rtd.), Department of Commerce, the University of Burdwan for assisting me in completing the present book. I am particularly thankful to Sri Debdas Rakshit, Lecturer, Department of Commerce, the University of Burdwan for helping me in 'Commerce Computer Lab'.

I express my gratitude to Mr. Mark Walsh, Principal, The Canadian Institute of Chartered Accountants for sending me valuable documents. I also thank Mr. Tomoe Kase of the Japanese Institute of Certified Public Accountants, International Affairs, for providing me with valuable information.

I acknowledge the immense help that I have received from the Librarians and members of the National Library, Indian Institute of Management (Joka, Kolkata) Library, Goenka College of Commerce and Business Administration Library.

I am also thankful to 'Dhar Brothers' for providing me with technical assistance.

Finally, I express my gratitude to my parents and my wife for bearing with me. My loving child Mst. Saumyorik deserve credit for at least not disturbing me off and on in spite of many lost hours of his covetable association with me.

**Subrata Kar**
Department of Commerce
The University of Burdwan
Burdwan - 713 104, West Bengal, India.

# Contents

# 1

# Introduction

Depreciation accounting has been, and still continues to be, a controversial issue in corporate financial accounting and reporting. Many scholarly studies have been conducted in the past in order to resolve controversies concerning depreciation accounting but problems still continue to persist. The leading accounting standard setters of the world have also spent considerable time and energy in developing effective solutions to depreciation accounting problems but this too has not changed the scenario very much. Solutions are now available but they can by no means be considered to be ideal ones.

Depreciation affects both the profit and loss account and the balance sheet. It affects the way in which net profit is computed and also the way in which the carrying values of depreciable assets are determined in the balance sheet. Depreciation provision has an important role to play in financing expansion and growth. In a manufacturing enterprise having huge investments in plant assets, depreciation charges can constitute a substantial element of the expenses to be matched against periodic revenue. Under the conventional historical cost-based system of accounting, depreciation is regarded as the periodic charge to profits that results from an allocation of cost or other basic input value over the life of a depreciable plant or other asset. According to the principle of matching, the cost or other basic input value of a tangible fixed asset is to be allocated to the different accounting periods expected to be benefited from its service. The principle further requires that yearly charges for consumption of asset services should reflect the benefits actually derived each year. In real practice, however, it often becomes difficult to ascertain the patterns of using up of asset services. Attempts are made to overcome the difficulty by assuming that the services of depreciable assets are used up at a constant rate over their useful lives. This, no doubt, eases the problems of accountants but impinges on financial arithmetic. Periodic profits are distorted and distortions also take place in the carrying values of the assets.

Problems of depreciation accounting stem not only from the inability to obtain realistic measures of the patterns of using up of asset services but also from several other sources. These include determination of true costs, estimation of useful service lives and estimation of residual selling values. With regard to cost determination, it may be possible to develop some objective bases but estimation of useful economic lives and residual values involve a good deal of uncertainty and subjectivity.

The problems of depreciation accounting tend to be complicated further when depreciable assets are subjected to a process of revaluation. When an item of depreciable assets is revalued it may be necessary to revise the base to be used for computing depreciation charges in periods subsequent to the date of revaluation. Another major problem which is encountered in depreciation accounting relates to the treatment of overhauling and repair costs.

There exists a controversy as to the inclusion of costs of funds tied up in fixed assets in periodic depreciation charges. It has been argued from several quarters that if depreciation is to reflect properly the value of consumption of asset services, it must include an interest element in it. Accounting standard setters have not yet been able to arrive at consensus as to how the interest issue should be resolved. Depreciation charges computed based on traditional practice do not embrace the interest cost. There is thus an understatement of the value of consumption of asset services.

Being unable to resolve the controversies which centre around depreciation accounting the rule makers have been rather forced to keep depreciation-related rules as flexible as possible. At present, companies are permitted to enjoy a great deal of freedom in designing their own depreciation policies. As a matter of fact, most companies take the benefit of the flexible rules to manage their profits and asset values.

## The Objective of the Present Study

The objective of the present study is to examine how companies in India account for depreciation in their published annual accounts. In order to do this it is at first necessary to know the regulatory framework within which the companies are to operate. The principal regulatory requirements relating to depreciation accounting are contained in the Companies Act and in the accounting standards and guidelines formulated by The Institute of Chartered Accountants of India. The requirements are not very rigid ones in that they permit companies to choose between procedures. In this study, an endeavour will be made to obtain an understanding of how companies in this country utilise the flexibility contained in prevailing depreciation accounting rules to compute their financial results. So far, no study has been conducted in this country on this aspect of preparation and presentation of company accounts. But corporate depreciation accounting behaviour is an important area of study because a knowledge of how companies make use of depreciation accounting flexibility in computing their financial results and of why they do what they do enables rule makers to adopt a more realistic approach to rule making.

Although the study is concerned with examining corporate accounting practices with regard to depreciation, efforts will also be made to judge the effectiveness of the rules themselves. For this purpose a comparative analysis will be made of the Indian corporate depreciation accounting rules and standards with those prevailing in some developed countries.

## Review of Literature

Depreciation accounting has attracted a great deal of attention from the researchers and recognised accounting bodies in the field of accounting and finance. Some of the noteworthy studies, which focus mainly on the conceptual aspects of the subject, include Matheson (1903)[1], Leake (1912)[2], Webb (1954)[3], Grant and Norton (1955)[4], NAA (1958)[5], Goldberg (1960)[6], Morrissey (1960)[7], Wright (1964)[8], Hogan (1967)[9], Roy (1977)[10], Baxter (1981)[11].

Matheson (1903) focused his work on capital invested in factories and the principles of depreciation and its incidence under varying circumstances. He pointed out the numerous causes of variation in the rates at which factories and plant depreciated and the absence of agreement in the practice of arriving at or assigning them. A successful attempt has been made in his work to systematise existing information with the help of diagrams and tables where needed and to make it possible to arrive at something like uniformity and accuracy in the practice of making up balance sheet for valuations. He also, through his work, supplied auditors and accountants with some valuable data to enable them to properly deal with facts and figures as to the fair allotment to capital or revenue of actual expenditure or estimated depreciation.

Leake (1912) defined the depreciation is a fall in exchangeable value of wasting assets, computed on the basis of cost expired during the period of their use in seeking profits. He defined wasting assets as both tangible and intangible fixed assets and all form of exchangeable value which inevitably diminish while applied to the purpose of seeking profits, increase, or advantage otherwise than by purchase and sales. He argued that depreciation is unaffected by market fluctuation in value of the assets used. In short, he termed depreciation as 'expired capital outlay'. He was an advocate of the straight line method and an adversary of the reducing balance method, but his principal objection was to spasmodic allocation of revenue account balances to reserve account to meet requirements of really unknown extent and rough and ready apportionment between capital and revenue account of large outlays on combined renewals and extensions. His unique contribution to accounting thought is the super profit theory of measuring goodwill.

Webb (1954) focused his work on an examination of existing theory and practice regarding depreciation of fixed assets in accountancy and economics with special reference to the effect that depreciation policies may have on replacement of plant, productivity of industry and employment. He highlighted the importance of depreciation both in economics and accountancy. An emphasis has been placed in his work on the reconciliation between accounting and economic views of depreciation. Certain of the difficulties as regards fixed assets, particularly the problem of fluctuation in the volume of replacement investment and fluctuation in the volume of expansion investment have been discussed in this thesis. The discussion in this study mainly related to Australia although some account was taken of the position in Great Britain, Canada and United States. He conducted a survey regarding the rate of replacement of capital equipment in Australia. The analysis revealed that 23 out of 67 companies surveyed, supplied actual figures in these regards. The result of survey has been shown that Australian manufacturer did not scrap or sell plant when it reached the stage of being fully depreciated and did not replaced it, but retained it in use for long periods.

Grant and Norton (1955) examined the treatment of depreciation for the purpose of Federal income taxation in the United States and on the accounting treatment of depreciation by individuals and corporations. They showed that the various types of business decisions that are related to the fact of decline in value of physical assets. They also examined the uses and limitations of figures which may be obtained from the depreciation accounts as a guide to such business decision. Since 1934, under the influence of income tax regulations depreciation accounting practices in the United States has been moving in the direction of straight line group depreciation accounting, with rates based on the best evidence of average service life. In the light of evidence available some concrete suggestions have been made for changes in the accounting and income tax treatment of depreciation in the final two chapters. The authors have realised that the changes in the income tax treatment of depreciation depend on action by the congress and by the Bureau of Internal Revenue in the United States.

National Association of Accountants (NAA) (1958) highlighted the practices followed in accounting for depreciation in the light of Federal income tax laws and regulation with reference to United States particularly after enactment of Revenue Code 1954. Before World War II, depreciation method mainly employed for income tax purpose but after World War II many of these conditions have been changed and trends towards new thinking and new depreciation practices seem to be emerging. As a consequence, the study were made by NAA was concentrated to ascertain the nature of different trends and to re-examine established depreciation accounting practices in view of Revenue Code 1954. NAA conducted a survey of 55 US companies and collected information regarding their practices and procedures in respect of accounting for depreciation. In this study, an emphasis was placed upon the purposes served by accounting for depreciation and how well the objectives were met by various depreciation practices.

Goldberg (1960) focused his thesis on different concepts held regarding depreciation and its treatment. He conducted a survey of 78 Australian corporations by using their published annual reports to find out the treatment or lack thereof regarding depreciation with consideration for legal requirements, standards of presentation propounded by professional bodies of accountants in Australia and those elements of tax legislation which influence accounting practices. His analysis revealed a general close adherence to statutory requirements for reporting with a wide spectrum of accounting procedure regarding depreciation in their published reports. He explained the fact that under conditions of increasing price levels in dealing with depreciation and capital erosion. He argued that depreciation accounting does not provide for replacement of fixed assets but he also explained the importance of depreciation for disclosure of income. He also highlighted the accounting for depreciation followed by Government of Australia.

Morrissey (1960), through his study, tried to present and analyse some of the problems relating to depreciation accounting with reference to the 1954 Revenue Code issued by US Treasury. These problems stimulated due to disagreement and uncertainty surrounding with relating to depreciation accounting. He considered only the two most popular accelerated method of depreciation namely declining balance method and sum-of-the-years'-digits method out of the methods authorised in the 1954 Code over the straight line method which was inconsistence with relating to depreciation of many assets particularly in inflationary situation. He also analysed many different aspects of the depreciation accounting in an attempt to clarify the issues and suggested how business' financial reports may be reconciled better with tax accounting.

In search of a general theory of depreciation Wright (1964) established a theory of depreciation whose foundation were laid by Hotelling and Canning. Canning developed the concept of opportunity value while Hotelling established his theory as 'theoretical selling price' as a function of time. He realised that a theory of depreciation should not be judged by its practical usefulness but rather by its theoretical soundness, its generality and the light it throws on accounting practice. He argued that traditional matching theory did not seriously attempt a justification, indeed it was developed largely for the purpose of by passing the valuation problem which lies at the root of most of our difficulties with depreciation. He further, argued that only the economic approach represents a theory of valuation and without a theory of valuation we cannot have a theory of depreciation. He emphasized the theory which based on the economic approach to the valuation of an asset i.e., discounting of expected net revenues from the asset. He considered that the opportunity value theory of depreciation is superior to the traditional matching approach because it is firmly grounded in valuation theory.

Hogan (1967) discussed the evaluation of depreciation policy and practice, and their effect on the economy with respect to capital replacement. He presented an analysis of the events leading up to the depreciation problem and its relationship to tax policies from the inception of the income tax laws prevailing at that time. He also examined the growth of depreciation reserves as a source of corporate funds and the importance role played by depreciation in business investment decisions. He conducted a thorough survey of the depreciation practices in different countries and reviewed the various methods proposed to reform the tax laws governing in USA. His study also focused on the evaluation of possible solutions particularly for the deficit between funds supplied by depreciation accruals and the amount needed to replace facilities at current price.

In India, the study of Prof. G.D. Ray (1977) is most notable. Besides the general concept of depreciation, an attempt has been made to reconcile provision with expenses for charging depreciation. He focused his work on method of ascertaining periodical depreciation under three heads viz. (i) allocation of cost resulting from expiration of cost, (ii) recovery of capital outlay and (ii) revaluation or appraisal methods or valuation method. All these methods, relevant to the pure theory of depreciation were discussed in his study. He established algebraic formulas for better understanding of depreciation methods. Apart from formulas, diagrams, and table were used where needed. He always suggested for alternative method for charging depreciation and modified the methods where needed to cope with related issues like cost of capital, interest etc. He justified the use of opportunity rate of cost of capital to be used as the discounting factor. He also used the concept of deprival value for replacement cost of asset. His unique contribution in this study was depreciation of human resources. He discussed from recognition of human asset to the factors affecting the process of human depreciation and replacement.

Baxter (1981) focused his work on identification of issues related to the problem of depreciation accounting irrespective of whether a cost-based accounting approach or value-based accounting approach is imposed and to suggest ways of testing depreciation methods in use. He favoured current value approach to depreciation including discounted value approach. He emphasized 'deprival value' as a standard against which validity of other depreciation methods is tested. He argued on interest methods of depreciation and suggested that all other methods would be enhanced by allowing for interest. An emphasis has been placed in his study on the relevance of cost packages i.e. depreciation and repairs and charges in cash flows.

Beside above studies, there are number of studies on depreciation. The notable studies are: Hotelling (1925)[12], Most (1957)[13], Meij (1961)[14], Lowe (1963)[15], Ma (1964)[16], Caplin and Klayman (1965)[17], Bierman (1966)[18], Brief (1967)[19], Burt (1972)[20] Jinnah (1989)[21], Kachelmeier & Granof (1993)[22], Dhameja (1997)[23] and Baxter (2000)[24].

Although the present study draws heavily on the above mentioned works, its main focus of attention is on the disclosure aspect of depreciation in the context of published company accounts. In India no comprehensive study has so far been made on how depreciation is actually accounted for by the companies in the country in preparing and presenting their external financial reports. The present study is a humble attempt to fill up this gap.

## Data Source and Methodology

This is basically a descriptive study. It aims to describe what is happening in the corporate accounting world with regard to depreciation accounting practices and to explain why things are what they are. The study does not involve any hypothesis testing in the real sense of the term. Analytical techniques have been, however, used to deal with conceptual issues.

Published company reports are the principal data source of the study. Since companies have a great deal of flexibility in computing periodic depreciation charges, they are required to explain in the policy section of the "notes to the accounts" as to how they have arrived at their depreciation numbers. Thus the present study focuses mainly on this section of published company accounts.

Other data sources for the study are:

(i) Companies Act

(ii) Income Tax Act

(iii) ICAI accounting standards and guidelines on depreciation accounting.

(iv) Accounting standards promulgated by the leading accounting standard setters of the world on the subject of depreciation accounting.

The present study also draws heavily on journal, articles, books and other published literature on this subject.

Although the study is concerned with examining corporate depreciation accounting practices in India, it is not possible to take into account the published accounts of all the companies currently operating in India. For the purpose of our study, we have taken a sample of 100 companies out of first 200 companies of 'ET 500' December 2004 edition published by Economic Times Intelligence Group (ETIG). For the purpose of this ranking, the Economic Times Intelligence Group has taken into account the average market capitalisations of companies for the period October 16 to 31, 2003 and companies being traded for six days or more [Source: ETIG Database]. The data has been collected from the Annual Reports of these 100 companies for the financial year 2003-04 having net turnover Rs. 100 crores or more. The purpose of our study is not to show the trend analysis of depreciation over a long period of time. Our sole object is to examine the corporate depreciation accounting practices in India. For this purpose we have considered only one financial year i.e., 2003-04. The companies belong to the manufacturing group only i.e., the companies either manufacturing goods or producing services having huge investments in tangible fixed assets. The selected company is either a company in the public sector or in the public limited companies. The sample has been drawn in a way as to cover all the major segments or divisions of Indian industries. That is cross section wise the sample companies have been selected. The companies selected are from automobile industry, oil and gas industry, chemical industry, iron and steel industry, pharmaceutical industry, infotech industry, cement industry, aluminium industry, paper industry, agro industry, hotel industry, cotton and textiles industry, shipping industry, engineering industry, fertilizers industry etc. Thus, the coverage of the industry is as wide as possible. Therefore, certain companies are obviously kept outside the purview of this study.

These companies are:

(i) Investment and Financing Company

(ii) Banking and Insurance Company

(iii) Trading and Export Company

(iv) Company which generates electricity i.e. the company which follows specific rules while preparing the annual report.

The study makes extensive use of tabulation, and accounting ratio particularly the fixed asset turnover ratio for analysing and interpreting the data collected from different sources.

## Limitation of the Study

The present study has some limitations.

- First, the study is based on the published annual reports of 100 companies. The size is too small with compared to the total number of companies that are currently operating and traded in India.
- Secondly, the study has considered the annual reports of different companies for the year 2003-04 only to examine the current depreciation accounting practices. Naturally, beyond 2003-04 we have not considered in our study.
- Thirdly, the study has considered companies within the manufacturing group. Companies belonging to non-manufacturing group are not under the jurisdiction of our study.
- Fourthly, no questionnaire has been administered to collect information in respect of depreciation practices adopted by the Indian companies.

## Plan of the Study

The study will be divided into eight chapters.

**Chapter I** is the introductory chapter. It will offer a detailed description of the aim, scope and methodology of the study. The chapter will also render a brief account of the literature available on this and other peripheral subjects.

**Chapter II** will explore the nature of accounting depreciation. It will also examine in detail the effects of charging depreciation—effect on net profit computation, effect on balance sheet valuation and effect on fund generation.

**Chapter III** will concentrate on the available methods of computing depreciation. It will discuss the effectiveness of the different methods of depreciation computation in the matter of realising the stated goals of depreciation accounting.

**Chapter IV** will be devoted to an enumeration of the regulatory requirements concerning depreciation accounting in India. The two important regulatory sources are Companies Act and standards and guidelines set forth by the ICAI. In this chapter, an endeavour will also be made to distinguish between tax accounting depreciation and financial accounting depreciation.

**Chapter V** will present a comparative study of depreciation accounting rules prevailing in some selected countries. The objective of doing this is to see how far Indian depreciation accounting rules are compatible with those prevailing elsewhere.

**Chapter VI** will present data relating to depreciation accounting practices of the Indian Companies covered in the sample. The issues involved in depreciation will be segmented and presented by means of suitable tables.

**Chapter VII** will provide analysis and interpretation of the data presented in Chapter VI. The analysis and interpretations will be done in the light of the concept of disclosure of financial information so for it relates to depreciation accounting.

**Chapter VIII** is the concluding chapter. It will bring out the final observations. It will also set forth the implications of the study for those responsible for regulating corporate depreciation accounting in India.

## REFERENCES

1. Ewing Matheson, *The Depreciation of Factories—Mines and Industrial Undertaking and Their Valuation,* London, E. & F.N. Spon Ltd., Third Edition, 1903.

2. P.D. Leake, *Depreciation and Wasting Assets and Their Treatment in Assessing Annual Profit and Loss*, Henry Good and Sons, 1912, Reprint Edition, Arno Press, New York, 1976.
3. G.T. Webb, *Depreciation of Fixed Assets—In Accountancy and Economics*, Australia, The Law Book Co. of Australasia Pty Ltd., 1954.
4. Eugene L. Grant and Paul T. Norton, Jr., *Depreciation*, New York, The Ronald Press Company, 1955.
5. National Association of Accountants, *Current Practice in Accounting for Depreciation, Research Series No. 33*, New York, NAA, 1958.
6. Louis Goldberg, *Concept of Depreciation*, Sydney, The Law Book Co. of Australasia Pty Ltd, 1960.
7. Leonard E. Morrissey, *The Many Sides of Depreciation*, New Hampshire, The Amos Tuck School of Business Administration, Dartmouth College, 1960.
8. F.K. Wright, "Towards a General Theory of Depreciation", *Journal of Accounting Research*, Vol. 2, No. 1, Spring 1964, pp. 80-90.
9. William Thomas Hogan, *Depreciation Policies and Resultant Problems*, New York, Fordham University Press, 1967.
10. G.D. Roy, *Anatomy of Depreciation*, Calcutta, The World Press Pvt. Ltd., 1977.
11. W.T. Baxter, *Depreciating Assets: An Introduction*, The Institute of Chartered Accountants of Scotland, Gee & Co. Ltd., 1981.
12. Harold Hotelling, "A General Mathematical Theory of Depreciation", *Journal of the American Statistical Association*", Vol. 20, September 1925, pp. 340-53.
13. Kenneth S. Most, "Scientific Estimation of Depreciation", *The Accountant*, Vol. CXXXVII, No. 4312, 10 August, 1957, pp. 153-56.
14. Jacob Louis Meij, *Depreciation and Replacement Policy*, Amsterdam, North-Holland Publishing Co., 1961.
15. Howard D. Lowe, "The Essentials of a General Theory of Depreciation", *The Accounting Review*, Vol. XXXVIII, No. 2, April 1963, pp. 293-301.
16. Ronald Ma, "Accounting for Depreciation", *Accountancy*, Vol. LXXV, No. 855, November 1964, pp. 978-82.
17. Mortimer M. Caplin and Robert A. Klayman, "Depreciation 1965 Model", *The Journal of Accountancy*, Vol. 119, No. 4, April 1965, pp. 34-42.
18. Harold Bierman, Jr., "A Further Study of Depreciation", *The Accounting Review*, Vol. XLI, No. 2, April 1966, pp. 271-274.
19. Richard P. Brief, "A Late Nineteenth Century Contribution to the Theory of Depreciation" *Journal of Accounting Research*, Vol. 5, No. 1, Spring 1967, pp. 27-38.
20. Oscar R. Burt, "A Unified Theory of Depreciation", *Journal of Accounting Research*, Vol. 10, No. 1, Spring 1972, pp. 28-57.

21. M.M. Jinnah, *Depreciation Accounting—A Study of Practices of Indian Business*, Delhi, Himalaya Publishing House, 1989.
22. Steven J. Kachelmeier and Michael H. Granof, "Depreciation and Capital Investment Decision: Experimental Evidences in a Governmental Setting", *Journal of Accounting and Public Policy*", Vol. 12, No. 4, Winter 1993, pp. 291-323.
23. Nand Dhameja, "Revaluation of Fixed Assets", *The Chartered Accountant*, Vol. XLV, No. 7, January 1997, pp. 10-11.
24. William Baxter, "Depreciation and Interest", *Accountancy* Vol. 126, No. 1286, October 2000, pp. 104-105.

# 2

# Nature of Depreciation

This chapter deals with the nature of depreciation. It has five sections viz., Definition of Depreciation, Causes of Depreciation, Effect of Depreciation, Practical Concept about Depreciation and Controversy relating to Fund Creation through Depreciation.

## Definition of Depreciation

Generally depreciation means the decrease in value of fixed assets arising out of wear and tear through use or for any other reasons.

Before mentioning different definitions given by different accounting bodies and the practical definition of depreciation it would be necessary to review the definitions of depreciation expressed by different Dictionaries and Encyclopaedias.

According to Dictionary for Accountants, "Depreciation is diminution of service yields from a fixed asset or fixed asset group that cannot or will be restored by repairs or by replacement of parts, caused by wear and tear from use, disuse, poor maintenance, obsolescence (progress of arts), and inadequacy (unsuitability to the particular enterprise)"[1].

According to Oxford Dictionary of Business English, Learners of English, "Depreciation is a gradual loss in the value of something, such as a vehicle, a machine or any asset that wears out with use and age."[2]

According to the Hand Book of International Financial Terms, "Depreciation is the recording of an expenses to represent the loss of value in a wasting asset over a period. Under the matching concept, depreciation should assign the total loss of value of an asset over its lifetime as express in the periods when the company benefits from its use."[3]

As per the Webters New Twentieth Century Dictionary, "Depreciation is a decrease in value of property through wear, deterioration or absolescence".[4]

In the Industrial Accountant's Encyclopaedia Dictionary, depreciation is defined as "the reduction in the value of a Fixed Asset because of wear and tear from use or disuse, obsolescence or accident".[5]

According to Encyclopaedia Britannica, "Depreciation is an accounting charge for the decline in value of an asset, spreads over its economic life. Depreciation covers wear and tear from use and physical deterioration from age and exposure to the elements. It also includes obsolescence, i.e. loss of usefulness arising from availability of newer and more efficient types of goods serving the same purpose. It does not cover losses from sudden and unexpected destruction of the usefulness of property as a result of fire, accident, theft, war, damage or adverse court decisions or from declining price levels".[6]

The term depreciation as defined in The New Columbia Encyclopaedia is "the accounting sense is a reduction in the value of fixed or capital assets as by use, damage, weathering or absolescence".[7]

As per the Encyclopaedia American, "Depreciation, in accounting, is a decrease in the value of, or loss of usefulness of, a fixed asset because of wear and tear, action of the elements, accidents, inadequacy or absolescence".[8]

Different worldwide eminent accounting bodies define the definition of depreciation on the basis of their own observation. Some of the definitions are as follows:

The American Accounting Association (AAA) Committee on Concepts and Standards 1957 stated that "Depreciation represents the decline in service potential of long term assets and that the decline in service potential may be the result of physical deterioration, consumption through use, or loss in economic value because of obsolescence or change in demand".[9]

The American Institute of Certified Public Accountants, Accounting Terminology Bulletin No. 1, 1953 defined depreciation accounting in the following manner, "Depreciation accounting is a system of accounting which aims to distribute the cost or other basic value of tangible capital assets, less salvage (if any), over the estimated useful life of the unit (which may be a group of assets) in a systematic and rational manner. It is a process of allocation, not of valuation. . . ."[10]

International Accounting Standard (IAS)-4 defined depreciation as—"the allocation of the depreciable amount of an asset over its estimated useful life. Depreciation for the accounting period is charged to income either directly or indirectly".[11]

According to Accounting Standard (AS)-6 issued by ICAI "Depreciation is a measure of the wearing out, consumption or other loss of value of a depreciable asset from use, effluxion of time or obsolescence through technology and market changes. Depreciation is allocated so as to charge a fair proportion of the depreciable amount in each accounting period during the expected useful life of asset. Depreciation includes amortisation of assets whose useful life is predetermined".[12]

Recommendation No. IX of the Institute of Chartered Accountants in England and Wales, issued in 1945 expressed the matter as—"Depreciation represents that part of the cost of a fixed asset to its owner which is not recoverable when the asset is finally put out of use by him. Provision against this loss of capital is an integral cost of conducting the business during the effective commercial life of the asset and is not dependent upon the amount of Profit earned...".[13]

The definition of depreciation whatever stated above are basically the accounting view of depreciation. Let us discuss, briefly the economic view of depreciation.

The economists' view regarding depreciation is that capital goods render services in producing goods for consumer satisfaction and such services should form a part of the cost of goods produced by utilising such services. The capital goods represent a fund from which a stream of services flow and by utilising such services the fund is exhausted. The totality of services available is represented by the value of the fund and cost or values appropriate to the services actually utilised should be charged to the cost of the goods that are produced by utilising the services. From other angle it can be said by utilising the capital goods in production, the value of capital goods or fund is gradually exhausted. So depreciation recognises as a flow of stream of services from the capital fund contributing to the cost the products or services properly chargeable against revenue earned.

The approach of the economist regarding fixed asset is different from that of modern accounting approach. Fixed assets to the economist are tangible instruments to be used in the production of goods both for consumer and for further production of goods for which there is an effective demand. The economist is not concerned with how they came into existence but to what use they will be put during their lifetime and whether they will be replaced at the end of such period.

The problem of depreciation is not discussed in the works of economists before Alfred Marshall. Adam Smith only mentioned to the fact that a manufacturer could not employ all his workmen on working up material, as he would need to employ some of the maintenance of machinery.[14] In fact, at that time, he wrote, the problem of depreciation provisions, rapid obsolescence of plant and machinery and need for replacement of plant and machinery over its lifetime did not concentrated.

Marshall referred to the question of depreciation in relation with the valuation of assets.[15] He did not discuss the effect of depreciation provisions or problems associated with the replacement of fixed assets. Regarding the advantages of the use of specialised machinery be explained that "a heavy allowance must be made for depreciation in consequence of its being probably improved upon before long."[16]

In modern accounting approach, depreciation is not concerned with the replacement of fixed assets. It does not seem to be recognised or discussed by economic writers. Economists appear to look upon the amount charged for depreciation as measuring the extent to which the value of fixed capital is used up in production. Instead the view that depreciation is concerned with the replacement of fixed assets will be found, expressly stated or implied, in most works on economics after Marshall, discuss the maintenance of capital. R.A.D. Egerton, in his articles stated that "depreciation is the amount which is set aside so that the equipment which is being currently used in production may be replaced when worn out".[17]

A similar view is taken by Mr. Fowler, who suggested that "most types of capital equipment wear out sooner or later, and have to be replaced if production is to continue. It therefore, becomes necessary to make provision for these replacements by creating depreciation or amortization reserves."[18] Professor Howtrey has stated that "depreciation may be regarded as a sinking fund to be accumulated at interest till replacement becomes due and then applied to the cost of replacement".[19]

Many economists assume that amounts provided for depreciation are set aside in a depreciation fund, and that when an asset is fully depreciated the cash so recovered through costs is available to replace it. In practice it is most exceptional for depreciation provisions to be paid into a depreciation fund but the depreciation provisions are used within the business as additional working capital for any purpose whatsoever. Lord Keynes, in his General Theory, examined the treatment of depreciation allowance relating to such investment. His views on the treatment of depreciation in production costs which arises out of debit side of the entry for the depreciation are the concern matter of accountants while he concerned mainly with the credit side of the entry for depreciation, the credit raised in the depreciation provision account.

The effect of excessive provisions for depreciation on employment was stressed by Lord Keynes and he pointed out that "the large the financial provision which it is thought necessary to make before reckoning net income, the less favourable to consumption, and therefore to employment, will a given level of investment prove to be."[20]

He pointed out that if the financial provisions for depreciation of existing capital equipment exceed the current expenditure on new equipment, in order to maintain a given level of employment, the amount of the excess would need "to be balanced by new investment, the demand for which has arisen quite independently of the current wastage of old equipment against which the financial provision is being made."[21] However, provided the 'excess' depreciation provisions are put to use by the business making them there need be no deflationary effect on employment. In this regard it is immaterial whether the additional funds obtained by charging depreciation into costs are used to purchase additional fixed assets, such as capital equipment or to finance increased non-liquid current assets such as trade debtors or inventory. It is when the 'excess' depreciation provisions pile up as idle funds that they become a danger to employment.

Though the term deprecation is widely used in accounting and finance but it should be viewed from the angle of Legal Experts (Lawyers). There are several case laws regarding depreciation. The Learned Judges expressed their opinions about depreciation and these judgement are very material for conceptualisation of the term depreciation. Some of the legal views concerning depreciation are described below in brief.

Lee Vs. Neuchatel Asphalte Co. Ltd (1989)[22]

The case was decided by Mr. Justice Lord Cotton, Lord Lindley and Lord Lopes in the Court of Appeal on 9th February, 1889.

It was held that a company may distribute dividend without making good the depreciation on wasting assets if it is authorised by its Articles of Association to do so. In this case the main fixed asset of the company was a natural bituminous deposit in Switzerland which eventually would be exhausted and the company wound up.

### *General Comments*

The resources extracted from a wasting asset causes depreciation of the asset through depletion. This depreciation is an essential charge against income which comes from such resources. If depreciation is not written off regularly neither the true profit nor loss of the business will be ascertained nor will fund be available for replacement of asset, after its resources are fully emptied. Again, this decision does not hold good at present in India with the inclusion of section 205 of the Companies Act, 1956.

Irish held that in the case of a company formed to work as wasting asset, such as a mine or timber right, there is no need, unless required by the Articles to provide for depletion before arriving at the profit available for dividend, even though such procedure may result in a partial return of capital with each dividend paid.[23]

Wilmer Vs. Mc. Namara & Co. Ltd. (1895)[24]

The case was decided by Mr. Justice Stirling in the Chancery Division on April 26, 1895.

The bone of contention of the case was depreciation on assets and divisible profit.

In course of delivering his judgement, the Hon'ble Justice remarked that a company can declare dividend out of current profits without making any provision for depreciation on fixed assets.

## *General Comments*

The decisions were given by the Court in favour of the defendant company. It is to be noted in this context that the decision of this case is quite ineffective in its application in India after the introduction of section 205 of the Companies Act, 1956.

Crabtree Thomas Vs. Crabtree (1912)[25]

The bone of contention of the case was provision for depreciation and divisible profit. The Hon'ble Justice gave his judgement as "In the ordinary course of ascertaining the profits of a business where there is a power machinery or trade machinery which is necessary in order to perform the work of the business, it is, in my opinion, essential that in addition to all sums actually expended in repairing the machinery or in renewing the parts there should also be written off proper sum for depreciation and that sum ought to be written off before you can arrive at the net profits of the business or at the profits of the business and it is not the profit until a proper sum varying with the class of machinery, has been written off for depreciation".

## *General Comments*

The decision still hold good at present that depreciation of plant and machinery is an essential charge against profit. In our country, it is obligatory for all the companies to charge depreciation on all depreciable assets since the Companies (Amendment) Act, 1960 has been enforced.

## Causes of Depreciation

All the definitions of depreciation are based on the causes of depreciation. An understanding of the cause of depreciation would facilitate identification of the characteristic of depreciation. Different eminent persons pointed out different causes of depreciation.

William Pickles defined the main causes of depreciation as:[26]

(a) Wear and tear

(b) Physical factors: evaporation of liquids, loss of potency of acids, erosion, dampness

(c) Obsolescence, due to invention or change of fashion

(d) Fall in market price (including foreign rates)

(e) Effluxion of time.

Eric Kohler expresses that the depreciation is a function of [27]

(a) Use

(b) Disuse

(c) Maintenance

(d) Change in production

(e) Restriction of production

(f) Decrease in demand

(g) Progress of the arts

(h) Obsolescence

(i) Inadequacy.

Montgomery divides the causes of depreciation into those which are more or less predictable at the time of installation and those due to unforeseen developments. Under the first group are[28]:

(a) Ordinary wear and tear from operation
(b) Physical deterioration resulting from time and the elements
(c) Inadequacy
(d) Obsolescence
(e) Diminution in supply of raw material
(f) Negligence.

Under the second group are those which may hasten the loss in service value of the property and necessitate replacement or complete abandonment.

(a) Structural defects
(b) Diseases, such as electrolysis, crystallization etc.
(c) Extraordinary wear and tear from operation
(d) Extraordinary obsolescence.

G.T. Ponsonby stated that the principal causes of depreciation in the value of assets may be considered under four broad headings namely: [29]

(i) Physical wear and tear resulting from use;
(ii) Physical deterioration resulting from exposure to the elements, essentially a function of time rather than use;
(iii) The expiration or running out of such legal rights as leases

and licences; and

(iv) The falling away over time of the demand for particular transport services provided by the assets. This item is of course, usually referred to as obsolescence.

M.M. Jinnah divided the causes of depreciation into four categories: physical causes, functional causes, other causes and contingent causes.[30] They are as follows:

1. Physical causes:
   - (a) Wear and tear from operation
   - (b) Efflux of time
   - (c) Poor maintenance
2. Functional causes:
   - (a) Inadequacy or supers cession: due to growth of business
   - (b) Obsolescence
     - (i) Inventions
     - (ii) Cessation of demand due to changes in fashion
     - (iii) Changes in the technology of production (either through the development of a more deficient asset or in the method of production i.e. automaton).
3. Other causes:
   - (a) Decrease in demand
   - (b) Restriction on production.
4. Contingent (contingencies) causes
   - (a) Accidents (due to negligence and structural defects)
   - (b) Disease (parasites, pollution of water, growths in water mains, electrolysis, crystallization, fisheries, dairy farming, sericulture, horticulture etc.)
   - (c) Natural calamities (fire, theft, war, damage storm, floods,

earthquakes etc.)
(d) Adverse court decision
(e) Decline in price level.

From the above discussion it becomes crystal clear that the experts do not express same view about causes of depreciation. Some of the causes explained briefly are as follows:

## (a) *Wear and Tear*

This is one of the common contributory factors for depreciation. The loss of value is due to the exhaustion of the potential utility of the asset as a result of continuous use. Although they are kept in order by providing for their repairs during the life-time of the asset, a time will come why they will be completely useless. The assets which are kept open in the nature also get normally exhausted due to natural causes like sun, rain, air etc. Plant, factory shed, building etc. are worn out in many causes due to such natural causes. Careless handling of an asset is also responsible for rapid loss of its value. E.L. Kholer states that a machine wears when operated from day to day and it is usually expected to wear out at least twice as fast when used sixteen hours a day. This loss of service-ability is commonly regarded as the primary cause of depreciation often being referred to as 'ordinary wear and tear'.[31]

## (b) *Efflux of Time*

With the passage of time, certain assets loose their workability. Assets like leasehold property, patent right, copyright etc. get exhausted not due to use but on account of efflux of time. It is quite true that if an asset is not used, even if the asset remains lying idle, depreciation occurs in its value with the passage of time because their value is contractual and time based. E.L. Kohler states that "a machine standing continuously idle became potentially less and less useful as time goes on; in fact, certain machine like farm implements standing in the open may age even more speedily from disuse than from use".[32]

## (c) *Obsolescence*

Due to the innovation of improved technology and invention of new asset, sometimes the old assets loose their utility, even the old one in good service potentiality, and are discarded. Such reduction in the value of any asset is known as loss due to obsolescence. For example, with the invention of new xerox machine the old one becomes obsolete and simultaneously discarded as the customers incline more and more on new xerox machine, so the loss in the value of the old xerox machine is the result of obsolescence. Obsolescence may also happen due to innovation, cessation of demand, changes in production technology and customers' taste, preference and need. John Mattews has truly mentioned that "the initial estimates of asset should not include any allowance for possible obsolescence. The impact of obsolescence does not occur immediately upon apprehension of the fact that there is improved equipment on the market or acquired by competitors. It comes when selling price has to be reduced; in the case when alternative cost is quoted at a lower amount. Which will immediately reduce contribution and also reduce the asset value derived from it".[33]

### (i) *Invention*

The literary meaning of invention is discovery of new thing or technical improvement of the existing product. Now, in both the cases the firm enjoys a reduction in cost i.e. cost effective position. For example, the new diesel rail engine made the old coal engine inoperative in service even though the old coal engine had remaining physical life. Moyer and Moutz discuss that "a distinction should be made between ordinary obsolescence and extraordinary obsolescence. Ordinary obsolescence deals with normal technical progress, while extra ordinary obsolescence relates to premature abandonment of asset for some sudden and unforeseen causes. To predict with reasonable accuracy the effect of the factor of obsolescence upon the history of any particular unit of plant is obviously quite difficult".[34]

### (ii) *Cessation of Demand*

Another major factor of obsolescence is cessation of demand for the product. Now the machine which produced goods may become obsolete either due to failure of the firm to compete with its competitor or shifting of consumer's tastes, preference and fashions. For example, the machine which produced old model telephone set become obsolete with the cessation of its demand.

### (iii) *Changes in Production Technology*

A firm adopts new production technology if it is cost effective. After adopting the new production technology with the help of new machine, the old machine looses its relative importance and discarded due to technical obsolescence. This types of obsolescence are often found in real life, for example, food processing industries, leather industries etc.

### (iv) *Customers Taste, Preference and Need*

With the change in the taste, preference and need of customers, a machine becomes obsolete and ultimately discarded. For example, with the shifting of customer's preference towards new model pen, the machine which produced the old model pen become obsolete and completely write off as a depreciation.

## (d) *Inadequacy*

Inadequacy is one of the causes of depreciation. It occurs when the asset retire due to growth of business. In order words, we can say that an inadequate condition results from increased demands made upon the facilities to such an extent that old machine is unable to produce a high volume of work as every machine suffering from capacity constraint. E.L. Kohler states that "inadequacy is loss of usefulness brought about by business charge; a building or machine may have to be replaced because it cannot be adjusted to an alteration in the character or rate of output".[35] The service life of an asset becomes limited due to changes in physical location of plant and machinery, changes of ownership of the business, expansion in the range of products manufactured or expansion of existing market. Inadequacy may occur due to Government decision not to use certain assets as they are not viable from the view point of control.

## (e) *Accident*

Depreciation may sometimes occur to the assets on account of various accidents. Due to different types of natural calamities like fire, earthquake, flood, volcanoes etc. different assets like plant, furniture, motor car etc. may be destroyed. As a result, depreciation occurs which is called as decrease in the value due to accident.

## (f) *Depletion*

In case of wasting assets like mines, quarries, oil-wells etc. the continuous extractions of mineral or oil reduces their stock and ultimately over the time the said stock gets fully exhausted, and the mine will become valueless.

### (g) *Exhaustion*

This type of depreciation is generally found relating to assets like plantations in the case of agriculture and horticulture, animal etc. They loose their value with the passage of time. They have their utility upto a definite period. After the expiry of the definite period, no utility can be derived from them. They will exhaust in value and become useless.

## Effect of Depreciation

It is very important to judge the effect of depreciation. In most of the cases the amount of depreciation is determined by managerial decision. Naturally, most of the firm use depreciation as an instrument of window dressing. Sometimes the organisation charged depreciation high or low according to their objectives taking the advantages of loopholes of law. According to Sidney Davidson, "it is impossible to state the effect of depreciation accounting unless it is compared with some other method of accounting for long lived physical assets".[36] The effect of depreciation can be discussed from the view point of balance sheet, profit and loss account, working capital and product cost determination.

### *Effect of Depreciation on Balance Sheet*

The result of depreciation accounting is to decrease the book value of the asset to which depreciation accounting applies. This may be done directly or by setting up an account 'Accumulated Depreciation' which is subtracted from the basic asset account on the Balance Sheet. Again if depreciation is not provided for, then fixed asset are shown in the Balance Sheet, at original cost. This lead to not only misstatement of fact but also overstated of fixed asset. This will distort exhibiting true and fair view of financial position of the business to the users of accounting information.

## *Effect of Depreciation on Profit and Loss Account*

An asset is purchased with a motive to earn revenue (profit) by using the asset. This asset causes wear and tear on account of its constant use. Thus, depreciation is charged to Profit and Loss Account like all other business expenses. The result of the depreciation expenses is a decrease in net income and in the retained earnings portion of the shareholder.

The decrease in net income i.e. the lower reported profits resulting from the recording of depreciation may decrease management's willingness to pay higher wages and may lower labour union pressure for wages increases and fringe benefits. The extent to which these possibilities will eventuate, will depend on the kind of labour market in which the firm is operating.[37]

Another possibility of lower reported profit is that dividends may be decreased. However there is no clear evidence that the dividends are a function of the reported income. In certain cases, depreciation accounting may decrease the amount of dividends which the company can legally pay.

Depreciation is a allowable expenses in the process of determining taxable income. So, the tax liability of the firm will be reduced. It is an advantageous position to the company. Again, lower reported profit may effect the credit rating of the firm. This leads to loss of confidence to the Banker, Investor, Creditor etc.

Finally, if depreciation is not charged to Profit and Loss Account, the correct profit cannot be ascertained. Now, under such circumstances, if the profit is distributed to the shareholders as dividend then it is nothing but to pay dividend out of capital. Again, if correct profit is not determined, as a result of depreciation, the profit and loss account obviously looses its True and Fair view position.

## *Effect of Depreciation on Working Capital*

It is a well known fact that the depreciation is a non-cash consuming expenses i.e. for charging depreciation no outflow of cash occurs to any firm. That means the amount which is charged as depreciation will remain in the business until and unless a new asset is purchased for replacement purpose. According to Sidney Davidson, "if a firm operates at a profit or break-even, if all the profits are paid by way of dividends, if no additional non current asset are purchased, and if no non-current liabilities are paid, the working capital will increase by the amount of depreciation."

### *Effect of Depreciation on Product Cost Determination*

Every firm recovers depreciation expenses through product pricing. That means depreciation is form a part of cost of a product. So if depreciation is not determined properly, then the true cost of production cannot be ascertained.

It is known to everyone that closing inventory (stock-in-trade) comprised of closing raw material, closing work-in-progress and unsold finished goods. Now, if the firm valued unsold finished goods at full cost, if depreciation is not charged properly and if closing inventory has a high proportion of finished goods, then closing inventory which is shown in the Balance Sheet does not reflect true and fair view of the firm's position.

## Practical Concepts About Depreciation

Once the different definitions of depreciation have been discussed it will be pertinent to examine how depreciation is viewed in actual practice. We start with the view of Louis Glodberg. According to Louis Goldberg depreciation is a (1) fall in market price, (2) physical deterioration, (3) fall in value, and (4) allocation of cost.[38]

Singer finds that depreciation has been referred to as meaning 1) the systematic amortization of cost without regard to value during life, (2) The exhaustion of service-units embodied in fixed assets (3) the loss in value due to wear and tear, deterioration and obsolescence, (4) physical deterioration and consequent loss in value, and (5) a means to keep real capital intact.[39]

Prof. G.D. Roy observed that the concepts of depreciation related to 1) cost, 2) capital outlay, and 3) value.[40] According to his opinion cost means 'cost less depreciation' where depreciation is merely a device for creating a provision of fund independently, as if, of what might have happened to the asset.[41] Capital outlay means expiration of capital outlay and value means diminution of value.

Eldon S. Hendriksen refers depreciation as a 1) the decline in service potential, (2) the maintenance of capital, and (3) the current cost of service consumed.[42]

Henry R. Hatfield stated that "there is considerable confusion about the nature of depreciation, as practiced by accountants. It has been described variously as a loss, a provision for loss, a recovery of a loss, a decrease in the value of the assets and a maintenance of assets".[43]

According to Bonbright, the technical meanings attached to the term depreciation are variants of four basic concepts: (a) impaired serviceableness, (b) fall in value, (c) difference in value, and (d) amortised cost.[44]

Ronald Ma argued that "the confusion may be traced to the difference between what the accountant is doing and what it is generally assumed that he is doing. He defined depreciation as: (a) measuring the decrease in the value of assets, (b) setting aside funds for the replacement of assets, and (c) charging cost to production."[45]

These views can be summarised into the following categories:

(i) A recognition of the physical or functional deterioration of a fixed asset

(ii) A process of allocation of cost of an asset

(iii) A measure of the maintenance of capital

(iv) A provision for replacement of depreciable assets

(v) A measure of decline in service potential

(vi) A current cost of service consumed.

### (i) *A Recognition of the Physical or Functional Deterioration of a Fixed Asset*

This concept is very popular in text books. These list physical causes consisting of wear, tear and the action of elements and functional causes consist of gradual obsolescence, inadequacy and all other causes. Obsolescence as considered here is that which is the gradual type and which is expected where improvement is constant. The aspect of deterioration has been historically important in gaining depreciation the recognition as a legitimate business expense. However, physical and economic serviceableness may influence the choice of a fixed asset's rate of depreciation but they do not identity the concept.

One point must be remembered that repair and maintenance do not enter the depreciation concept. A firm's standard of maintenance affects an asset's efficiency and life but depreciation accounting may differ from engineering figures, using an asset does not necessarily mean using it up. Although many firm coordinate depreciation and maintenance accounting by aligning depreciation method with estimated future maintenance and repairs.

George A. Mac Farland and Robert D. Ayars explain that depreciation is an expenses arising out of the continuous lessening in the value of fixed assets caused chiefly by wear and tear the effect of the elements and gradual absolescence.[46] K. Mukherjee and S.

Sengupta State that depreciation is often characterised as diminution of value. The common-sense view also relies on the idea. The concept implies that depreciation is the reduction in value of a fixed asset occasioned by physical wear and tear, obsolescence or the passage of time.[47] C. Rollin Niswanger states that all plant assets except land loose their usefulness with the passage of time. The several factors that contribute in varying degrees to this decline in utility are wear, the action of the elements, inadequacy and obsolescence. Accordingly the cost of such assets should be charged to expense in a systematic manner during their useful life. This cost expiration which is periodically matched against revenue is called depreciation.[48]

### (ii) *A Process of Allocation of Cost of an Asset*

The classical definition of the aforesaid concept is that of the AICPA. "Depreciation accounting is a system of accounting... distribute the cost ...over the estimated life... in a systematic and rational manner. It is a process of allocation not of valuation..."[49] Sidney Davidson and James S. Schindler suggest that the central purpose of the depreciation accounting process is to allocate the cost of the asset used to the periods of their use in a reasonable orderly fashion.[50] Montogomery states depreciation is an allocation of the entire cost of depreciable assets to the operating expenses of a series of fiscal periods.[51] According to Harold Bierman, depreciation accounting is generally defined as a systematic procedure for allocating cost of a long lived asset over its useful life.[52]

### (iii) *A Measure of the Maintenance of Capital*

Maintenance of capital means keeping intact the same amount of capital (monetary or physical) at the end of a period as the period's beginning so that the entity may be at 'break-even' or have zero income. Here the decrease in value of the assets should be considered as the appropriate measure of depreciation and provision made for it helps the maintenance of capital.[53] Here, depreciation has been defined as a means of measuring whether capital is retained intact for further use. Three comments can be made in respect of this definition. First, depreciation cost does not differ from other costs as cause of the retention of capital both with respect to dividend policy and otherwise. Retaining capital intact is the role of revenue i.e., recovering costs and expenses. Second, capital and costs must be stated in the same rupees as revenue in order to make the measurement of capital maintenance meaningful and capital must signify not merely an aggregate of historical money amounts but the purchasing power of the business. Third, assuming absence of price-level changes, a period's plant cost consumption is fully recovered by revenue if the period shows a profit and is partly recouped in case of a loss.[54]

## (iv) *A Provision for Replacement of Depreciable Assets*

Depreciation accounting has been adopted mainly for two purposes: one is economic and the other one is accounting. The economic purpose is one of providing for the replacement of capital goods consumed in operations, the accounting purpose is the one of income determination. Replacement may mean physical replacement, replacement of output capacity and value, although a concern sometimes is to restore to current assets, through the depreciation provision, the amount diverted earlier to non-current assets.[55] According to G.T. Webb, there is no objection to the use of depreciation provisions within a business as working capital to finance an increase in current assets or to purchase additional fixed assets until such time as the depreciating fixed assets require replacement.[56]

Replacement of depreciable assets by way of depreciation may mean either (1) that depreciation is taken in order to reserve funds for asset replacement, or (2) that depreciation itself reserve funds by designating them for replacement purchases, or that depreciation provides funds. A study published by the National Association of Accountants in 1958 reveals that generally management is concerned with the effect of depreciation policy on the flow of cash to fixed assets and back but that for various reasons it has not adopted a policy of using special depreciation procedures in order to reserve replacement funds.[57]

### (v) *A Measure of Decline in Service Potential*

Another important opinion regarding depreciation is a periodic decline in the value of the fixed assets which provides service to the firm. Historical cost of an asset is practically equal to the aggregated of all the services or benefits that are expected to be generated over its working life. Here, it is assume that the cost of the assets represents the "store of expected flows of service that will be derived throughout the life of it". This store of expected services decreases due to various economic reasons such as use, decrease in demand, obsolescence etc.[58] So a part of its historical cost which is equal to its decrease in value of asset should form a part of the production cost termed as depreciation and deducted from the revenue of the corresponding period. Committee on Concepts and Standards on Depreciation, of the American Accounting Association (AAA) also expressed same view.

### *(vi) A Current Cost of Service Consumed*

Under this concept the current cost of the service consumed in a year practically equals depreciation for the period. This concept stresses on charging depreciation on current replacement cost instead of historical cost of fixed asset. Sprouse and Moonitz in

Accounting Research Study (ARS)-3 expressed that depreciation represents an allocation of current costs and the depreciation charge for a period is the current cost of services consumed in that period.[59] This concept similar to that of process of allocation of cost concept with the only difference that the later method concerned with original cost but the former concept stressed on replacement cost of the asset. This concept is more realistic when replacement is needed even at the time of inflation but measurement of replacement cost of fixed asset is a troublesome job.

## Controversy Relating to Fund Creation Through Depreciation

Depreciation is the value of service received from the fixed assets in the process of generating revenue out of operation. It is one of the areas of controversy because of it's strange characteristics. It is the expired cost of capital. It is a valid expense and charged against profit. On the other hand, it is not a cash consuming expense i.e. though profit is determined after charging depreciation but no cash has to be paid to the outside agencies for charging depreciation. The amount of depreciation remains in the business in the form of current asset, untill and unless new assets are purchased by the company. So sometimes a question is raised whether depreciation is a source of fund or not. Some argue that it is surely a source of fund while others say depreciation cannot be a source of fund. Let's examine both of their opinions.

### *Depreciation: A Source of Fund*

Finance managers consider that depreciation plays a vital role in financing the fund. As per their opinion, in most of the cases depreciation alone constitutes a major portion of inflow of fund or sources.

According to G.D. Roy, "the source of fund may be understood in the sense that increases fund from what it was in the beginning of a period".[60] There are, in general, three recognised sources of fund: i) issue of shares, debentures and long term loan, ii) sale of unused fixed assets and long term investments and iii) net profit from operation. In connection with the third source of fund, it may be generally said that operation generate funds through sales or revenue but the entire sales do not add to fund during a period under consideration. From sales all actual and expected expenses are deducted to find out profit from operation. But the depreciation provision made against revenue during the period is a non-cash item, hence added back to net profit and accordingly fund set aside equivalent to this provision makes an additional source of funds over and above net profit. According to E.W. Walker, "Depreciation can constitute a source of fund only when it is supposed that every fund returned to the business—whether from depreciation or from any other expenses and available for use are considered a source of fund".[61] According to B. Banerjee, "Depreciation when charged to revenue as an expenses also sets aside or segregates in the same way, a fund equal to it out of revenue".[62]

Sale of an asset either fully or partially is treated as a source of fund. Now, as within the sale price of the goods produced, depreciation is definitely added, so sale price includes depreciation. As a matter of fact, then, when the sale price is realised, the amount of depreciation on assets is also realised. And, depreciation is a part-value of the asset. So it appears as if a part of the asset is sold and the amount is realised. If the sale of any asset or part of any asset is treated as a source of fund, then this recovery of capital in the form of flow of depreciation back to the business should be treated as a source of fund. E.W. Walker observed that "the contemplated loss of a part of the fixed asset for cash easily compares with cash-sales of fixed assets which is always treated as a source of fund".[63]

According to ICAI "As a fixed asset may be converted into cash through sales so as excess provision may be converted into reserve by transfer".[64]

Fund usually refers to working capital and money received in exchange of both profit and depreciation enhances working capital. But how much of closing working capital is contributed by profit and how much by depreciation cannot be separately demarcated. Hence, if money earned from net profit is considered a source then money from depreciation should also be treated a source of fund.

## *Depreciation: Not a Source of Fund*

The idea that depreciation is a source of fund is according to many academics, nothing but misleading and erroneous as well.[65] In accounting, depreciation is a allocation of cost of fixed asset over the useful life. If must therefore, be remembered that depreciation is the accountant's of matching cost of fixed assets with the benefits derived from those assets, so depreciation is not a source of fund.[66] According to Anthony, Robert and James "The funds flow occur when fixed assets are acquired, moreover at that time the flow is a use (investment) of funds not a source. Depreciation simply spreads that outflow over the life of the assets for purpose of measuring result of operations".[67]

Like wages and other overhead expenses, depreciation is one kind of expenses. As with wages and other expenses depreciation is recovered through sale of manufactured goods. Hence if depreciation a source, wages and other expenses should be similarly treated. For funds, it needs an external connection. Truly speaking, depreciation has no external connection. It is just an internal adjustment. So depreciation cannot be accepted as a source of fund. Harold Bierman and Allan R. Drebin rightly observed that "Funds are not generated by charging or occurring depreciation;

they are created by sales". According to ICAI "Depreciation does not generate funds as the funds actually flow from the sales revenue".[68]

Ronald Ma pointed out that "depreciation, of course, does not 'provide funds'. The confusion here is, firstly, between a book keeping entry and a separate financial transaction. Secondly, the object of the capital maintenance rule is to maintain intact the invested in the enterprise, in money terms at least, and not the individual assets. The point, however, might have been over emphasized. Admittedly, only trading revenue can provide funds, but a charge for depreciation does not retain funds which might otherwise have been distributed."[69]

The fact that depreciation is added to net profit for computation of fund from operations cannot be considered a sound judgement for treating depreciation a source of fund. It is added to on the logic that it is a non-cash expenses i.e. an expenses for which money did not flow out. Non-cash expenses deflate sources since they are deducted from sales, the main source of fund to have a measure of net profit. Again if production occurred but no sales are made during fiscal period, no funds are derived from operation whatever and how big is the annual depreciation charge. In the opinion of Lester E. Heitager and Serge Matulich, "Depreciation expenses reported on the income statements does not require the use of either cash or working capital, because no current assets or liabilities are affected by the recording of depreciation. Depreciation is therefore known as a non fund item on the income statement, it neither provides nor uses funds".[70]

W.A. Paton rightly observed that "many people appear to believe that the process of depreciation accounting—occurring depreciation—automatically provides funds, and that all that is necessary to obtain more money is to accrue more depreciation. This is a completely mistaken view. Accounting is an important instrument of business administration but fortunately or unfortunately it has no magic power. Funds are provided by the delivery of product to customers at a price, not by accounting. Moreover, there is very little realism in the notion that the flow of funds from customers can be increased merely by increasing the amount of plant cost charged to current operations. No doubt there are some roundabout relationships between cost accounting and the volume of receipts from customers, but it is day-dreaming to imagine that such receipts increase or decrease automatically as depreciation cost is increased or decreased."[71]

If depreciation is considered a source of fund, it logically follows that when necessary, fund may be collected by charging depreciation at higher rate. In other words, in needs the management may adopt this technique and can avoid the trouble of issuing shares, debentures or accepting loan to collect fund. It is ridiculous and fanciful. Charles T. Horngren express his view that "if depreciation is really a source of fund, a firm may double or triple its depreciation charges when funds are badly needed".[72]

Unlike other operating expenses, depreciation does not use cash or working capital. However, it can in directly influence the flow of funds by affecting the firm's tax liability. Depreciation, calculated as per income tax rules is tax deductible, thus the tax liability of the firm will be reduced. There will be less outflow of cash to the income tax authority. Except through its impact on tax liability depreciation expenses has no effect on working capital.[73]

Richard Brealey and Steward Myers observed that "depreciation tax shields contribute to project cash flow but they are not valued separately; they are just folded into project cash flow along with dozens or hundreds of other specific inflows and outflows".[74]

The claim that depreciation serves as a source of fund mainly steams from the reality that depreciation is a non-cash cost expense and provision for depreciation therefore makes available an amount of fund out of current flow of revenue for replacement leaving aside the question of the impact of price changes on the adequacy fund for replacement. Now the question is even if we accept that depreciation is a source of fund. Can it work as such under all the circumstances? The answer to this question depends on whether the fund is operating at: (1) above break-even point (BEP), (2) at BEP, and (3) below BEP on the one hand; and on the amount of depreciation charged against revenue and amount of revenue flow on the other. The possible consequences at different activity levels may, therefore, be summed up as follows:

### (1) *Above BEP (i.e., revenue > total cost)*

Depreciation, being charged against revenue as an expenses is treated as a source of fund. Because it is free, unlike other cash-consuming expenses, a fund that is not required to recover any past loss of liquid assets or fund or cash and this free cash easily compares with cash-sales of fixed assets which is always treated as a source of fund.

### (2) *At BEP (i.e., revenue = total cost)*

Depreciation is fully recovered and it accordingly sets aside a fund out of revenue. The position does not change even when activity increases.

### (3) *Below BEP (i.e., revenue < total cost)*

Where loss > depreciation, whole of depreciation charged remains unrecovered and accordingly charging depreciation is such a situation cannot set aside any fund out of revenue.

When loss < depreciation, only a part of depreciation can be recovered out of revenue and the portion recovered will represent yielding of fund out of revenue.[75]

## REFERENCES


1. Eric L. Kohler, *Dictionary for Accountants*, New Jersey, Prentice-Hall Inc, 1957, p. 165.
2. *Oxford Dictionary of Business English for Learners of English* Edited by Allene Trck, Calcutta, Oxford University Press, 1994, p. 128.
3. Peter Males and Nicholas Terry, *The Hand Book of International Financial Terms*, Oxford, Oxford University Press, 1999.
4. *Webster's New Twentieth Century Dictionary*, Second Edition, 1977.
5. *Industrial Accountant's Encyclopaedia Dictionary*, Prentice-Hall Incorporation, Prepared by Editorial Staff of Prentice-Hall, p. 207.
6. *Encyclopaedia Britannica*, London, Encyclopaedia Britannica Inc., Vol. 7, 1973, p. 268.
7. *The New Columbia Encyclopaedia*, London, Columbia University Press, 1975, p. 748.
8. *The Encyclopaedia Americana*, New York, American Corporation International, Lexington Avenue, Vol. 8, H-Q 575.
9. *The American Accounting Association (AAA) Committee*, Concepts and Standards, 1957, p. 4, 6, *cited from*, L.S. Porwal, *Accounting Theory—An Introduction*, New Delhi, Tata McGrow—Hill Publishing Company Limited, 1996, p. 246.
10. *The American Institute of Certified Public Accountants (AICPA)*, Accounting Terminology Bulletin No. 1, 1953, *cited from*, Gokul Sinha, *Accounting Theory*, Calcutta, Book World, 1986, p. 143.
11. *International Accounting Standard Committee (IASC)*, International Accounting Standard—4, *cited from*, John Blake, *Accounting Standards*, London, Longman, 1981, p. 199.
12. The Institute of Chartered Accountant of India (ICAI), *Compendium of Statements and Standards Accounting*, New Delhi, 1993 p. A-35.
13. *The Institute of Chartered Accountants of England and Wales*, Recommendation No. IX, 1945, *cited from*, M.M. Jinnah, *Depreciation Accounting—A Study of Practices of Indian Business*, Bombay, Himalaya Publishing House, 1989, p. 32.
14. Adam Smith, *The Wealth of Nations (Everyman edition)*, London 1910, Vol. 1, p. 252.

15. Alfred Marshall, *Principles of Economics*, Eighth Edition, London 1920, p. 237.
16. *Ibid.*, p. 279.
17. R.A.D. Egerton, "The Capital Coefficient and the Rate of Depreciation" *The Economic Journal, cited from* G.T. Webb, *Depreciation of Fixed Assets*, Australia, The Law Book Co. of Australia Pvt. Ltd., 1954, p. 115.
18. R.F. Fowler, *The Depreciation of Capital—Analytically Considered*, London 1934, pp. 10, 1 and 8.
19. R.G. Hawtrey, *Capital and Employment*, London 1937, pp. 41, 80 and 95.
20. J.M. Keynes, *The General Theory of Employment Interest and Money*, London, 1936, pp. 98-99.
21. *Ibid.*, p. 99.
22. Lawrence R. Dicksee, *Auditing—A Practical Manual for Auditors*, London, Gee & Co. (Publishers) Ltd., Tenth Edition, pp. 656, 659.
23. Irish, *Auditing Theory and Practice, cited from* G.T. Webb, *Depreciation of fixed Assets*, Australlia, The Law Book Co. of Australia Pvt. Ltd., 1954, p. 66.
24. Lawrence R. Dicksee, *op. cit.*, p. 674.
25. Walter W. Bigg, *Spicer & Pegler's Practical Auditing*, Indian Edition by S.V. Ghatalia, New Delhi, Allied Publishers Pvt. Ltd, 1999, pp. 628-624.
26. William Pickles, *Accountancy*, London, The English Language Book Society, 1960, p. 168.
27. Eric L. Kohler, *op. cit.*, p. 164-65.
28. Montogomery, *Auditing Theory and Practice,* cited from, M.M. Jinnah, *op. cit.,* p. 13.
29. G.J. Ponsonby, "Depreciation with Special Reference to Transport", in W.T. Baxter and Sidney Davidson Edited, *Studies in Accounting Theory*, Sweet & Maxwell Ltd., 1962, p. 259.
30. M.M. Jinnah, *op. cit.,* p. 17.
31. Eric L. Kohler, *op. cit.*, p. 165.
32. *Ibid.,* p. 166.
33. John Matthews, "Yield—Value Depreciation", *The Accountant*, Vol. 162, No. 4975, April 23, 1970, p. 598.
34. Moyer and Mautz, *Intermediate Accounting, cited from*, M.M. Jinnah, *op. cit.*, p. 21.
35. Eric L. Kohler, *op. cit.*, p. 166.

36. Sidney Davidson, *Handbook of Modern Accounting*, New York, Mc. Graw-Hill Book company, p. 18-3.
37. *Ibid.*, p. 18-3.
38. Louis Goldberg, *Concepts of Depreciation*, Sydney, The Law Book Company of Australsia Pty. Ltd., 1969, p. 4.
39. Frank A. Singer, "Depreciation—Better Left Unsaid", *Accounting Review*, Vol. 32, July, 1957, P. 406, *cited from*, Levis D. Mc Cullers and Richard G. Schroeder, *Accounting Theory Text and Reading*, Santa Barbara, John Wiley & Sons, p. 252.
40. G.D. Roy, *Anatomy of Depreciation*, Calcutta, The World Press Private Limited, 1977, p. 45.
41. *Ibid.*, p. 22.
42. Eldon S. Hendiksen, *Accounting Theory*, Homewood, Richard D. Irwin Inc., 1977, p. 390-91.
43. Henry R. Hatfield, "What They Say about Depreciation", *Accounting Review*, Vol. XI, No. 1, March 1936 pp. 18-26, *cited from*, Ronald Ma, "Accounting for Depreciation," *Accountancy*, Vol. LXXV, No. 855, November 1964, p. 978.
44. James C. Bonbright, *The Valuation of Property*, New York, Mc Grow Hill, 1937, P. 183, *cited from*, Ronald Ma, *op. cit.*, p. 978.
45. Ronald Ma, *op. cit.*, p. 979.
46. George A. Mac Farland, Robert D. Ayars and Willard E. Stone, *Accounting Fundamentals*, New York, Mc. Grow Hill Book Company Inc., 1957, p. 241.
47. K. Mukherji and S. Sengupta, "Depreciation—Theory and Its Uses", *Studies in Accounting Theory*, Edited by K. Mukherji and G.D. Roy, p. 208.
48. C. Rollin Niswanger and Philip E. Fess, *Accounting Principles*, Chicago, South Western Publishing Co., Ninth Edition, p. 253.
49. AICPA, *op. cit.*, p. 25.
50. Sidney Davidson, James S. Schindler and Roman L. Weil, *Fundamental of Accounting*, Illinois, The Dryden Press, Hinsdale, p. 409.
51. Montogomery, *Auditing Theory and Practices, cited from*, M.M. Jinnah, *op. cit.*, p. 28.
52. Harold Bierman, *Managerial Accounting—An Introduction*, New York, the Macmillan Company, 1959, p. 118.
53. Gokul Sinha, *Accounting Theory*, Calcutta, Book World, 1986, p. 145.

54. Levis D. Mccullers and Richard G. Schroeder, *Accounting Theory Text and Readings*, Santa Barbara, John Wiley & Sons, p. 258.

55. *Ibid.*, p. 254.

56. G.T. Webb, *Depreciation of Fixed Assets*, Australia, The Law Book Co. of Australia Pvt. Ltd., 1954, p. 19.

57. NAA, Current Practice in Accounting for Depreciation Research Report No. 33, April, 1958, pp. 10-13 *cited from*, Levis D. McCullers and R.G. Schroeder, *op. cit.*, p. 254.

58. Gokul Sinha, *op. cit.*, p. 144.

59. Sprouse and Moonitz, *Accounting Research Study (ARS) No. 3, Published by AICPA cited from*, Eldon S. Hendriksen, *op. cit.*, p. 391.

60. G.D. Roy, *op. cit.*, p. 4.

61. E.W. Walker, *Essentials of Financial Management*, New Delhi, Prentice-Hall of India Ltd., 1978, p. 157.

62. B. Banerjee, *Financial Policy and Management Accounting*, Calcutta, The World Press Private Ltd., 1999, p. 259.

63. E.W. Walker, *op. cit.*, pp. 157-58.

64. The Institute of chartered Accountant of India, *A Guide to Company Audit, cited from* G.D. Roy, *op. cit.*, p. 4.

65. B. Banerjee, *op. cit.*, p. 260.

66. I.M. Pandey, *Financial Management*, New Delhi, Vikas Publishing House Pvt. Ltd., 1998, p. 62.

67. Anthony, Robert and James, *Management Accounting Principles, cited from*, I.M. Pandey, *op. cit.*, p. 62.

68. Harold Bierman and Allan R. Drebin, *Financial Accounting—An Introduction, cited from*, M.M. Jinnah, *op. cit.*, p. 64.

69. Ronald Ma, *op. cit.*, p. 979.

70. Lester E. Heitger and Serge Matulich, *Managerial Accounting*, New York, McGraw-Hill Book company, Second Edition, p. 830.

71. W.A. Paton, "Significance of Depreciation Accounting—With Special Reference to Plant Replacement" in W.T. Baxter and Sidney Davidson Edited, *op. cit.*, p. 275.

72. Charles T. Horngren, *An Introduction to Management Accounting*, New Delhi, Prentice-Hall of India Pvt. Ltd., 1984, p. 578.

73. I.M. Pandey, *op. cit.*, p. 62.

74. Richard Breaby and Stewart Myers, *Principles of Corporate Finance*, Auckland, McGraw-Hill International Book Company 1985, p. 559.
75. B. Banerjee, "Depreciation as an Internal Source of Fund: A Conceptual Problem", *Business Studies*, Vol. VI, No. 2 July 1980, p. 50.

# 3

# Methods of Depreciation

Depreciation is a allowable expenses in general accounting purposes and income tax accounting purposes. But it differ categorically from other conventional expenses because depreciation charge does not occur any outflow of business fund. This chapter deals with the different methods of depreciation with their merits and demerits so that a firm is in a position to choose the best method.

The periodical amount of depreciation is affected by the following factors[1].

1. the cost of the asset;
2. the life of the asset;
3. the expected residual value of the asset;
4. and, by the method of depreciation selected for amortisation of the asset which must be systematic and rational.

Cost of asset means the basic acquisition cost of the asset plus all incidental expenses which are required to the asset into use. The incidental expenses like freight, import duty, Brokerage, legal expenses and installation charges are also form a part of cost of asset. There are some controversies regarding repairs and maintenance cost. In general, heavy repairs and maintenance cost which increases the life of the asset or keep the asset in its usable state[2] are also to be capitalised.

The useful life of an asset is the period of time during which the firm expects to use the asset for earning revenue[3]. It is not an easy task to estimate an accurate life of the asset. The useful service life of an asset may come to an end whether as a result of physical causes or as a result of changing economic significance or both[4]. Ronald Ma observed that "the life of the asset is the shorter of the life determined by (a) physical wear and tear, taking the maintenance policy of the firm into account, (b) obsolescence, and (c) where a machine has been installed to exploit a wasting asset, the period of exploitation or in the case of a machine with a specialised function the period determined by the effective and sufficient demand for its products."[5] The physical, engineering life of the asset can be determined with a fair degree of accuracy, but technological obsolescence and demand for a product cannot be determined easily. So, instead of exact working life only the probable useful period may be assumed through rational approach like, past experience, quality of asset, expert's opinion, consulting asset's manual, statistical tools for forecasting etc.

Salvage value of an asset refers to the amount that can be expected to realise from disposal of the asset at the ends of its useful life. That means it is the difference between the cost of the asset and the total depreciation during its life. Expecting a few cases, salvage values of retired assets are not of any great significance. Still an incorrect estimate of the salvage value, however small it may be cannot but result incorrect measure of the periodical depreciation[6].

Once the cost of the asset, useful lives and the salvage value are determined the problem of depreciation is reduced to one of finding a suitable basis of allocation of the cost of the asset less salvage value over the periods that use services of the asset. In general accounting practice, the choice of method of allocating the cost of a tangible fixed asset over its effective life i.e. depreciation should depend upon the patterns of expected benefits obtainable in each period from its use. The main problem of this approach is that there is no dependable way to measure the quantum of service that can be received from the asset over its expected service life. In actual practice what happen is that the accountant selects a method to be used as the basis for allocating the depreciable cost.

Sometimes, accountant are guided by a management's policy relating to the allocation of cost of fixed asset. In all the cases, however, the problem boils down to the question of selecting a method which has to be systematic and rational[7].

An interim report on an AICPA accounting research study on depreciation by Charles W. Lamden[8], reported that the focus of much of the dissatisfaction is on the variety of cost allocation methods admissible under generally accepted accounting principles. The only requirement is that the allocation method be 'systematic and rational'.

There is a wide variety of depreciation method in use and all these methods are based upon certain implicit assumptions though they all seek to distribute the cost of the asset over its useful life. These methods can be classified under the following groups[9]:

### (i) Constant Charge Method

This method is based on the assumption that depreciation is a function of time and the service potential which is assumed to decline by an equal amount in each period. Straight line method falls under this category.

### (ii) Variable Charge Method

It is based on the assumption that depreciation is a variable charge rather than a fixed cost. Under this method, it is assumed that the value of an asset declines as a function of use rather than through the passage of time[10]. Usage method e.g. service-hours method, output method fall under this group.

## (iii) Declining Charge Method

Depreciation under this method assumes that the amount of service potential of an asset declines each year. This method is called accelerated method of depreciation[11]. Here the pattern of allocation of cost is such that higher amount of depreciation is charged in the initial years and lower amount of depreciation in the later years. This is based on the assumption that there is larger cash inflows in the earlier years than it is in later years. Higher depreciation in the initial years has a plus point in it. Since it acts as a greater tax shield. Diminishing balance method, sum-of-years'-digits method, double declining balance method are all fall under this category.

## (iv) Increasing Charge Method

This method is based on present value of future cash flow taking into account the time value of money[12]. This method is characterised by the compound interest on the investment of the amount charged for depreciation for ensuring cash flow to meet the replacement cost of the asset. Another assumption under this method is the maintenance of capital. Annuity method, sinking fund method are included under this group.

## (v) Miscellaneous Method

This method comprises those which do not fall within the ambit of the above stated categories. It depends on arbitrary methods of allocation or any combination of time or use basis. Group or composite method, replacement method, revaluation method are included in this group.

Charles W. Lamden[13] indicated that the systematic and rational criteria might have allowed a wide variety of methods. In practice, however, four basic approaches have been followed:

(i) Straight-line apportionment overtime, that is a uniform amount of amortised cost for each period in the estimated life of the property unit.

(ii) Reducing charge methods which produce decreasing amount of amortised cost over the life of the property unit.

(iii) Production and revenue methods which amounts of amortised cost that vary directly with the volume of production or the amount of revenue.

(iv) Compound interest methods which produce increasing amounts of amortised cost over the life of the property unit.

Accountants' Encyclopaedia[14] classified depreciation method under the following categories:

1. Methods producing a uniform charge in each final year
   (a) Straight line method
   (b) Annuity method
2. Methods producing a decreasing charge in each fiscal year (accelerated methods)
   (a) Fixed percentage on declining balance—scientific methods
   (b) Fixed percentage on declining balance—unscientific method (Income tax method)
   (c) Sum-of-years'-digits method or Reducing fraction method
3. Methods producing a fluctuating charge in each fiscal year viz.
   (a) Unit or production method
   (b) Working hours method
   (c) Inventory or Revolution Method
4. Method producing on increasing charge each fiscal year
   (a) Sinking fund method

Grant and Norton classified the depreciation accounting method other than straight line method in the following categories: [15]

1. Consistent methods based on time
   (a) Methods giving smaller writes-off than straight line in early years of life.
      (i) Sinking fund or present worth method
      (ii) Retirement method
      (iii) Replacement method
   (b) Methods giving larger write-off than straight line in early years of life.
      (i) Declining balance method
      (ii) Sum-of-years' digits method
      (iii) Multiple straight-line method
2. Consistent methods based on use
   (a) Production method
   (b) Combination of the production and straight line method
3. Irregular methods
   (a) Retirement reserve method
   (b) Arbitrary write-offs determined annually by management
   (c) Per cent of revenue methods
   (d) Periodic appraisals.

Thus in the accounting literature several methods of allocation of cost (depreciation) have been suggested. In actual practice however, the following methods are in use[16].

1. Straight line method

2. Usage method
   (a) Output method
   (b) Working-hours method
   (c) Mileage method
3. Decreasing charge method
   (a) Diminishing balance method
   (b) Double declining balance method
   (c) Sum-of-the-years'-digits method
4. Interest methods
   (a) Annuity method
   (b) Sinking fund method
5. Other methods
   (a) Revaluation method
   (b) Group or composite method
   (c) Discounted cash flow method
   (d) Replacement method.

Some of the well known methods of depreciation accounting are briefly explained in the discussion that follows:

## Straight Line Method

Under this method, an equal amount is provided each year for depreciation of each asset until the asset has been written down to nil or its scrap value at the end of the estimated life of the asset[17]. The name of this method is derived from the fact if the successive annual depreciation over the life of the asset are plotted on a graph, the result will be a straight line with a slope equal to the annual depreciation. This method is also called 'Fixed Installment Method' because a uniform amount of depreciation is charge each year[18]. The formula of the annual depreciation under the method is:

$$D = \frac{C-S}{n}$$

Where,

D = Annual depreciation.

C = Cost of the asset

S = Salvage or scrap value

n = Estimated life of years.

This method can be recommended only when the following conditions are satisfied.

(a) The asset is expected to render an uniform service through out its estimated useful life[19].

(b) Annual repairs and maintenance costs are assumed to remain constant over its life[20].

(c) The asset is expected to earn an equal amount of revenue each year throughout its life.

(d) The amount of depreciation is a function of time only.

## *Repair Cost*[21]

To mollify, the higher shut down and repair costs in the later part of the asset's life, a partial rectification of this method is possible by estimating the total amount of repair cost over the life of the asset. The depreciation and repairs are accounted for as a unit. The annual cost would then be:

$$\frac{\text{Cost} - \text{Estimated Salvage Value} + \text{Repair Cost}}{\text{Estimated Life in Years}}$$

### *Merits*

There are several merits of the method:

(a) This method is not only simple to understand but also easy to calculate.

(b) The book value of an asset can be fully written off.

(c) The life of the certain assets sometimes depend on contracts like leasehold property, patents, trade marks etc. In such case this method is very much appropriate.

(d) Effective life of an assets, scrap value, repairs and maintenance cost, rate of interest etc. cannot be measured with certainty. So, no single method can weight all the factors at a time with equal importance for fixing the amount of depreciation. From this view point, this method appears most reasonable as some favourable impact of some factors are offset by unfavourable effects of others.

### *Demerits*

As against the advantages enumerated above, the straight-line method has some disadvantages also. Some of the disadvantages are:

(a) This method does not take into account the interest on capital invested on the assets[22].

(b) Under this method the amount of depreciation can never be equal to the value of services rendered from the asset. An asset is expected to render more effective services during earlier period than later period of its useful life as it's efficiency decreases over times.

(c) The charge for depreciation remains constant year to year but the repair and maintenance expenses may go up with the asset growing older and older.

(d) The recovery of 'Real Capital' is not possible under this method as the amount of depreciation remains the same year after year. Only the historical cost is recovered.

(e) This methods ignores the time value of money[23] and inflation factor.

## Diminishing Balance Method

In this method, depreciation is charged at a fixed percentage each year to the net asset balance (i.e. cost less accumulated depreciation). The depreciation charges is higher at the early stages than the later stages i.e. the amount of depreciation decreases gradually although the depreciation rate is fixed. This method is also known as 'Declining Balance Method', 'Written Down Value Method'[24] etc.

### *Formula*

Let,

C = Original cost of the asset.

D = Depreciable value i.e. total depreciation during the service life of asset.

S = Scrap value or residual value (S = C – D).

n = Estimated life of the asset.

r = Rate of depreciation in decimal term

V = Book value (i.e. cost less depreciation) (i.e. $V_1$, $V_2$, $V_3$ ..... $V_n$ be respectively, the book value at the end of the period 1, 2, 3.........n)

$d_1$, $d_2$, $d_3$ ...............$d_n$ be respectively the amount of depreciation at the end of period 1, 2, 3, ..............n

Thus in the first year

$d_1 = C \times r$ ... (1)

$V_1 = C — d_1$ ... (2)

From (1) and (2) we get,

$V_1 = C - C \times r$

or, $V_1 = C (1 - r)$ ... (3)

In the second year,

$d_2 = V_1 \times r$ ... (4)

From (3) and (4) we get,

$d_2 = C (1 - r) \times r$

or, $d_2 = C \times r (1 - r)$ ... (5)

And, $V_2 = V_1 - d_2$ ... (6)

From (3), (5) and (6) we get,

$V_2 = C (1 - r) - Cr (1 - r)$

or, $V_2 = C (1 - r) (1 - r)$

or, $V_2 = C (1 - r)^2$ ... (7)

In the third year,

$d_3 = V_2 \times r$ ... (8)

From (7) and (8) we get,

$d_3 = C (1 - r)^2 \times r$

or, $d_3 = Cr ((1 - r)^2$ ... (9)

And, $V_3 = V_2 - d_3$ ... (10)

From (7), (9) and (10) we get,

$V_3 = C (1 - r)^2 - dr (1 - r)^2$

Or, $V_3 = C (1 - r)^2 (1 - r)$

Or, $V_3 = C (1 - r)^3$ ... (11)

If we follow the equation no. (1), (5) and (9) we can easily determine $d_4$, $d_5$ and so on i.e.

$d_1 = C.r.$

$d_2 = Cr (1 - r)$

$d_3 = Cr (1 - r)^2$

$d_4 = Cr (1 - r)^3$

.................

$d_n = Cr (1 - r)^{n-1}$

Similarly, if we follow the equation no.(3) (7) and (11) we can easily determine the value of $V_4$, $V_5$ and soon i.e.

$V_1 = C (1 - r)$

$V_2 = C (1 - r)^2$

$V_3 = C (1 - r)^3$

$V_4 = C (1 - r)^4$

................

$V_n = C (1 - r)^n$

It appears from the above, both depreciation and the book value of the asset are reducing at a constant rate.

$d_n = Cr (1 - r)^{n-1}$

and $V_n = C(1 - r)^n$

In general terms,

and $d_t = Cr(1 - r)^{t-1}$

and $V_t = C(1 - r)^t$

Where t ranging from 0 to n

Adding periodic depreciation we get

$$D = d_1 + d_2 + d_3 + \ldots\ldots\ldots\ldots\ldots\ldots\ldots + d_n \qquad \ldots (12)$$

By substituting the value $d_1$, $d_2$, $d_3$ etc.

$$D = Cr + Cr(1-r) + Cr(1 - r)^2 + \ldots.. + Cr.(1 - r)^{n-1} \qquad \ldots (13)$$

Multiplying both side of the equation by (1 – r), we get

$$D(1 - r) = Cr(1 - r) + Cr(1 - r)^3 + \ldots\ldots Cr(1 - r)^n \qquad \ldots (14)$$

Subtracting (13) from (14), we get

$$-Dr = -Cr + Cr(1 - r)^n$$

Dividing both side by '– r'

$$D = C - C(1 - r)^n$$

$$\text{or, } D = C[1 - (1 - r)^n]$$

$$\text{or, } \frac{D}{C} = 1 - (1 - r)^n$$

$$\text{or, } (1 - r)^n = 1 - \frac{D}{C}$$

$$\text{or, } 1 - r = \sqrt[n]{1 - \frac{D}{C}}$$

$$\text{or, } 1 - r = \sqrt[n]{\frac{C - D}{C}}$$

$$\text{or, } 1 - r = \sqrt[n]{\frac{S}{C}} \quad (\text{As, } S = C - D)$$

$$\text{or, } r = 1 - \sqrt[n]{\frac{S}{C}} \qquad \ldots (15)$$

To find out the value of $d_1$, $d_2$, $d_3$ etc. directly, we have already shown in terms of general equation i.e.

$d_t = Cr\,(1 - r)^{t-1}$

Where t = Estimated life of the asset which is ranging from 0 to n

It may be written either as $d_t = [\, r\,(1 - r)^{t-1}] \times C$

Thus instead of applying a fixed rate on the diminishing balances of the asset, it is also possible to compute depreciation by applying fluctuating rates on the original cost of the asset.[25]

Diminishing balance method is characterised generally by predetermined fixed rate say 20 per cent, 15 per cent or 10 per cent on the diminishing balance to charged depreciation in each year. But the same result may be obtained under this method by charging depreciation on variable rate on the initial cost of asset. What is needed for the purpose is some mathematical adjustment.

It is observed from the above that a negative acceleration[26] is achieved under diminishing balance method.

## *Merits*

The diminishing balance method of depreciation has some advantages. These are mentioned below:

(a) Under this method, depreciation is calculated according to the service yielding capacity of the asset. As amount of depreciation decreases gradually with the decrease in service potential of asset.

(b) This method can be proved very helpful in adopting the better matching of revenue and expenses as in the first few years depreciation being heavy and repairs light and in the last few years repairs being heavy and depreciation light. The combination of depreciation with the cost of repairs and maintenance is resulted more or less even charge against revenue over the whole life time of the asset.

(c) There is no danger that asset will be over-depreciated since no matter how high the rate of depreciation is taken (less than 100%) there is always something left in the relative ledger account to which the rate would be applied in the next year.[27]

(d) This method is consistent with the principle that book value of an asset should be considered equal to the present value of its remaining service potentials because asset value decrease at higher rate in the earlier parts than in the later parts of the life.

### *Demerits*

There are certain objections to the use of this method. The main objections are as follows:

(a) There is no certainty that the service yielding ability of depreciable assets will always reduce by a constant rate.

(b) This method puts too much emphasis on the historical cost. Proper emphasis is not given on the recovery of capital invested on the asset. Similarly interest on capital invested is also ignored here.

(c) The use of this method mitigates against accurate costing." It has been observed in practice that sometimes the assets can earn more or less the same amount of revenue for a long period of time. In that case, different amount are charged for the use of same assets in different periods cannot be justified.

(d) This method does not give acceptable depreciation charges in either practice or theory where disposal costs of an asset are taken into account for purposes of determining the periodic rate.[28]

(e) If the salvage value is relatively small the methods demands a very high rate of depreciation per annum. Again if the salvage value of the asset becomes zero or negative in that case, the formula has no applicability.

(f) This method requires a good deal of mathematical calculation.

## 'Sum-of-the-Years'—Digits Method

This is another accelerated depreciation method which was introduced by the US Internal Revenue Code of 1954[29]. Under this method the cost less salvage value is charged to different years in the ratio of capital blocked in the asset in the year concerned to the total blockage over its life. This method assumes that depreciation of the first year should be the highest as no portion of the capital has been recovered till then and the depreciation of the last year should be the least of all years because a major portion of the invested capital has been already recovered.

Since depreciation is measured according to the volume of blocked investment, its magnitude is expressed by means of a fraction. The denominator of the fraction, which remains constant is the total of the digits representing the useful life of the asset. The numerator, on the other hand, measuring the blockage of capital in the reverse weighted digits of each year.

***Formula*[30]**

Let,

$D_t$ = Depreciation in period t

C = Cost of the asset

S = Estimated salvage value of the asset

n = Estimated life of the asset in years

t = The year of life of the asset (i.e. 1 is the first year, 2 is the second year and so on)

$\sum_{i=1}^{n} Y_i$ = The sum of the digits from 1 to n = $\frac{n(n+1)}{2}$

The formula for measuring depreciation for a particular year is:

$$D_t = (C - S) \times \frac{n+1-t}{\sum_{i=1}^{n} Y_i}$$

***Merits***

The merits of the method are as follows:

(a) In this method, the quantum of depreciation is greater in the earlier years in comparison with the later years because the benefits received from the use of the asset are greater in the early years than in the later years.

(b) In the earlier year repairs are light but depreciation is heavy but in the later year, as the asset gets older the repairs are heavy but depreciation is light. So depreciation plus repairs will more or less constant every year and the charge to Profit and Loss Account should be uniform.

(c) If the asset is retired earlier than anticipated as result of unforeseen obsolescence, the loss upon retirement will be less than if straight line depreciation were used, because, asset are recovered at a higher rate in the earlier years where as only a small fraction remains left for recovering them in the later years.

(d) For tax accounting purposes, these methods have a clear advantage over the straight line method. The larger deductions in the early years mean that at the very least tax payments are postponed for a considerable period. On the other hand, this method gives a tax postponement with the greatest present value.

(e) In this method nearly three-fourth of total depreciation is charged within half of its life. That means three-fourth of blocked investment recovered within short span.

(f) This method is very simple to understand and simple to calculate.

(g) This method is preferable for assets with services lives of eight years or more.

### *Demerits*

Although this method is considered to be a great innovation in the field of depreciation accounting but it has some disadvantages which are given below:

(a) This method also ignored the cost of capital on invested fund.

(b) In the earlier year greater depreciation is charged at a result less profit is available for declaring dividend in the earlier year. This may created serious problem for organisation to attract new investor. As dividend is one of the motivating factors for investment. Again more depreciation in the earlier year may resultant the high cost of production in the competitive market.

## Double Declining Balance Method

In the USA the Internal Revenue Code of 1954[31] permitted the tax payers who were using a declining balance method to charge depreciation for tax purpose a maximum of double the rate allowed under straight line method. This method of calculating depreciation was called double declining balance method. This method may be identified as a combination of straight line and diminishing balance method. Like diminishing balance method here the depreciation is charged on the opening written down value of the fixed asset. Like straight line method a fixed rate of depreciation is charged in this method. But the rate used is twice the straight line rate.

It is important to mention here that under this method an over depreciated cost of the asset at the end of the life of asset than its anticipated salvage value. In that case there may be two options to deal with the problem. Depreciation charge for the last year may be adjusted to make salvage value equal to its anticipated salvage value. Alternatively, in the last year the firm may opt out for straight line depreciation for written off the over depreciated salvage value. Again, under most circumstances, the entire depreciation would not be allocated during the life of the asset i.e. the amount of the asset would exceed the salvage value. So that at a point some where near the mid point of the life of the asset, a change is made to the straight line method. If salvage value is zero and the life is an odd digit, the years of change will be n/2 + 1½; if the life is a even digit, the year of change will be n/2 + 2. If the salvage is greater than zero, the year of change will be later than this.[32]

### *Merits*

The advantages of this method are as follows;

(a) In the earlier year more depreciation is charged than later years, so by adopting this method a firm can save tax by lowering its tax liability.

(b) In the initial year high depreciation accompanied with low repairs and maintenance cost and in the later part of asset's life low depreciation accompanied with high repairs and maintenance cost will be tend to make a uniform equitable year after year during the asset's life.

(c) A firm will generate more interest if it invest the depreciation outside the firm. It helps to create more fund at the time of replacement of asset.

(d) The firm will face minimum loss at the time of disposal of asset due to innovation as a large part has already changed to profit and loss account by way of depreciation.

### *Demerits*

Every methods has its own limitation. The main objections against adopting the method are as follows:

(a) This method shows lower profit in the earlier year as high depreciation is charged. It will depict poor performance in the initial year.

(b) The investors are unhappy as they get low dividend in the earlier year for generating lower profit by the firm.

(c) Though it is popular among tax payer but sometimes they face high cost of production due to higher depreciation.

(d) Under this method the asset value can never be reduced to zero.

## Sinking Fund Method

Under this method, depreciation is a provision by charging out of revenue for replacement of an asset and a means of maintaining capital. This method is based on the assumption that a fund is to be built up and that the amount of this fund should equal the total amount of the depreciation at the end of the useful life of the depreciable asset. An equal amount by way of depreciation is set aside by charging to the profit and Loss Account at the end of every accounting period, so that, all such equal installments if allowed to accumulate at a compound interest[33] would equal to the depreciable cost of the asset at the expiry of its useful life. Under all other methods of depreciation liquid cash may not be available to the firm at the time of replacement of asset because in those cases the amount of depreciation is retained in the business. In this method annual equal installment set off as depreciation is regularly invested outside the business in interest bearing easily marketable securities. Interest yielded on such securities is compounded or reinvested in each year. When the life of the asset expires, investments are disposed off and the proceeds are utilised for replacing the old asset. This method is also known as 'Depreciation Fund Method' or 'Redemption Fund Method'.[34]

### *Formula*

Let,

d = Sinking Fund Depreciation.

C = Cost of the asset.

S = Salvage value

i = Rate of interest in decimal term

n = Years

Let it be assumed that the salvage value equal to zero. The

accumulated amounts should then be equal to the cost of the existing asset. The accumulated amount can be obtained from the following:

$$C = d\,(1+i)^{n-1} + d\,(1+i)^{n-2} + d\,(1+i)^{n-3} + \ldots\ldots\ldots + d\,(1+i)^{n-(n-1)} + d\,(1+i)^{n-n}$$

$$\text{or, } C = d\,(1+i)^{n-1} + d\,(1+i)^{n-2} + d\,(1+i)^{n-3} + \ldots + d\,(1+i) + d \quad \ldots (1)$$

Multiplying both side of the equation by (1+i)

$$C\,(1+i) = d\,(1+i)^{n} + d\,(1+i)^{n-1} + d\,(1+i)^{n-2} + \ldots\ldots\ldots + d\,(1+i)^{2} + d\,(1+i) \quad \ldots (2)$$

Subtracting equation (1) from equation (2), we get,

$$C \times i = d\,(1+i)^{n} - d$$

$$\text{or, } C \times i = d\,[(1+i)^{n} - 1]$$

$$\text{or, } d = \frac{C \times i}{(1+i)^{n} - 1} \quad \ldots (3)$$

## *Merits*

The main advantages of this method are as follows:

(a) Under this method, at the end of the specified time, a definite sum is available in cash to replace the old asset.

(b) Since the amount is invested outside the business there is no need to drawn money from the business for replacement purpose at the end of the life of the asset. This helps to avoid pressure on working capital.

## *Demerits*

There are some weaknesses of this method and these are as follows:

(a) From the management view point the method is inefficient. Generally the internal rate of return of the firm is higher than the return on investment. As a result this causes substantial loss to the firm.

(b) There is always a risk factor about the loss on realisation of investments. That means if the market price of the investment in which depreciation is invested fluctuate in that case the amount realised may be less than cost of the asset.

(c) The firm may face the difficulty of finding suitable investments which provide the desired rate of return per annum.

(d) It is difficult to estimate the exact working life of the asset which will be replaced.

(e) The effect of price level change is not considered at all. Since the amount of available fund at the end of the asset does not exceed the historical cost of the asset, the claim that fund invested outside the business will effectively replace the asset, remains doubtful.

(f) Under this method, the amount of depreciation charge does not bear any relation to the intensity of the use of the asset.

(g) This method does not consider the salvage value of an asset, at the end of its working life. It is truly unjustified.

## Annuity Method

The principle underlying this method is that in calculating depreciation regard should be held, not only to the cost of an asset but also to the interest[35] which the capital blocked in that asset would have earned had it been invested outside the business. So under this method, a fixed installment of depreciation is charged against revenue for each year of the life of the asset in such a way that at a given rate of interest the present value of the sum of all those installments equals to the cost of the asset. Stated otherwise, depreciation for each year is made to include an interest on unrecovered capital outlay but the interest which is credited annually to Profit and Loss Account, gradually diminishes. On the other hand, depreciation excluding interest i.e. net depreciation goes on increasing. It may also be noted that Annuity Method of depreciation recovers more than the original cost of the asset. The excess being interest on investment.

## *Formula*

Let,

A = Annuity depreciation

C = Cost of the asset

S = Salvage value

i = Rate of interest in decimal term

n = Estimated life of the asset

It also assume that salvage value is equal to zero.

Then, the present value of A due in 1 year = $\frac{A}{(1+i)}$

the present value of A due in 2 years = $\frac{A}{(1+i)^2}$

So, the present value of A in n year = $\frac{A}{(1+i)^n}$

The sum of the present value of future annuity depreciation is to be equal to the cost of the asset.

$$\text{Then, } C = \frac{A}{(1+i)} + \frac{A}{(1+i)^2} + \frac{A}{(1+i)^3} + \dots\dots\dots + \frac{A}{(1+i)^n} \qquad \dots (1)$$

Multiplying both side of the equation by (1+i)

$$C\,(1+i) = A + \frac{A}{(1+i)} + \frac{A}{(1+i)^2} + \frac{A}{(1+i)^3} + \dots\dots\dots + \frac{A}{(1+i)^{n-1}} \qquad \dots (2)$$

Subtracting equation (1) from equation (2), we get,

$$C \times i = A - \frac{A}{(1+i)^n}$$

$$\text{or, } C \times i = A\left[1 - \frac{1}{(1+i)^n}\right]$$

$$\text{or, } C \times i = A\left[\frac{(1+i)^n - 1}{(1+i)^n}\right]$$

$$\text{or, } A = \frac{C \times i \times (1+i)^n}{(1+i)^n - 1} \qquad \dots (3)$$

## *Merits*

A number of merits can be claimed for this method:

(a) In this method depreciation includes not only the recovery of invested capital but also the interest on capital outlay. So this is more logical and realistic than other methods.

(b) At the time of inflation, it is possible for the firm to replace the asset as total depreciation charged is more than cost of the asset.

(c) This method is most appropriate for the intangible such

as leasehold rights, patents etc. In this cases depreciation varies with the passing of time rather than with the intensity of use.

### *Demerits*

The method has some demerits and these demerits are as follows:

(a) The use of the asset or its service rendering capacity is not at all considered for measuring depreciation. The cost of waiting time rather than the cost of physical deterioration is given more importance in such a case.

(b) In this method, it is assume that the rate of interest on unrecovered capital outlay is equal to its cost of capital but in real world it is hardly happen.

(c) The scrap value of the asset is not considered which is not justified.

(d) Annual repairs and maintenance cost are assumed to remain constant throughout the life of an asset, but it is not so happen.

(e) This methods creates difficulty in measuring depreciation if replacement of old asset with new asset occurs during the life of old asset.

## Insurance Policy Method

This method is similar to the sinking fund method except that instead of investing the money in securities an insurance policy[36] is taken to produce the amount required at the end of asset's life. Here a fixed amount is charged each year to the Profit and Lost Account, but unlike the sinking fund method, the amount is paid to the insurance company as premium at the beginning of each year. As the Insurance Company requires to be paid for the risk it undertakes and it follows that the insurance policy method is a little more expensive than the sinking fund method, but it provides a definite amount at the end of the asset's life.

### *Merits*

The merits of this method are as follows:

(a) In this method, there is a certainty that the guaranteed amount will be received from the insurance company. There is no such risk due to fluctuation in the market price of securities.

(b) There is no need to judge the merit of different securities for investment. Fund is made by paying the premium on insurance policy.

### *Demerits*

Some of the demerits of this method are as follows:

(a) As the insurance company takes the risk and it also makes some profit naturally the interest on insurance policy is less than the rate of interest prevailing in the market. So depreciation charge in this method becomes more expensive.

(b) If new asset is acquired during the life of the old asset this method cannot be used effectively because the contract with the insurance company cannot be changed.

## Discounted Cash Flow Method of Depreciation[37]

Under this method the value of an asset is computed by discounting the future cash flows attributable to the asset. Here depreciation is a measure of change in the discounted value of the asset. This means depreciation is measured the difference between the value of the asset based on the discounted future cash flow at the beginning of the period and the discounted future cash flow at the end of the period. This method is widely used in the field of economics.

### *Formula*

Let,

V = Present value of future cash flows

D = Periodic depreciation

R = Periodic Cash Flows (i.e. $R_1$, $R_2$, $R_3$ ..........$R_n$ be respectively the cash flow at the end of the period 1, 2, 3 ..........n).

i = Rate of interest in decimal term

n = Life of the assets in years

This the value of the asset at the beginning

$$V_o = \frac{R_1}{(1+i)} + \frac{R_2}{(1+i)^2} + \frac{R_3}{(1+i)^3} + \ldots\ldots\ldots + \frac{R_n}{(1+i)^n}$$

$$\text{or, } V_o = \sum_{J=1}^{n} \frac{R_j}{(1+i)^j} \qquad \ldots (1)$$

Then, the value of the asset at the end of 1st year

$$V_1 = \frac{R_2}{(1+i)} + \frac{R_3}{(1+i)^2} + \frac{R_4}{(1+i)^3} + \ldots\ldots + \frac{R_n}{(1+i)^{n-1}}$$

$$\text{or, } V_1 = \sum_{j=2}^{n} \frac{R_j}{(1+i)^{j-1}} \qquad \dots (2)$$

$\therefore$ Depreciation in year 1

$$D_1 = V_o - V_1$$

$$\text{or, } D_1 = \sum_{j=1}^{n} \frac{R_j}{(1+i)^{j-}} - \sum_{j=2}^{n} \frac{R_j}{(1+i)^{j-1}}$$

Similarly, depreciation in year 2

$$D_2 = V_1 - V_2$$

$$\text{or, } D_2 = \sum_{j=2}^{n} \frac{R_j}{(1+i)^{j-1}} - \sum_{j=3}^{n} \frac{R_j}{(1+i)^{j-2}}$$

And, depreciation in year 3

$$D_3 = V_2 - V_3$$

$$\text{or, } D_3 = \sum_{j=3}^{n} \frac{R_j}{(1+i)^{j-2}} - \sum_{j=4}^{n} \frac{R_j}{(1+i)^{j-3}}$$

In this way we can calculate the depreciation in respect of any period. In general term the period is denoted as $D_t$.

$$\therefore D_t = V_{t-1} - V_t$$

$$\text{or } D_t = \sum_{j=1}^{n} \frac{R_j}{(1+i)^{J-t+1}} - \sum_{j=t+1}^{n} \frac{R_j}{(1+i)^{j-t}}$$

$$\text{Again, } V_t = \sum_{J=t+1}^{n} \frac{R_j}{(1+i)^{J-t}}$$

$$\text{or, } V_t = \frac{R_{t+1}}{(1+i)} + \frac{R_{t+2}}{(1+i)^2} + \frac{R_{t+3}}{(1+i)^3} + \ldots\ldots.. + \frac{R_n}{(1+i)^{n-t}} \quad \ldots (3)$$

$$\text{And, } V_{t-1} = \sum_{j=t}^{n} \frac{R_j}{(1+i)^{j-t+1}}$$

$$\text{or, } V_{t-1} = \frac{R_t}{(1+i)} + \frac{R_{t+1}}{(1+i)^2} + \frac{R_{t+2}}{(1+i)^3} + \ldots\ldots.. + \frac{R_n}{(1+i)^{n-t+1}} \quad \ldots (4)$$

Multiplying both side of the equation (4) by (1+i), we get,

$$V_{t-1}(1+i) = R_t + \frac{R_{t+1}}{(1+i)} + \frac{R_{t+2}}{(1+i)^2} + \ldots\ldots.. + \frac{R_n}{(1+i)^{n-t}} \quad \ldots (5)$$

Subtracting equation no (3) from equation (5), we get

$V_{t-1}(1+i) - V_t = R_t$

or, $V_{t-1} + i.V_{t-1} - V_t = R_t$

or, $V_{t-1} - V_t = R_t - i.V_{t-1}$

or, $D_t = R_t - i.V_{t-1}$ [As, $D_t = V_{t-1} - V_t$]

So, the new formula for getting the depreciation at 't'th period:

$D_t = R_t - i.V_{t-1}$ ... (6)

Putting the value t (1, 2, 3..............n) we can easily determine the depreciation for period 1, 2, 3.................. and so on.

$D_1 = R_1 - i.V_o$

$D_2 = R_2 - i.V_1$

$D_3 = R_3 - i.V_2$

.................

$$D_n = R_n - i.V_{n-1}$$

### *Merits*

The merits of this method are as follows:

(a) Under this method depreciation is based on the service potentiality of an asset. So this method in the ideal method for charging depreciation.

(b) This method is widely used in the field of economics.

(c) This method may be used effectively where the firm depends on single asset.

### *Demerits*

Weaknesses of this method are as follows:

(a) Future cash flow may not be correctly known from previous. So this method depends on the expected cash flow.

(b) Forecasted cash flow and actual cash flow may differ, in that case this method gives some unrealistic picture of business.

(c) Cash flow of a business is a joint product of many factors. So, it is difficult to find out the separate cash flow generated by individual asset.

(d) Under this method, it is difficult to forecast the future services of the asset; to value those future services and to determine the appropriate rate (or rates) of discount.[38]

(e) This method needs a good deal of mathematical calculation.

## Use-base Method

Under this method depreciation charge is made a function of usage rather than a function of time. The basic assumption of this method is that with every unit of product the value of the asset reduces proportionately. So depreciation under this method becomes a true variable cost of the product. This method is suitable where individual output can easily be identified, the rate of wage varies from period to period and total usage of the asset over its life can be established reliably.

There are three methods based on this concept:

(i) Output method (ii) Working hours method, and (iii) Mileage method.

### (*i*) *Output Method*

Under this method depreciation charge for the year is made to vary with the number of units produced during the years. To find out depreciation, the cost less salvage value of the asset is divided by the number of units expected to be produced by the asset during its service life.

$$\text{So, Depreciation cost per unit} = \frac{\text{Cost of Assets} - \text{Salvage Value}}{\text{Estimated Number of Units}}$$

Periodic depreciation = Number of units produced during the period X Depreciation cost per unit.

### (*ii*) *Working Hours Method*

This method is suitable where the life of asset is measured by its service hours rather than units produced. To find out depreciation, under this method cost of asset less salvage value is divided by the total working hours during its life.

$$\text{So, Depreciation cost per hour} = \frac{\text{Cost of Assets} - \text{Salvage Value}}{\text{Total Working Hours of the Assets}}$$

Period depreciation = Number of hours worked during the period X Depreciation cost per hour.

## *(iii) Mileage Method*

This method is used in transport industries. The working life of the vehicles like asset is expressed in mileage or kilometers. Depreciation per kilometer is calculated by dividing the cost of the vehicle by the estimated running kilometers it can travel in its life time.

So, Depreciation cost per mile/kilometer =

$$\frac{\text{Cost Less Salvage Value}}{\text{Estimated Miles / Kilomertres Run During the Service Life}}$$

Periodic depreciation = Actual miles or kilometers run by the vehicle during the period X depreciation cost per mile or kilometer.

## Other Methods of Depreciation

### *Depletion Method*

This method is generally applied in case of wasting assets e.g., mines, quarries and natural resources. Here the rate of production is measured by the rate of exhaustion of the asset. Under this method the total reserve of asset is measured by an expert valuer. After that the cost per unit of reserve asset is ascertained by dividing the cost of acquisition of the asset by the total reserve of that asset. Periodic depreciation is calculated by multiplying the reserve of assets exhausted during the period by the cost per unit of reserve asset. The asset reduced to zero at ends of the total exhaustion, so the method is known as depletion method.

### *Revaluation Method*

This method is generally applied to assets like small tools, container, crockery etc. which are not material significance to the business. This method depends solely on the market value of the asset. The basic assumption of this method is that reduction in value of the asset in particular year is its depreciation. Depreciation is calculated here as the difference between the book value as at the beginning of the period and the reappraised value as obtained at the end of the period.[39] In any year, if closing market value exceeds the opening value of the asset, the excess amount is not taken into account.

### *Group or Composite Method*

This method is applied where assets having relatively lower values and keeping separate account is expensive and laborious job. Under this method, depreciation is not calculated individually on different items of asset belonging to the same group or different group of different rates, rather than a average group or composite rate of depreciation is preferred. When the asset are of same characteristic, the method is called group depreciation method and when the asset are of different characteristic the process is called composite depreciation method.[36] The rate of depreciation is calculated by dividing the sum of each assets annual depreciation by the cost of the entire group. For this purpose the average working life of all the assets of group is taken as the base. The disadvantages of this method are that the rate of depreciation is to be changed frequently with the addition of asset and it does not consider the intensity of use of the assets.

### *Selection of a Best Depreciation Method*

Charles W. Lamden[40], on his study, pointed out that 'systematic and rational' ultimately permits almost any method. Fortunately, in practice only a relatively few methods have been used. The choice among even these few methods, however, can have a significant effect on reported income. Without criteria for choosing among the alternatives, companies are almost completely unrestricted in their choice of method and they do choose different methods under apparently similar circumstances. It is also not uncommon for companies to change methods and thereby significantly change reported net income which also affects comparisons between periods.

He again asserted that neither the original choice nor subsequent changes in methods are motivated predominantly by any real effort to report underlying economic circumstances. The proponents of unrestricted choice recognise that such freedom is sometimes abused, but they deny that such abuse is typical. They contended that management most often makes a sincere effort to choose methods which best reported economic reality. To date, this controversy has not been resolved.

It is important that the method selected reflects economic reality. It is also important that the criteria for the choice be clearly understood so that the method be the same in all cases where the circumstances are the same. Most important, arbitrary shifts between methods should be eliminated.

His study also observed that the end objective is to confine variations in methods of accounting for depreciable assets to those justified by substantial differences in circumstances. Further, it could be argued that reducing the acceptable alternatives may not improve the usefulness and comparability of financial statements. There is a substantial group that feels that diversity of practices is needed if depreciation accounting is to reflect the existing diversity to economic circumstances in a truly comparable and useful way, even if a variety of practices is desirable, it does not necessarily follow that the decision to use given methods must be unrestricted. Rather, sufficient criteria should be established so that the choices among alternatives will be based on valid differences in relevant circumstances.

Depreciation is a mandatory charge. The management of a firm must select a depreciation method for income tax purposes and for financial accounting purposes. The firm needs not, however choose the same depreciation method for both income tax purposes and financial reporting purposes. In both cases, the selection is subject to constraints. For income tax purposes, the method must be one of these that are approved by Income Tax Rules. For financial accounting purposes, the method must be one that falls within the purview of generally accepted accounting principles (GAAP). Specially for Indian Company, for financial accounting purposes, the method is guided by the Companies Act 1956. So in both the cases, the selection of a suitable method is limited by law.

If the firm selects same method of depreciation both for income tax accounting purposes and for financial accounting purposes, only one set of depreciation records need to be maintained and hence the cost of the accounting process will be lower. Despite this fact, some firms select to use approved depreciation method for income tax purposes and other method for financial accounting purposes.

## REFERENCES

1. L.S. Porwal, *Accounting Theory*—An Introduction, New Delhi, Tata McGraw—Hill Publishing Company Limited, 1996, p. 251.
2. G.D. Roy and A.K. Basu, "The Methods of Depreciation", *Studies in Accounting Theory*, Edited by K. Mukherji and G.D. Roy, The World Press Pvt. Ltd., 1981, p. 267.
3. L.S. Porwal, *op. cit.*, p. 252.
4. G.D. Ray and A.K. Basu, *op. cit.*, p. 266; Sidney Davidson, *Handbook of Modern Accounting*, New York, McGraw-Hill Book Company, p. 18-5.
5. Ronald Ma, "Accounting for Depreciation", *Accountancy*, Vol. LXXV, No. 855, November 1964, p. 978.
6. G.D. Roy and A.K. Basu, *op. cit.*, p. 267.
7. Sidney Davidson, *op. cit.*, p. 18-9.
8. Charles W. Lamden "Depreciation—A Reliability Gap", reprinted in *The Journal of Accountancy*, Vol. 133, No. 4, April 1972, p. 68.

9. L.S. Porwal, *op. cit.*, p. 254.
10. Eldon S. Hendriksen, *Accounting Theory*, Delhi, Khosla Publishing House, 1984, p. 395.
11. G.D. Roy, *Anatomy of Depreciation*, Calcutta, The World Press Private Limited, 1977, p. 51.
12. L.S. Porwal, *op. cit.*, p. 254.
13. Charles W. Lamden, *op. cit.*, p. 70.
14. Accountants' Encyclopaedia, Vol. I, p. 177, cited from, M.M. Jinnah, *Depreciation Accounting—A Study of Practices of Indian Business*, Bombay, Himalaya Publishing House, 1989, p. 77.
15. Eugene L. Grant and Paul T. Norton Jr., *Depreciation*, The Ronald Press Company, New York, 1955, p. 185.
16. L.S. Porwal, *op. cit.*, p. 253.
17. G.T. Webb, *Depreciation of Fixed Assets*, Australia, The Law Book Co. of Australia Pvt. Ltd., 1954, p. 24.
18. Gokul Sinha, *Accounting Theory*, Calcutta, Book World, 1986, p. 147.
19. Gokul Sinha, *op. cit.*, p. 147.
20. Eldon S. Hendriksen, *op. cit.*, p. 396.
21. Sidney Davidson, *op. cit.*, pp. 18-10.
22. Gokul Sinha, *op. cit.*, p. 148.
23. Sidney Davidson, *op. cit.*, pp. 18-10.
24. M.M. Jinnah, *op. cit.*, p. 94.
25. G.D. Ray and A.K. Basu, *op. cit.*, p. 272.
26. G.D. Ray, *op. cit.*, p. 64.
27. G.T. Webb, *op. cit.*, p. 26.
28. D.J. Brown, "Time to Abandon Reducing Balance Method?", *Accountancy*, Vol. LXXXII, No. 938, October 1971, p. 586.
29. Sidney Davidson, *op. cit.*, pp. 18-11.
30. *Ibid.*
31. M.M. Jinnah, *op. cit.*, p. 89.
32. Sidney Davidson, *op. cit.*, p. 18-13.
33. G.D. Roy, *op. cit.*, p. 74.
34. M.C. Shukla and T.S. Grewal, *Advanced Accounts*, New Delhi, S. Chand & Company Ltd., 1989, p. 217.
35. G.D. Roy, *op. cit.*, p. 77.
36. William Pickles, *Accountancy*, London, The English Language Book Society, 1960, p. 175.
37. Eldon S. Hendriksen, *op. cit.*, p. 373.
38. G.D. Roy, *op. cit.*, p. 101.
39. Gokul Sinha, *op. cit.*, p. 160.
40. Charles W. Lamden, *op. cit.*, pp. 68-70.

# 4

# Regulatory Requirements Concerning Depreciation Accounting in India

This chapter deals with the regulatory requirements concerning depreciation accounting in India. It has three sections viz., Depreciation under Companies Act 1956, Accounting Standard on Depreciation (AS-6) and Depreciation under Income Tax Act 1961. The methods of depreciation discussed earlier in Chapter-III reveal that the amount of depreciation provided in a year on an asset by a firm differs according to the method of depreciation followed. A firm can choose any one of the different methods for charging depreciation. The only exception is a company, for financial accounting purposes in India, the choice of selecting a method is regulated by the Companies Act, 1956. Thus, in case of companies, section 205 and 350 of the Companies Act, 1956 with Schedule XIV, govern the provisions regarding charging of depreciation for the purpose of divisible profit, computation of managerial remuneration etc. Compliance with accounting standards has been made mandatory according to subsection (3A) to section 211 of the Companies (Amendment) Act 1999. It requires that every profit and loss account, and balance sheet shall comply with accounting standards. Accounting standards mean the standards of accounting issued and recommended by the Institute of Chartered Accountants of India (ICAI) and prescribed by the Central Government in consultation with the National Advisory Committee on Accounting Standards (NACAS) constituted under section 210A(1) of Companies (Amendment) Act, 1999. A company, for tax accounting purposes has to follow the provisions of Income Tax Act, 1961 for charging depreciation. So for discharging the tax liability a company is bound to follow the section 32 of the Income Tax Act 1961. The provisions of Companies Act, AS-6 and Income Tax Act as aforesaid are discussed briefly in the following sections.

## Depreciation Under Companies Act, 1956[1]

Section 205 of the Companies Act 1956 prescribes the methods of charging depreciation. Section 205 of the Companies Act requires that no dividend shall be declared or paid by a company except out of the profits of the company arrived at after providing for depreciation in accordance with the provisions of sub-section 2 of that section. The relevant extracts of section 205 (2) thereof are as follows:

... depreciation shall be provided either

(a) to the extent specified in section 350; or

(b) in respect of each item of depreciable asset, for such an amount as is arrived at by dividing ninety-five per cent of the original cost thereof to the company by the specified period in respect of such asset; or

(c) on any other basis approved by the Central Government which has the effect of writing off by way of depreciation ninety-five per cent of the original cost to the company of each such depreciable asset on the expiry of the specified period; or

(d) as regards any other depreciable asset for which no rate of depreciation has been laid down by this Act or any rules made thereunder, on such basis as may be approved by the Central Government by any special order in any particular case.

Provided that where depreciation is provided for in the manner laid down in clause (b) or clause (c), then, in the event of the depreciable asset being sold, discarded, demolished or destroyed the written down value thereof at the end of the financial year in which the asset is sold, discarded, demolished or destroyed, shall be written off in accordance with the proviso to section 350.

According to clause (a) of section 205 (5)

*"Specified period" in respect of any depreciable asset shall mean the number of years at the end of which at least ninety-five per cent of the original cost of that asset to the company will have been provided for by way of depreciation if depreciation were to be calculated in accordance with the provisions of section 350.*

Section 205 (2) with section 205 (5) (a) allows the company to provide for depreciation either in the manner specified in section 350 of the Act or in the alternative manners specified in 205 (2) section itself. Section 350 deal with the ascertainment of depreciation. According to section 350 -

*The amount of depreciation to be deducted in pursuance of clause (K) of sub-section (4) of section 349 shall be the amount calculated with reference to written-down value of the assets as shown by the books of the company at the end of the financial year expiring at the commencement of this Act or immediately thereafter and at the end of each subsequent financial year at the rate specified in Schedule XIV.*

Provided that if any asset is sold, discarded, demolished or destroyed for any reason before depreciation of such asset has been provided for in full the excess, if any, of the written-down value of such asset over its sale-proceeds or as the case may be, its scrap value, shall be written off in the financial year in which the asset is sold, discarded, demolished or destroyed.

An important changes has been made by Amendment Act of 1988 delinking the rates of depreciation under Income Tax Act and specifying the rates in the Act itself by way of Schedule XIV. This Schedule equally applicable to section 205 relating to computation of depreciation.

Now companies are required to provide for depreciation as per the rates prescribed in Schedule XIV for purposes of this Act. The rates of depreciation under Schedule XIV have come into force from 02.04.1987. It may be noted that for purposes of payment of managerial remuneration, depreciation to be calculated at written down value rates, irrespective of the fact that the company is charging depreciation on straight line method rates in its annual accounts for the purpose of section 205.

Schedule XIV provided the different categories of asset and its rate of depreciation under different method and shift. For the purpose of the Companies Act, depreciation has to be calculated in accordance with the rates specified in Schedule XIV. The salient features of the Schedule are as follows:

1. Assets have been divided into four categories, viz., (i) building, (ii) plant and machinery (iii) furniture and fittings and (iv) ships. Under each of the above categories, several items of assets have been included and for each of them or group of them depreciation rates have been prescribed under two alternative methods i.e. the written down value method (WDV) and straight line method (SLM). A company may adopt any of the said two methods of depreciation and apply appropriate rate of depreciation. The concept of 'specified period' laid down in clause (a) of section 205 (5) is therefore no longer relevant on adoption of straight line method of depreciation under clause (b) of section 205 (2).
2. In respect of plant and machinery, two sets of depreciation rates, general rate and special rate have been prescribed, under WDV method and SLM method. General rate is applicable in respect of items of plant and machinery and continuous process plants i.e. designed to operate 24 hours a day. The items of plant and machinery, which are covered by special rates have been put under four categories and for each of the said categories separate rates of depreciation have been laid down.

3. In respect of furniture and fittings, there is a general rate apart from a special rate for furniture and fittings used in specified business and/or for specified purposes.

4. In respect of ships there are two categories viz., ocean going ships which is sub-divided into three categories and vessels ordinarily operating on inland waters which is again sub-divided into two categories and a general rate is given for each under two methods.

5. The Schedule provides for three separate rates of depreciation for single shift, double shift and triple shift working under each of the aforesaid two methods viz., the WDV method and SLM method.

6. The rates of depreciation for double shift and triple shift working have been laid down only for assets covered under the head plant and machinery and not for any other assets. Even, in respect of plant and machinery, the rates of depreciation for double and triple shift working have not been prescribed for all the items. As for plant and machinery which is covered by general rate of depreciation, extra shift depreciation is not required to be charged in respect of several items as stated in Para 6 of Notes to the Schedule.

7. Where, during any financial year, any addition has been made to an asset, depreciation thereon shall be calculated on a pro rata basis from the date of such addition.

Similarly, where an asset has been sold, discarded demolished or destroyed during any financial year, depreciation shall be calculated on pro rata basis up to the date on which such asset has been sold, discarded etc. Excess if any of the written down value of such asset over its sale proceeds or, as the case may be its scrap value, shall be written off in the financial year in which the asset is sold, discarded etc.

8. Depreciation on the basis of rates provided for double or triple shift working shall have to be provided only when the concern has actually so worked during the financial year. In case the concern has not worked on single, double or triple shift uniformly throughout the financial year, the calculation for extra depreciation for double or triple shift working as required to be made separately in the proportion which the number of days for which the concern worked double or triple shift as the case may be, bears to the normal number of working days during the year, For this purpose, the normal number of working days during the year shall be deemed to be:

   (a) in the cases of seasonal factory or concern, the number of days on which the factory or concern actually worked during the year or 180 days whichever is greater;
   (b) in any other case, the number of days on which the factory or concern actually worked during the year or 240 days whichever is greater.

No extra shift depreciation has to be charged under category 'D' for which 100 per cent depreciation is chargeable on single shift basis.

9. Depreciation on assets whose actual cost does not exceed Rs. 5000/- shall be provided at the rate 100 per cent. Where however the aggregated actual cost of individual items of plant and machinery casting Rs. 5000 or less, constitutes more than 10 per cent of the total actual cost of the plant and machinery, rates of depreciation applicable shall be the rates as specified in item II of Schedule XIV. [Notification GSR No. 101(E), dated 01.03.1995]

10. As regards to the disclosure of depreciation policy, the depreciation method followed and also the depreciation rates or the useful lives of the assets as adopted by a company, if

they are different from the rates of depreciation specified in Schedule XIV have to be disclosed in the annual accounts.

11. As regards depreciable assets, for which no rates of depreciation has been laid down in the Schedule, depreciation is required to be provided on such basis as may be approved by the Central Government—vide clause (d) of sub-section 205 (2).

Department of Company Affairs under Ministry of Industry of Government of India issued several clarifications time to time regarding depreciation. The most relevant clarifications are as under:

## (1) *Charging Higher Rates of Depreciation*

The rates as contained in Schedule XIV should be viewed as the minimum rates, and therefore, a company shall not be permitted to charge depreciation at rates lower than those specified in the Schedule in relation to assets purchased after the date of applicability of the Schedule. However, if on the basis of a bona fide technological evaluation, higher rates of depreciation are justified, they may be provided with proper disclosure by way of a note forming part of annual account (Circular 2 of 1989, dated 07.03.1989).

## (2) *Recomputation of Specified Period*

Specified period once computed need not be recomputed. The companies may, therefore, continue to charge depreciation at the old straight line method rates (in spite of new rates of depreciation prescribed under Schedule XIV) in respect of the already acquired assets against which depreciation has been provided in earlier years on straight line method (SLM) basis. (Circular No. *ibid*).

## (3) *Immovable Property Acquired for Investment Purpose*

The Department has opined that as such immovable properties unless they are acquired for resale represent fixed assets, it would be obligatory to provide depreciation thereon (Circular No. 10-CL-VI/61 dated 27.09.1961). These views of the department may not be applicable where a property has been acquired merely as investment and is not being used for any business purpose.

### (4) *Adoption of Different Methods for Different Types of Assets*

A company may adopt more than one method of depreciation. Thus, it is permissible to follow different methods for different types of assets provided the same methods are consistently adopted from year to year in accordance with section 205 (2). Also units in different geographical locations can follow different methods of depreciation provided the same are consistently followed (Circular No. *ibid*).

### (5) *Depreciation When WDV is Already 5 Per cent*

A company following the SLM need not provide any depreciation on assets the WDV when it is already 5 per cent of the original cost (Circular No. *ibid*).

### (6) *Charging Depreciation Whether Assets Used or Not*

The Department has opined that according to accepted accounting principles, depreciation also arises from efflux of time, and so, it would be necessary for the purpose of section 205 to provide for depreciation even on the assets which were not in use during the financial year (Circular No. ibid).

### (7) *Depreciation in Respect of Multiple-shift Working*

If the asset concerned are used for more than one shift, the shift allowance will have to be taken into consideration for the purposes of section 205 (5) (a) and section 350. (Circular No. 10 (1) CL-VI dated 27.09.1961).

## *(8) Can Straight Line Method (SLM) Rates be Different than Those Specified Under Schedule XIV ?*

It is clarified that a company must necessarily provide SLM at the rates prescribed under Schedule XIV and the interpretation that fractions of years cannot be taken into account is not correct (Circular No. 2 of 1989, dated 07.03.1989).

## (9) *Revision of Rates of Depreciation-Schedule XIV*

Notification No. 756 (E), dated 16.12.1993 has made three basic changes; firstly a new category of machinery called 'continuous process plant' will carry a higher rate of depreciation on straight line method basis and written down value basis. However, no extra shift depreciation will be allowed. Secondly the furniture and fixture used for hotels and other entertainment industry will carry higher rate of depreciation. Thirdly, the assets upto value of Rs. 5000 can be written off in the year of purchase entirely.

The changes made in Schedule XIV as per the amending notification shall apply in respect of accounts of the companies closed on or after the date of issue of the notification. The revised rate of depreciation shall apply to assets acquired by the companies on or after that date. As regards applicability of these changes to existing asset, the companies are advised to follow the recommendation of the Institute of Chartered Accountants of India contained in its Guidance Notes on the "Accounting for Depreciation in Companies." (Circular No. 14/93, date 20.12.1993)

## (10) *Disallowed of 'Unit of Production' Method*

The Department of Company Affairs has stated that it disapproves use of 'unit of product' based computation of deprecation for the purpose of section 205 (2) (b) of the Companies Act, 1956, as the same ignores the impact of time element in depreciation and has a potential to be manipulative. Further, if allowed it may prolong the life of the asset beyond its specified life.

Part I of Schedule VI to the Companies Act shows the form of balance sheet. Regarding fixed assets this Schedule clarifies specified that under each head the original cost, and the additions thereto and deductions there from during the year and the total depreciation written off or provided up to the end of the year to be stated.

As per the requirements of Part II of Schedule VI to the Companies Act, the company will have to provide the depreciation on the total book value of the fixed asset. Para 3(iv) of Part II of the Schedule VI to the Companies Act requires disclosure of the amount provided for depreciation, renewals or diminution in value of fixed Assets. If such provisions is not made by means of depreciation charge, the method adopted for making such provision should be disclosed. If no provision for depreciation is made the fact that no provision has been made shall be stated and the quantum of arrears of depreciation computed in accordance with section 205(2) of the Act shall be disclosed by way of a note.

'Revaluation Reserve' which is created by a company by transferring the difference between the revalued figure and the book value of the fixed assets. Depreciation is required to be provided with reference to the total value of the fixed assets as appearing in accounts after revaluation. In this circumstance, the additional depreciation related to revaluation may be adjusted against 'Revaluation Reserve' by transfer to Profit and Loss Account. Such a disclosure would appear to be in consonance with the requirement of Part I of Schedule VI to the Companies Act, prescribing disclosure of write-up in the value of fixed assets for the first five years after revaluation.

## Accounting Standard on Depreciation Accounting (AS-6)

The Institute of Chartered Accountants of India (ICAI) not being a regulatory body cannot on its own force company to follow mandatory accounting standards unless they are backed by relevant statutory approval. If a company does not follow the mandatory accounting standards, the auditors who are the members of ICAI, have to qualify their audit reports, failing which they will be guilty of professional misconduct. According to subsection (3) of section 227 requires the auditors to report whether, in his opinion, the profit and loss account and balance sheet comply with the accounting standards referred to in section 211(3c). SEBI and the Indian Companies Act made the implementation of accounting standards by prepares of financial statements compulsory for listed companies and the corporate sector respectively. According to clause 50 of the Listing Agreement it is mandatory for the companies listed in a recognised stock exchange to comply with all applicable accounting standards in the preparation and presentation of financial statements. Section 217(2AA) of the Companies Act also held a responsibility on the Board of Directors to comply with mandatory accounting standards. As per this section, the Boards report shall include a director's responsibility statement indicating therein[2] (a) the applicable accounting standards have been followed with proper explanation relating to material departure if any; (b) the director's had selected such accounting policies and applied them consistently and made judgements and estimates that are reasonable and prudent so as to give a true and fair view of the state of affairs of the company; (c) that the directors had taken proper sufficient care for the maintenance of adequate accounting records in accordance with the provisions of this Act for safeguarding the assets and for preventing and detecting frauds and other irregularities, and (d) that the directors had prepared the accounts on a going concern basis.

According section 211(3B) of the Companies Act, where the financial statements do not comply with the accounting standards, such companies shall disclose (a) the deviation from the accounting standards; the reasons for such deviation; and (c) the financial effect, if any, arising out of such deviation. For the purpose of this section, the expression accounting standards mean the accounting standards recommended by ICAI, as may be prescribed by the Central Government in consultation with the National Advisory Committee on Accounting Standards established under section 210A(1). Provided that the standards of accounting specified by ICAI shall be deemed to be the accounting standards untill the accounting standards are prescribed by the Central Government under this section. Before discussing As-6, let us discuss briefly the objectives of accounting standards and the formation and function of Accounting Standard Board (ASB) in India.

Accounting standards usually mean the set of official rules pronounced by accounting bodies from time to time to guide their members to tackle the problems they face in their practice[3]. Accounting standards may be viewed as a method of resolving potential conflicts of interest between the various user groups which have access to company accounts and reports. The basic objectives of accounting standards are as follows:

(i) To provide uniformity in preparation of the companies annual financial statements. In other words, the standards are developed to harmonize the diverse accounting policies and practices adopted by different companies. The harmonization process makes accounting information comparable across different companies which enables the financial statements users to properly interpret the information contained in the financial statements of different companies for their investment decisions[4].

(ii) To disclose the accounting bases in order to guide judgement of professional accountants to ensure that the bases of measurements involved and qualities of presentation of data are consistently manifested in the information disclosed[5].

(iii) To improve the quality of 'Annual Report' to enable present and potential investors in making rational investment, credit and similar decisions[6].

The motivation and explicit encouragement for standard setting by ICAI in India has primarily come from external influences, such as the International Accounting Standards Committee (IASC). Prior to 1970, there are virtually no effort, systematic or otherwise, on the part of accounting profession to even initiate the standard setting process. It was in 1976 that because of impetus from the membership of the IASC, the Institute of Chartered Accountants of India (ICAI) decided to undertake the task of setting the accounting standards. Recognising the need to harmonize the diverse accounting policies and practices used by the companies in India and also by keeping in mind the international developments in accounting, the council of the Institute established the Accounting Standards Board (ASB) on 21st April, 1977[7]. The main functions of ASB are[8].

(i) To formulate, Accounting Standard after considering the laws, customs, usages and business environment in India and with reference to International Accounting Standards;

(ii) To propagate the Accounting Standards and persuade the concerned parties to adopt them in the preparation and presentation of financial statements.

(iii) To issue guidance notes on the Accounting Standards and give clarification on issues arising there from.

(iv) To review the Accounting Standards at periodical intervals.

The ICAI issued Accounting Standard on Depreciation (AS-6) under the caption 'Depreciation Accounting' in November, 1982[9]. This standard deals with the accounting for depreciation and the disclosure requirements in connection therewith. In the initial years, this accounting standard will be recommendatory in character. During this period, this standard is recommended for use by companies listed on a recognised stock exchange and other large commercial, industrial and business enterprises in the public and private sectors[10].

In the context of insertion of Schedule XIV in the Companies Act in 1988 the ICAI brought out a Guidance Note on accounting for Depreciation in Companies which came into effect in respect of accounting periods commencing on or after 1st April, 1989. The Guidance Note differs from AS-6 in respect of accounting treatment of (a) change in the method of depreciation and (b) change in the rates of depreciation. It was clarified in the Guidance Note, with regard to the matter under (a) that AS-6 would be revised to bring it in line with the recommendations of the Guidance Note[11].

On the basis of recommendations of the ASB, the council of the ICAI at its meeting held on 26-29, 1994 decided to bring AS-6 in line with the Guidance Note in respect of both of the aforementioned matters. Accordingly, it was decided to modify paragraphs 11,15,22 and 24 and delete paragraph 19 of AS-6. Similarly, in the contest of delinking of rates of depreciation under the Companies Act from those under the Income Tax Act as per Companies (Amendment) Act, 1988, the council decided to suitably modify paragraph 13 of AS-6. An announcement to this effect was published in due course. The accounting standard on depreciation i.e. AS-6 has been made mandatory in respect of accounts for period commencing on or after 01.04.1995.

The accounting standard in respect of Depreciation Accounting occurs in paragraphs 20-29 of this statement. Preface to the statements of Accounting Standard occurs in paragraph 1-19[12]. On minute reading of the Accounting Standard (AS-6), it is found that

Introduction, definitions, explanation and disclosure have been stated in paragraph 1-19.

Introduction consists of paragraph 1 and 2. Certain types of assets which are not under the purview of depreciable assets are stated in paragraph 1.

Definitions regarding depreciation, depreciable assets, useful life and depreciable amount are given in paragraph 3.1,3.2,3.3 and 3.4 respectively.

Explanation comprises of paragraph 4-16. Some general information like determination of cost of asset, useful life, residual value have been explained in the paragraph 4 to 10. These information and clarification are similar to that of information which is included in Companies Act and Income Tax Act.

Paragraph 11 is very relevant in this context. According to paragraph 11 "The quantum of depreciation to be provide in an accounting period involves the exercise of judgement by management in the light of technical, commercial, accounting and legal requirements and accordingly may need periodical review. If it is considered that the original estimate of useful life of an asset requires any revision, the unamortised depreciable amount of the asset is charged to revenue over the revised remaining useful life."

According to paragraph 12, in the context of paragraph 11, the standard gives an open hand to management for selecting a suitable 'depreciation method' at their own choice.

According to paragraph 13 of the standard if the rate of depreciation laid down in Companies Act differs with the rates revised by the management based on estimated useful life, the difference is to be accounted for properly.

Disclosure of net surplus due to disposed, discarded etc. is included in paragraph 14.

Paragraph 15 is very important. It deals with the change in the method of providing depreciation.

This paragraph is similar to that of paragraph 21 which is discussed later on.

Disclosure relating to, amount of depreciation, depreciation on revalued assets and any change in the method of depreciation is stated in paragraph 17 to 19.

The main text of this standard is discussed in the paragraph 20 to 29. The paragraphs are as under:

*Paragraph* 20: The depreciable amount of a depreciable asset should be allocated on a systematic basis to each accounting period during the useful life of the asset.

*Paragraph* 21: The depreciation method selected should be applied consistently from period to period. A change from one method of providing depreciation to another should be made only if the adoption of the new method is required by statute or for compliance with an accounting standard or if it is considered that the change would result in a more appropriate or presentation of the financial statements of the enterprise. When such a change in the method of depreciation is made, depreciation should be recalculated in accordance with the new method from the date of the asset coming into use. The deficiency or surplus arising from retrospective recomputation of depreciation in accordance with the new method should be adjusted in the accounts in the year in which the method of depreciation is changed. In case the change in the method results in deficiency in depreciation in respect of past years, the deficiency should be charged in the statement of profit and loss. In case the change in the method results in surplus, the surplus should be credited to the statement of profit and loss. Such a change should be treated as a change in accounting policy and its effect should be quantified and disclosed.

*Paragraph* 22: The useful life of a depreciable asset should be estimated after considering the following factors:

(i) expected physical wear and tear;

(ii) obsolescence;

(iii) legal or other limits on the use of the asset.

*Paragraph* 23: The useful lives of major depreciable assets or classes of depreciable assets may be reviewed periodically. Where there is a revision of the estimated useful life of an asset, the unamortised depreciable amount should be charged over the revised remaining useful life.

*Paragraph* 24: Any addition or extension which becomes an integral part of the existing asset should be depreciated over the remaining useful life of the asset. The depreciation on such addition or extension may also be provided at the rate applied to the existing asset. Where an addition or extension retains a separate identity and is capable of being used after the existing assets is disposed of, depreciation should be provided independently on the basis of an estimate of its own useful life.

*Paragraph* 25: Where the historical cost of a depreciable asset has undergone a change due to increase or decrease in long term liability on account of exchange fluctuations price adjustment, changes in duties or similar factors, the depreciation on the revised unamortised depreciable amount should be provided prospectively over the residual useful life of the asset.

*Paragraph* 26: Where the depreciable assets are revalued, the provision for depreciation should be based on the revalued amount and on the estimate of the remaining useful life of such assets. In case the revaluation has a material effect on the account of depreciation, the same should be disclosed separately in the year in which revaluation is carried out.

*Paragraph* 27: If the depreciable asset is disposed off, discarded or demolished, the net surplus or deficiency if material should be disclosed separately.

*Paragraph* 28: The following information should be disclosed in the financial statements:

(i) the historical cost or other amount substituted for historical cost of each class of depreciable assets,

(ii) total depreciation for the period for each class of assets; and

(iii) the related accumulated depreciation.

*Paragraph* 29: The following information should also be disclosed in the financial statements along with the disclosure of other accounting policies:

(i) depreciation methods used; and

(ii) depreciation rates or the useful lives of the assets if they are different from the principal rates specified in the statute governing the enterprise.

The Guidance Note on 'changing of depreciation in case of revaluation of assets' is very important on the subject of accounting for depreciation because there is no clear cut policy either in Companies Act or in AS-6 in this respect. So as per recommendation issued by ICAI, a 'Revaluation Reserve' is created by a company by transferring the difference between the revalued figure and the book value of the fixed assets. Depreciation is required to be provided with reference to the total value of the fixed assets as appearing in the accounts after revaluation. In these circumstances, the additional depreciation relating to revaluation may be adjusted against 'Revaluation Reserve' by transfer to Profit and Loss Account. Therefore, a company can transfer an amount equivalent to the additional depreciation from Revaluation Reserve. Such transfer from Revaluation Reserve should be shown in the Profit and Loss Account separately and an appropriate notes by way of disclosure would be desirable. The Revaluation Reserve is not available for payment of dividends.

Paragraph 5 of Guidance Note on Accounting for Depreciation in Companies stated that a company may adopt more than one method of depreciation. Thus, it is permissible to follow different methods for different types of assets provided the same methods are consistently adopted from year to year in accordance with section 205 (2). Also units in different geographical location can follow different methods of depreciation provided the same are consistently followed.

Paragraph 12 of the Guidance Note on Accounting for Depreciation in Companies recommended Schedule XIV requires that where the company has worked extra shift, the multiple or extra shift depreciation will have to be provided on the plant and machinery, wherever applicable. In this regard, various units/departments/mills/ factories should be taken as separate concerns.

The most interesting point to note is that even the revised version of AS-6 permits the use of 'any method' for calculating depreciation. The flexibility provided by the AS-6 to management in choosing the depreciation method will affect the comparability of accounting information across different companies if the "diversity" in the depreciation methods selected by the management is not narrowed[13].

## Depreciation Under Income Tax Act, 1961[14]

Depreciation under section 32 (1) of Income Tax Act is allowed as a deduction at a prescribed rate on tangible and intangible assets subject to certain conditions.

### *Tangible Assets Which are Eligible for Depreciation*

The following are the assets on which depreciation is allowed: (a) building, (b) machinery, (c) plant and (d) furniture.

(a) *Building*: The word 'building' is not defined in the Act. Its meaning has, therefore, to be taken in its ordinary sense after taking into consideration of judicial pronouncements on building.

- Building does not include land
- A structure with or without a roof to be regarded as a building.
- Building includes roads, bridges, culverts, wells and tube-wells.

(b) *Machinery*: Like 'building' the word 'machinery' has not been defined anywhere in the Act. Therefore, one has to depend upon natural meaning and decided cases.

- Machinery need not be self-contained unit capable of being put to use by itself and may be part of a bigger machinery.
- Machinery is a complex combination of mechanical parts.

(c) *Plant*: The word 'Plant' is defined under section 43(3) to include ships, vehicles, books, scientific apparatus and surgical equipment used for the purpose of the business or profession but does not include tea bushes or livestock or "buildings or furniture and fittings".

(d) *Furniture*: As the word 'furniture' is not defined in the Act, its meaning in common parlance has to be ascertained. Furniture includes all articles of decoration or convenience use for the purpose of furnishing an office or place of trade or manufacturing.

## *Condition to be Satisfied to Claim Depreciation*

One should satisfy the following conditions to avail depreciation.

(a) asset must be owned by the assesses.

(b) it must be used for the purpose of business or profession; and

(c) it should be used during the relevant accounting year.

(a) *Asset Must be Owned by the Assessee*: In order to claim depreciation allowance, the assessee has to show that such assets are owned by him or the assessee is the co-owner of the asset. Only the owner of the assets is entitled to claim depreciation on them. The Supreme Court in its judgement held that the real test was to ascertain whether the assessee was entitled to the income from the property and hence, the owner must be the person who can exercise the rights or the owner not on behalf of the owner but it has own right.

The following points are important regarding ownership.

(i) Registered owner Vs. Beneficial owner: There are two types of owner, one registered owner and another beneficial owner. Registered owner is that owner who has a registered document conferring legal title. Beneficial owner for the purpose of claiming depreciation is a person who can exercise the rights of owner.

(ii) Property taken on Lease: Lessee cannot avail depreciation as he is not the legal owner of the leased assets. The lesson, on the other hand, is entitled for depreciation in respect of such asset. There is however, one exception to this rule. If an assessee carries on business or profession in a building not owned by him but in respect of which he holds a lease or other right of occupancy, he is entitled to depreciation in respect of capital expenditure incurred by him after March 31, 1970 on construction of any structure or any work in relation to the building by way of improvement, renovation or extension.

(iii) Property of partnership firm: The partnership firm is entitled to claim depreciation on immovable assets brought by partners as their capital contribution, even if such assets are not registered in the name of the firm under the Transfer of Property Act.

(iv) Property taken on Hire Purchase: If an assessee makes use of any such asset in his business without being the legal owner of the asset as under the hire-purchase agreement, he is not entitled to depreciation allowance for the same. Mortgage of an asset or its after as security for payment to the balance of purchase consideration subsequent to the transfer of ownership will not deprive the purchaser of his right to depreciation.

(v) Depreciation on Fractional Ownership: After the amendment in section 32(1) by the Finance (No. 2) Act 1996, depreciation will be admissible even in respect of fractional ownership of an asset with effect from the assessment year 1997-98.

(b) *Asset Must be Used for the Business or Profession*: To claim depreciation, the assets must have been used for the purpose of business or profession. Actually control determines, who is using it. 'User' means not only getting benefit, but also controlling, running, stopping, repairing, replacing etc.

Following points are relevant in this context:

(i) *Passive Vs. Active User*: The use of the asset should be understood in a wide sense as to embrace passive as well as active user. If a machine is kept ready for use at any moment in a particular factory, under an express agreement, from which taxable profits are earned, the machine can be said to be 'used' for the purpose of the business which earned profits, although in fact it had not worked during the year.

(ii) *Assets Used Partly for Business Purposes*: Under section 38 (2) where any building, machinery, plant or furniture is not exclusively used for the purpose of the business or profession, the deduction under section 32 (1) (ii) shall be restricted to a fair proportionate part thereof which the Assessing officer may determine, having regard to the user of such building, machinery, plant or furniture for the purpose of the business or profession.

(c) *Asset Must Used During the Relevant Accounting Year*: Depreciation is allowed only if the asset is used for the purpose of business or profession at least for sometime during (not necessarily throughout) the previous year. Even user during any part of the year would be sufficient to enable the assessee to claim depreciation for the whole year. However from the assessment year 1992-1993, where an asset is acquired and put to use for the purpose of business or profession for less than 180 days during the previous year in which it is acquired, depreciation there on shall be allowed at 50 per cent of the depreciation allowable according to the percentage prescribed in respect of the block of assets comprising such asset.

The Indian Income Tax Act, 1961 as amended up to date also specified the cases where depreciation as a charge against revenue is not permissible. These are stated below:

(i) In case a car (use on hire for tourists) is acquired between 01.04.1967 and 28.02.1975, depreciation will not be allowed in respect of cost in excess over Rs. 25,000 as per section 43 (1).

(ii) According to section 32(1)(ii), foreign car acquired after 28.02.1975 but before 01.04.2001 is not available for depreciation. However, depreciation will be allowed if the car is used as a taxi on hire for tourists (Indian or foreigner) or is used by the assessee outside India in his business or profession carried on in another country and where a foreign made car is acquired after 31.3.2001 and used for business purposes in India.

(iii) Any machinery or plant if actual cast thereof is allowed as a deduction in one or more years under agreement entered into by the Central Government under section 42.

The Income Tax Act incidentally also specified the factor to be reckoned in the determination of an amount as an allowance for depreciation charges. These are stated below:

1. Method of depreciation
2. Rates of depreciation
3. Block of assets
4. Actual Cost
5. Written down value.

1. *Method of Depreciation:* Depreciation is allowed on the basis of actual cost in the first year and written down value in subsequent years in respect of all assets. In other words, reducing balance method is used under the Income Tax Rules.

But from the assessment year 1998-99, an undertaking engaged in generation or generation and distribution of power can claim depreciation (in respect of assets acquired after March 31, 1997) in case of tangible assets according to any one of the following methods:

(i) Depreciation can be claimed according to straight line basis at the percentage specified rate to the Income Tax Rules.

(ii) Alternatively, such undertaking can claim depreciation, at its option, according to written down value method like any other assessee on the basis of block of assets.

It is important to mention here that in the case of power generating unit, depreciation is available on straight line basis method in respect of tangible assets acquired after March 31, 1997. To claim depreciation on written down basis under the block system, an option has to be exercised before the due date of furnishing the return of income under section 139 (1).

So a power generating unit can have straight line basis method only in respect of tangible assets acquired after March 31, 1997. For assets acquired before April 1, 1997, a power generating unit does not have any option but to claim depreciation on the basis of written down basis under block of assets system.

2. *Rates of Depreciation*: Depreciation is computed at the specified rates on the closing balance of each 'block of assets' under different categories of assets. The main features of the rate of depreciation as per Income Tax Rules are as follows:

(i) Assets have been divided into four categories, viz., (1) building, (2) furniture and fittings, (3) machinery and plants and (4) ships. Under each of the above categories several items of assets have been included and for each of them or group of them, depreciation rates have been prescribed under written down value method.

(ii) Depreciation at the rate of 100 per cent is to be charged for certain categories of assets under building and machinery and plants.

(iii) No extra-shift allowance will be available from assessment year 1988-89 onwards.

(iv) In respect of building, there are four categories of asset, depreciation is ranging from 5 per cent to 10 per cent, in special case it is 100 per cent.

Furniture and fittings are in single category, depreciation is prescribed at the rate of 15 per cent.

Under the head machinery and plants assets are subdivided into nine categories and the rate of depreciation ranges from 20 per cent to 100 per cent.

When the asset concerned is a ship. Ships are classified into three distinct categories and the rate of depreciation is 25 per cent for each category.

A flat rate of 25 per cent is prescribed for intangible assets.

In case of power generating unit, depreciation is available on straight line basis method in respect of tangible assets acquired after March 31, 1997. Tangible assets, in case of power unit, have been divided into sixteen categories from (a) to (p). Under each of the categories one or more item(s) of assets have been included and for each of them or group of them depreciation rates have been prescribed under straight line method basis and the rate of depreciation varies from 1.95 per cent to 33.40 per cent of actual cost.

*Computation of Additional Depreciation*: Section 32 has been amended with effect from the assessment year 2003-04 to provide for a additional depreciation. To claim additional depreciation the following conditions should be satisfied.

(a) The assessee should be engaged in the manufacture of production of any article or thing (may be priority sector item or even non-priority sector item given in the Eleventh Schedule)

(b) Additional depreciation is available only in respect of new plant and machinery acquired and installed after March 31, 2002.

(c) Any plant and machinery which has been acquired and installed after March 31, 2002 by an assessee is qualified for additional depreciation. However certain assets are not eligible for additional depreciation for example, ships and aircrafts, any office appliances or road transport vehicles.

(d) Additional depreciation will not be available unless the assessee furnishes the details of machinery or plant and increase in the installed capacity of production in Form No. 3AA along with the return of income and the report of a chartered accountant, certifying that the deduction has been correctly claimed in accordance with the provisions.

*Rate of Additional Depreciation*: Additional depreciation shall be available @ 15 per cent of actual cost. If, however, the asset is put to use for less than 180 days in the year in which it is acquired the rate of additional depreciation will be at the rate of 7.5 per cent of actual cost.

3. *Block of Assets*: For charging depreciation on tangible assets used is a business are classified in various blocks depending on the class of assets i.e, building, furniture, plant and machinery and the rate of depreciation allowed in respect thereof. The term 'block of assets' has been defined by section 2 (11) to mean a group of assets falling within a class of assets comprising.

(a) tangible assets being building, machinery, plant or furniture.

(b) intangible assets being know-how, patents, copy rights, trademarks, licences, franchises or any other business or commercial rights of similar nature, in respect of which the same percentage of depreciation is prescribed.

A taxpayer may have 18 different block of assets out of which block 1 to 11 are in respect of tangible assets and block 12 to 18 are in respect of intangible assets.

For the purpose of out study, we only concentrated on the blocks 1 to 11, which are meant for tangible assets:

(i) First three blocks i.e. block 1, 2 and 3 are related with the building and the rate of depreciation are 5 per cent, 10 per cent and 100 per cent respectively.

(ii) Block 4 is related with furniture and the rate of depreciation is 15 per cent.

(iii) Block 5 to block 11 are related with the plant and machinery including ships but with separate classes of assets and separate rate of depreciation. The rate of depreciation applicable to these blocks are—15 per cent for block 5, 20 per cent for block 6, 40 per cent for block 7, 50 per cent for block 8, 60 per cent for block 9, 80 per cent for block 10 and 100 per cent block 11.

4. *Actual Cost*: It will be recorded that actual cost is factor in the fixation of the amount to be charged against revenue as depreciation. Actual cost for this purpose means the actual cost of an asset to the assessee as reduced by that portion, which has been met directly or indirectly by any other person or authority. The accepted accounting rules for determining cost of fixed asset is to included all expenses directly relatable to acquisition of the assets, expenses necessary to bring the asset to site, install it and make it fit for use and expenses incurred to facilitate the use of the asset and expenses on insurance, power and fuel, incurred before commencement of business.

Section 43 (1) as stated above is followed by thirteen explanations enumerating the cases where actual cost of an asset is determined at a notional figure.

(i) *Assets Used for Scientific Research*: Where an asset is used in the business after it ceases to be used for scientific research related to that business and depreciation is to be allowed in respect of that asset, the actual cost of asset to the assessee shall be the actual cost to the assessee as reduced by the amount of any deduction allowed under section 35 (1) (iv).

(ii) *Assets Acquired by Way of Gift or Inheritance*: Where an asset is acquired by the assessee by way of gift of inheritance, the actual cost of the asset to the assessee shall be the actual cost to the previous owner as reduced by the following amounts.

(a) the amount of depreciation actually allowed under this Act in respect of any previous year relevant to the assessment year commencing before 1st April, 1988 and

(b) the amount of depreciation that would have been allowable from the assessment year 1988-89 onwards as if that asset was the only asset in the relevant block of assets.

*(iii)* *Second Hand Assets*: Where, before the date of acquisition by the assessee, the assets were at any time used by any other person for the purpose of his business or profession and the Assessing Officer is satisfied that the main purpose of the transfer of such assets directly or indirectly to the assessee was the reduction of tax liability, the actual cost to the assessee shall be such an amount as the Assessing Officer may, with the previous approval of the Deputy Commissioner, determine having regards to all the circumstances of the case.

(iv) *Re-acquisition of Assets*: According to the explanation 4 to section 43(1), where a business asset is transferred by the assessee to another person and is subsequently re-acquired by him, the actual cost, would be actual cost to the assessee when he first acquired it as reduced by the amount of depreciation or actual cost at the time of re-acquisition which ever is less.

(v) *Sale and Lease Back*: Explanation 4A has been inserted in section 43(1) with effect from October 1, 1996 to determine the written down value in a case, where the assets which have previously been used by a person (hereinafter referred to as 'first person') and on which depreciation has been allowed to him are acquired by any other person and the assets have been let, hired or leased to the sellers. Actual cost of such assets shall be the same as the written down value of the said asset at the time of transfer thereof (by the first person).

(vi) *Building Which was Used for Non-business Purpose Earlier*: Where a building previously the property of the assessee, is brought into use for the purpose of business or profession, the actual cost of the asset to the assessee will be the actual cost of the building to the assessee, as reduced by depreciation, calculated at the rates in force on that date, that would have been allowable had the building been used for the purposes of business or profession since the date of its acquisition by the assessee [As per explanation 5 to section 43 (1)].

(vii) *Asset Transferred Between a Holding Company and Its 100 Per cent Subsidiary Company*: Where any capital asset is transferred by a holding company to its 100 per cent subsidiary Indian Company or vice-versa, then the actual cost of the transferred asset to the transferee company shall be taken to be the same as it would have been if the transferor company had continued to hold capital asset for the purpose of its business provided that the transferee company is an Indian company.

(viii) *Scheme of Amalgamation*: According to the explanation to section 43(1), where in a scheme of amalgamation, any capital asset is transferred by the amalgamating company to the amalgamated company and the amalgamated company is an Indian company, the actual cost of the transferred capital asset to the amalgamated company shall be taken to be the same as it would have been if the amalgamating company had continued to hold the capital asset for the own business.

(ix) *Interest Payable*: According to the explanation 8 to section 43 (1) any amount paid or payable as interest in connection with the acquisition of an asset and relatable to a period after the asset is first put to use will not form part of actual cost of the asset.

(x) *Adjustment of MODVAT*: Explanation 9 clarifies that in cases where duty of excise or additional duty leviable under the Customs Tariff Act 1975 and duty leviable under Central Excise Rules, 1944 has been paid and has been included in actual cost of the asset acquired on or after March 1, 1994 such duty shall be excluded as and when any credit by way of MODVAT is allowed to the assessee under the Central Excise Rules, 1944.

(xi) *Subsidy*: Explanation 10 provides that where a portion of the cost of an asset acquired by the assessee has been met, directly or indirectly, by the Central Government or State Government or any authority established under any law or by any other person in the form of subsidy or grant or reimbursement, then in a case where the subsidy is directly relate to the asset, such subsidy shall not be included in the actual cost of the asset.

(xi) *Asset Brought into India by a Non-resident*: Accordingly to explanation 11 to section 43 (1), where an asset is acquired outside India by an assessee, being a non-resident, such asset is brought by him to India and used for the purposes of his business or profession, the actual cost of the asset to the assessee shall be the actual cost of the asset to the assessee as reduced by an amount equal to the amount of depreciation calculated at the rate in force that would have been allowable had the asset been used in India for the said purposes since the date of its acquisition by the assessee.

(xiii) *Transfer in the Case of Corporatisation of a Recognised Stock Exchange*: Where any capital asset is acquired by the assessee under a scheme of corporatisation of a recognised stock exchange in India, the actual cost of the asset shall be deemed to be the asset shall be deemed to be the amount which would have been regarded as actual cost had there been no such corporatisation.

(5) *Written Down Value*: The written down value of any asset for the assessesment year 2004-05 will be determined as under in accordance with the section 43 (6):

(i) Find out depreciated value of the block of assets on April 1, 2003.

(ii) To this value add 'actual cost' of the asset (falling in the block) acquired during the previous year ending March, 31, 2004 relevant for the assessment year 2004-05.

(iii) From the resultant figure, deduct money received/receivable (together with scrap value) in respect of that asset (falling within the block of asset) which is sold discarded, demolished or destroyed during the previous year ending March 31, 2004 relevant for the assessment year 2004-05. However, the amount of reduction cannot exceed the value of block of asset as computed in (ii)

The resulting amount is the written down value of the block of assets on March 31, 2004 relevant for the assessment year 2004-05.

From the assessment year 1988-89, depreciation is admissible on the basis of block of assets. To ascertain the amount of depreciation, one should charged rate of depreciation on written down value of block of assets. However, there are certain exceptions to the rule:

(i) No depreciation is admissible where written down value has been reduced to zero. Though, the block of assets does not cease to exist on the last date of the previous year.

(ii) No depreciation is admissible if a block of asset cease to exist or if all assets of the block have been transferred and the block of asset is empty on the last day of the previous year.

(iv) No depreciation is admissible in respect of any motor car, manufactured out of India, where such car is acquired by the assessee after February 28, 1975 but before April 1, 2001.

(v) No depreciation is admissible if there is a charge of ownership of asset due to succession, amalgamation, business reorganisation or demerger.

(v) If in the first year in which an asset is acquired and it is put to use for less than 180 days, the deduction in respect of such asset shall be restricted to 50 per cent of the amount calculated at the percentage prescribed in the case of block of asset comprising such asset.

As per Explanation 5 to section 32 (1) (ii) from the assessment year 2002-03, depreciation under section 32 will be available whether or not the assessee has claimed the deduction for depreciation in computing his total income i.e. claim of depreciation is not optional.

## Comparison with Companies Act and Income Tax Act Regarding Depreciation

It has been observed that depreciation as an expense and charged against revenue in the case of corporate undertakings are regulated by two sets of Act Viz., the Indian Companies Act and Indian Income Tax Act. It will therefore be pertinent to see how these provisions compare among themselves.

1. Companies Act permit two methods, viz. straight line method (SLM) and written down value method (WDV) for charging depreciation. Whereas Income Tax Act permit mainly written down value method for charging depreciation except for an undertaking engaged in generation or generation and distribution of power where straight line method may be adopted from the assessment year 1998-99.
2. Double shift, triple shift depreciation rates for certain categories of assets under plant and machinery prescribed under Schedule XIV of Companies Act with some restriction i.e., extra shift depreciation allowance is permitted by Companies Act. Whereas there is no provision for extra shift depreciation allowance under Income Tax Act.
3. Depreciation rates prescribed under Schedule XIV of the Companies Act are generally lower than those specified in the rules framed under Income Tax Act. For example, general rate of depreciation for plant and machinery other than continuous process plant on WDV basis is 13.9 per cent under the Schedule, while it is $33^1/_3$ per cent under the Income Tax Rules.
4. As per Income Tax Rules, the cost of an asset purchased during the accounting years added to the depreciated value of relevant block of assets and it qualifies for full year's depreciation irrespective of date of purchase. Except where the assets put in used for 180 days or less, the rate of depreciation will be 50 per cent of prescribed rate, whereas under Companies Act the depreciation is to be charged on individual assets only from the date of purchase i.e. pro rata basis.
5. Under the Income Tax Act, proceeds of assets sold, discarded etc. during a year is deducted from depreciated value of block of assets, where as under the Companies Act normal depreciation has to be provided till the date of sale etc. of

the particular asset and the shortfall in recovery of the written down value thereof has to be further written off in that financial year.

6. Under Companies Act, depreciation is to charged in the books of account in respect of assets which are not in use of the whole or part of the year. Here it is assume depreciation arises from efflux of time. Whereas one of the conditions to be satisfied to claim depreciation under Income Tax Act that it must be used for the purpose of business or profession. So, as per Income Tax Act no depreciation is allowed if the asset is not used for sometime during the financial year.

7. As per Companies Act, the rate of depreciation as contained in Schedule XIV should be viewed as the minimum rates. So, a company will not be permitted to charge depreciation below the rates prescribed in the Schedule but can charge higher rate of depreciation on the basis of bona fide technological evaluation, provided proper disclosure in annual accounts, whereas no higher rate of depreciation than specified rate is admissible under Income Tax Act.

8. Under Companies Act no additional depreciation is allowed over the rate specified in Schedule XIV or the rated determined by management. But from the assessment year 2003-04, under Income Tax Act, additional depreciation over the normal depreciation is allowed to an assessee after fulfilling some conditions.

The auditor who is conducting the audit of a company here to first check depreciation which is computed as per Companies Act 1956 to find out divisible profit and again for computing the taxable income, the auditor hare to recheck the depreciation allowance which is computed as per Income Tax Act 1961. Even Companies following written down value method for charging depreciation in their books of accounts cannot avoid double calculation.

## REFERENCES


1. Companies Act, 1956; A. Ramaiya, Guide to the Companies Act, Agra, Wadhwa & Company, 1998; A.K. Majumdar and G.K. Kapoor, *Company Law and Practice*, New Delhi, Taxmann Publication (Pvt.) Ltd., 2003.
2. Dolphy D'Souza, *Indian Accounting Standards & GAAP*, Mumbai, Snow White Publication Pvt. Ltd., 2005, Vol. 1, p. 17
3. Gokul Sinha, "Anatomy of Accounting Standards", *Business Studies*, Vol. XIX, Nos. 1 and 2, January and July, 1996, p. 125.
4. Bhabatosh Banerjee and Bikki Jaggi, "Accounting Standards and Standard Setting Process in India—An Appraisal", *Indian Accounting Review*, Vol. I, No. 1, June 1997, p. 63.
5. P.R. Chowdhury and J.B. Sarkar, "Accounting Standards and Indian Accounting", *Unpublished Paper Presented at the Seminar of Indian Accounting Association, Calcutta Branch*, Held in Department of Commerce, University of Burdwan, 1984.
6. A.K. Basu, "The International Accounting Standards Committee—A Twenty Year Perspective", *Business Studies*, Vol. XVII, Nos. 1 and 2, January and July, 1994, p. 1.
7. Sanjiv Agarwal, *Accounting Standards and Corporate Practices*, New Delhi, Snow White Publications Pvt. Ltd., 1998, p. 854.
8. The Institute of Chartered Accountants of India, *Compendium of Statements and Standards Accounting*, New Delhi, ICAI, p. A-1.
9. A Ramaiya, *op. cit.*, p. 4796.
10. ICAI, *op. cit.*, p. A-35.
11. A. Ramaiya, *op. cit.*, p. 4796.
12. ICAI, *op. cit.*, p. A-39; A Ramaiya, *op. cit.*, p. 4798.
13. Bhabatosh Banerjee and Bikki Jaggi, *op. cit.*, p. 67.
14. Income Tax Act 1961; V.K. Singhania and Kapil Singhania, *Direct Taxes—Law and Practice*, New Delhi, Taxmann Publication (Pvt.) Ltd., 2004.

# 5

# Depreciation Accounting Requirements in Some Selected Countries

This chapter will make a comparative study of fixed assets with depreciation accounting rules prevailing in some selected countries along with international accounting standards issued by International Accounting Standard Board (IASB). Fixed assets and depreciation are very much co-related. Discussion of depreciation accounting without fixed assets is fruitless and aimless because depreciation always depends on nature and volume of fixed assets. Moreover, in many countries accounting standard on depreciation is included in accounting standard on fixed asset. The objective of this chapter is to examine how far India depreciation accounting rules are compatible with those prevailing elsewhere. The countries that have been brought under the purview of the analysis are the United States, Canada, the United Kingdom, Germany, France, the Netherlands, Brazil, South Africa, Australia, Japan and China. Apart from these countries the international accounting standard issued by IASB is taken into consideration. The requirements regarding fixed assets and depreciation for the purpose of preparation and presentation of annual financial statements in India are not considered under this chapter. It has been discussed in details in chapter IV. These countries have been chosen to represent all the major accounting models that are currently in operation. It is important to mention here that the selected countries are the leading countries in their respective continent.

The United States is the leading country in the North America both in term of economic development and accounting development.

This country has a very exhaustive, rule-oriented accounting system. The financial statement disclosure requirements are geared toward regulatory bodies and also considered to be the ideal one in serving the needs of active securities market. On the other hand, Canada has very strong accounting system. But Canadian GAAP has always been influenced by the US GAAP although the style and form of Canadian standards are generally quite similar to International Financial Reporting Standards (IFRSs) issued by IASB.[1] Canadian accounting requirements primarily govern by the Handbook Section and Guidelines. Moreover Canada has long been a strong advocate of international accounting standards. From 1966 to 1977, along with the United Kingdom and the United States, it was a member of the Accountants International Study Group.

In Europe, no doubt, the United Kingdom (UK) is the leading country with a long history of accounting development. There are some significant accounting systems (principle-oriented) in the UK in respect of the form and content of their corporate annual reports. The reports of the UK are geared toward sophisticated users (shareholder) rather than regulatory bodies like the USA. Both Germany and France belong to continental European accounting model are governed by very high degree of legalistic orientation. The another feature of this camp is that the financial accounts are required to comply with tax requirements. The German accounting system is based on law and tax code and is extremely conservative. The reporting system is geared to the workers and investors. On the other hand, the French has an elaborate system based on tax law. The French accounting system is promulgated by the ministry of economics and the system of taxation is upheld by the ministry for the budget. The Netherlands is a continental European country but the accounting system currently being used in this country is different in many respects from that being used in most other continental European countries. The Netherlands places a heavy emphasis on economics and applies an integral approach to the business environment. Dutch accountants are innovative and far from conservative in their accounting practices. The widespread use of replacement values by Dutch companies as the basis of measurement of expenses to be match against revenue is a testimony to Dutch accounting's affinity to business economics.

In South American continental, Brazil has a very unique system of accounting. The main feature of this accounting system is the adjustment of accounts for changes in the level of prices. The country has shown a remarkable ability to live with such a hyper inflationary environment. The Brazilian accounting system has also been able to learn the technique of responding effectively to the problems that are caused by persistent inflation.

South Africa is the most developed country in African continental having a strong accounting framework. The South African Institute of Chartered Accountants (SAICA) established itself as one of the leading institutes in the world playing its effective role in a highly dynamic business sector. The structure of South African GAAP (SA GAAP) is well designed to satisfy the requirements of different parties. In addition to the Companies Act requirements, SA GAAP requires the disclosure of information concerning the company's accounting policies, details of taxation, extra ordinary items, prior-year adjustment in the income statements and other matters. Additional disclosure requirements apply to companies listed on JSE Securities Exchange which is similar to that of the United States' Securities and Exchange Commission.

In Oceania continental, Australia, no doubt the leading country in terms of economic development as well as accounting development. Australian Accounting Standards Board (AASB) prepares accounting standards under the overall guidance of the Financial Reporting Council. The AASB recently issued 40 new or revised Accounting Standards referred to as Australian equivalents to International Financial Reporting Standards (A-IFRS) applicable for all financial year begaining on or after 1 January, 2005.[2]

Japan is not only a major force in Asian continental but also in the world. It has maintained a fairly impressive rate of growth for a long period of time. Japanese companies have become technological leader and differentiators in a wide range of modern industries. A sizeable portion of Japanese revenue comes from international trade and cross-border direct investments. The inclusion of China is justified on the ground that its rapid economic growth in the last two decades has stunned the rest of the world. Since China opened its door to foreign investments in 1979 the rapid growth of its economy, international trade and securities market has shaped new objectives for financial reporting. At the same time, China has reached out to the international community to form joint venture and gain greater access to the latest technologies and the world's capital markets.

Since, International Accounting Standards/International Financial Reporting Standards are gaining increasing popularity, it will be logical to consider International Accounting Standard in this regard. Actually, the International Accounting Standards Board (IASB) is a private-sector organisation and as such it has no authority of its own to enforce the standards formulated by it. It must depend on others for ensuring compliance with its standard. There are many third world countries that have adopted IAS as their own national standards (e.g. Zimbabwe, Kuwait) and many third world countries use the standards formulated by the IASB as a starting point in formulating their domestic accounting requirements (e.g. India, Singapore). On the other hand, in some countries IAS/IFRS are recommended in those cases where there are no corresponding domestic requirements (e.g. Nigeria).[3]

This comparative study reflects the accounting practices followed and standard regarding depreciation and fixed assets that were issued prior to 31 December 2004.

## The United States

The United States has a very detailed framework of generally accepted accounting principles (US GAAP). This is based on accounting standards and guidance ofThe Financial Accounting Standards Board and those of its predecessor bodies, Statements of Position and interpretations from the American Institute of Certified Public Accountants (AICPA) and consensuses reached by the Emerging Issues Task Force (EITF). In addition, listed companies must follow the rules, regulations and releases issued by the Securities and Exchange Commission (SEC)[4].

The United States is also a leading country in the sphere of accounting development. Economic development in the country has always been matched by expansion of accounting services. The accounting regulatory framework that has been built up in the country is considered to the most ideal one in serving the needs of active securities markets. In this country, both the government and the accounting profession have important roles to play in regulating corporate financial accounting and reporting. The most important governmental regulatory agency in the sphere of corporate financial accounting and reporting is the Securities and Exchange Commission (SEC). This agency has been entrusted with power to formulate accounting standards but it has delegated most of its power to Financial Accounting Standard Board (FASB). Company legislation has actually no role to play in this country in determining the form and context of published accounting reports of companies. The US Uniform Commercial Code does not contain any provisions relating to how companies should maintain their accounting records. State laws have specifications relating to accounting, but they are concerned only with some elementary issues.

Companies in the United States are required to prepare their external financial statements in conformity with generally accepted accounting principles (GAAP). The body of accounting principles known as GAAP we their origin to a number of sources, the most important of which being the Securities and Exchange Commission (SEC), the FASB and its predecessors bodies such as the Accounting Principles Board (APB), the Committee on Accounting Procedures (CAP) and Emerging Issues Task Force (EITF). Prevailing industry practices have also a significant role to play in providing a source of GAAP.

*Accounting Principles Board*: The profession's response was to substitute the Accounting Principles Board (APB) for the Committee on Accounting Procedure (CAP) in order to facilitate the development of principles based primarily on the research of the Accounting Research Division. Moreover, formal approval of Board issuances by the Securities and Exchange Commission (SEC) gave additional support to its activities.

*Financial Accounting Standards Board* (FASB): The FASB is recognized as authoritative though Financial Reporting Release 1 by the Securities and Exchange Commission and through Rule 203, Rules of conduct by the AICPA. The Board issues several type of pronouncements. Statements of Financial Accounting Standards and Interpretations are the most important of these because they are category A GAAP.[5]

*American Institute of Certified Public Accountants* (*AICPA*): The Accounting Standards Executive Committee (AcSEC) is the senior technical committee of the AICPA. AcSEC is authorized to set accounting standards and to speak for the AICPA on accounting matters. The accounting standards that AcSEC issues are prepared largely though the work of AICPA committee and task forces. AcSEC issues Statement of Position (SOPs) and industry audit and accounting guides, which are reviewed and cleared by the FASB and thus are category B GAAP.[6]

*Emerging Issues Task Force* (*EITF*): The EITF was formed in 1984 by the FASB in order to assist the Board in identifying current or emerging issues and implementation problems before divergent practices become entrenched. The guidance provided is often on narrow issues that are of immediate interest and importance. The SEC believes that a Task Force Consensus is GAAP for public companies and they will question any accounting that differs from it. Although EITF pronouncements are technically category C GAAP.[7]

The requirements regarding fixed assets and depreciation for the purpose of preparation and presentation of annual financial statements are as follows[8]:

(i) Fixed Assets should be recorded at historical cost. Any reasonable cost involved in bringing the asset to the buyer and incurred prior to using the asset in actual production is capitalised..

(ii) Major inspection and overhaul costs are generally charged to expense with certain exception. Extraordinary repairs and maintenance increase the value (utility) of the asset or increase the estimated useful life of the asset should be recorded as increase asset amount i.e. capitalised. If there costs able to extend the useful life of the asset should decrease accumulated depreciation.

(iii) The future cost to retire (including dismantling and removing) an asset is measured and recognised in the financial statements as a liability and correspondingly, as a part of the depreciable cost of the assets (SFAS 143).

(iv) Financing costs directly attributable to the construction of the property, plant and equipment should be capitalised.

(v) For self-constructed asset, all direct costs of constructing an entity's own fixed assets should be capitalised. However a controversy exists regarding the proper treatment of fixed overhead.

(vi) Revaluation above historical cost is not permitted except in connection with business combinations accounted for using the purchase method.

(vii) When the carrying amount of a long-lived asset (or asset group) exceeds its fair value, the condition is called as impairment. Impairment losses are only recognised when the carrying amount of the impaired asset (or asset group) is not recoverable (SFAS 144). Fair value is determined using quoted market prices in active markets when available. Otherwise, the entity estimates fair value based on the best information available such as market prices for similar assets (or groups of assets) or using valuation techniques such as the expected value of future cash flows as set forth in FASB concepts statement 7.

(viii) If the carrying amount of long-lived asset less than its fair value i.e. if the carrying value is recoverable, no impairment loss is recognised (SEAS 144).

(ix) After recognition of impairment losses, the adjusted carrying amount of the impaired long-lived assets constitute their new cost basis. Depreciation is recognised prospectively over their remaining estimated useful lives.

(x) If the entity commits to a plan to abandon the asset before the end of its previously estimated useful life, the depreciable life is revised in accordance with APB 20 and depreciation of the asset continues until the end of its shortened useful life.

(xi) Gain or loss recognition due to exchange of similar non-current asset is prohibited.[9]

(xii) As asset may be disposed off individually or a port of a disposal group. A disposal group is a group of assets to be disposed off in a single transaction as a group and the liabilities directly associated with those assets that will be transferred with those assets.

(xiii) Long-lived assets (disposal groups) classified as held for sale are measured of the lower of their carrying amount or fair value less cost to sell. A loss is recognised for any initial or subsequent written down to fair value less cost to sale. A gain is recognised for any subsequent increase in fair value less cost to sale but recognised gains may not exceed the cumulative losses previously recognised. Long-lived assets that are classified as held for sale are presented separately on the balance sheet. This kinds of assets are not to be depreciated.

(xiv) Different depreciation method (e.g. straight line method, declining balance method, sum-of-the-years'-digits method, present value method, depreciation method based on actual physical usage etc) are permitted to depreciate tangible capital assets as long as the method chosen is systematic and rational with the exception of annuity method.

(xv) When on asset is either acquired or disposed off during the year, the full year depreciation calculated is prorated between the accounting periods involved. As an alternative to proration an entity may follow any one several simplified conventions:

(a) Record of full year's depreciation in the year of acquisition and none in the year of disposal;

(b) Record one-half year's depreciation in the year of acquisition and one-half year's depreciation in the year of disposal.

(xvi) Gains and losses are not recognised on the disposal of an asset but are netted into accumulated depreciation.

(xvii) A change in depreciation method (but not of useful life or residual value) is dealt with as a change in accounting policy, for which the cumulative effect to date is put through the current year income statement after extraordinary items.

(xviii) The cost of an asset should include all the costs necessary to get the asset set up and functioning properly for its intended use including interest and interest cost should be capitalised as a part of the historical cost.

## Canada

Canadian requirements are based on the standards issued by Accounting Standard Board (AcSB) of the Canadian Institute of Chartered Accountants.[10] The Accounting Standard Board and The Public Sector Accounting Board (PSAB) both develop and establish standards and guidance governing financial accounting and reporting in Canada. The AcSB sets standards for profit-oriented enterprise and not-for-profit organisation while the PSAB sets standards for public sector entities.

Canada has long been a strong advocate of international accounting standards. From 1966 to 1977 along with the United Kingdom and the United States, it was a member of the Accountants International Study Group, a body that issued comparative studies on 15 topics of mutual interest.[11]

Canadian GAAP has always been influenced by the US GAAP although Accounting Standard Board of the Canadian Institute of Chartered Accountants has made significant contribution in developing accounting standards. Canadian market is very linked to the US market. For the Toronto Stock Exchange and Alberta Stock Exchange, all registrants must submit financial statement that follow Canadian GAAP. The Canadian Securities Administrators (CSA), on the contrary appears to believe that accounting standards issued can be evaluated independently.[12]

The reporting issuers in Canada increasingly using US GAAP as over the past decade growing number of Canadian companies have accessed to US capital market. In Canada, two approaches have emerged:

(a) These companies issue financial statement, prepared in accordance with the Canadian GAAP including an audited reconciliation statement with the US GAAP;

(b) Alternatively, large Canadian companies issue financial

statements, prepared as per US GAAP and use it as primary basis for public communication and file financial statements prepared as per Canadian GAAP with provincial securities regulators.[13]

The definition Canadian GAAP is given in the CICA Handbook. Accounting Standards in the CICA Handbook are set by the Accounting Standard Board (AcSB) of the Canadian Institute of Chartered Accountants (CICA). CICA Handbook Section 3061 deals with 'Property, Plant and Equipment'.

The requirements regarding property, plant and equipment and depreciation for the purpose of preparation and presentation of annual financial statements are as follows.[14]

(i) An item of property, plant and equipment should be recognised at historical cost. Cost includes all costs directly attributable to the acquisition including site preparation costs, testing, and preparation charges necessary for its intended use.

(ii) The cost of replacement and betterments are to be included in the cost of the asset i.e. capitalised.

(iii) The estimated cost of asset retirement including cost of the dismantling and removing the asset are capitalised.

(iv) The cost of an item of property plant and equipment includes direct construction or development costs (such as material and labour) and overhead costs directly attributable to the construction or development activity.

(v) The revaluation of asset is not permitted.

(vi) When the carrying value of an item of property, plant and equipment exceeds both cash flows it is capable of generation and its fair value is called impairment. It impairment has occurred; an impairment charge is recognised immediately in the income statement. Review the carrying value of property, plant and equipment on a regular basis and where it exceeds fair value consider the asset to be impaired.

(vii) When at the time of acquisition a portion of the acquired item of property, plant and equipment meets the criteria in Disposal of Long-Lived Assets and Discontinued Operation (Section 3475) to be classified as held for sale at the acquisition date, that portion of the item is measured at fair value less cost to sale. The remainder of the acquired item is measured at cost of acquisition of the entire item less the amount assigned to the portion to be sold. When at the time of acquisition, a portion of the acquired item of property, plant and equipment is not intended for use because it will be abandoned, its cost and any costs of disposal, net of any estimated proceeds, are attributed to that portion of the acquired asset which is intended for use.

(viii) Depreciation should be recognised in a rational and systematic manner appropriate to the nature of an item of property, plant and equipment with limited life and its use by the enterprise.

(ix) Different methods of depreciating an item of property, plant and equipment result in different patterns of charges to income. The objective is to provide a rational and systematic basis for allocating the depreciable amount of an item of property, plant and equipment over its estimated life and useful life. A variety of methods of depreciation are allowed e.g. straight line method, increasing charge method, decreasing charge method etc.

(x) The depreciation method and estimated of the life and useful life of an item of property, plant and equipment should be reviewed on a regular basis and if expectations differs from previous estimates, the change(s) should be accounted for as a change in an accounting policy (in accordance with Accounting Changes, Section 1506)

(xi) Significant events that may indicate a need to revise depreciation method or estimated of the life and useful life on an item of property, plant and equipment include:

(a) a change in the extent the asset is used
(b) a change in the manner in which the asset is used
(c) removal of thc asset from service for an extended period of time
(d) physical damage
(e) significant technological developments
(f) a change in the law, environment or consumer styles and tastes affecting the period of time over which the asset can be used

(xii) Borrowing costs that are directly attributable to the acquisition, construction or development of asset are capitalised.

## The United Kingdom

Accounting in the United Kingdom is based on Companies Act that are laid out by parliament and enforced by the secretary of state for trade. In August 1990, the UK's accounting body, Accounting Standards Board (ASB) replaces the ASC with statutory authority to issue accounting standards without the need to seek approval from the six accounting bodies that make up the Consultative Committee of Accountancy Bodies.[15] The Urgent Issues Task Force (UITF) was established by the ASB in 1991. It assists the ASB in areas where an accounting standard or Companies Act provision exists, but where unsatisfactory or conflicting interpretation have developed or seem likely to develop. The results of the UITF's deliberations on a subject are promulgated by means of published Abstracts. UK's requirements are based on the Companies Act 1985 as amended for EU Directives. The Act states that disclosure should be made as to whether accounts have been prepared in accordance with applicable accounting standards. Prior to December 2004, the ASB has adopted and issued 27 Financial Reporting Standard (FRS). Accounting standards issued by Accounting Standard Board and its Urgent Issues Task Force are applicable for the purpose of this Act.

The UK has a long history of wide share ownership, with not only multinationals but also medium-sized domestic companies obtaining listing on London Market. The requirements of shareholders and the desire of companies to demonstrate continuously upward profit trends have, as a result influenced significantly, the development of UK accounting practice.

The requirement for all companies, both private and public, to prepare annual financial statements giving a true and fair view, to appoint auditors (the very smallest companies are exempt from audit) and to file such financial statements with the Registrar of Companies, comes from Companies Act. Holding companies of a certain size must file consolidated financial statements in addition to the individual company financial statements.

The Companies Act 1989 amended the Companies Act 1985 introducing into it a definition of 'accounting standards' along with a requirement for companies over a certain size to disclose in financial statements whether or not they have been prepared in accordance with applicable accounting standards and if not particular and reasons for any departure. Auditor's are required by regulation and professional standard to have regard to all applicable accounting standards in reaching a true and fair opinion. UK accounting practices have developed separately from tax law and reconciliations between tax accounting and statutory accounting are often complex. Financial Reporting Standard (FRS) 15 deals with Tangible Fixed Assets.

The requirements regarding tangible fixed assets and depreciation for the purpose of preparing the annual financial statements are as follows:[16]

(i) Tangible fixed assets initially recorded at cost, which includes only directly attributable costs necessary to bring the asset to working condition. Cost includes end of life dismantling provisions.

(ii) Subsequent expenditure is capitalised if it enhances economic benefits beyond that originally assessed replaces or restores a component which has been depreciated or relates to major maintenance that has been charged through depreciation.

(iii) The law permits tangible fixed assets to be recorded at a valuation generally current cost or market value at the date of the last valuation (Companies Act 1985, Schedule 4).

(iv) Assets should never be carried at more than their recoverable amount.

(v) Where a tangible fixed asset is revalued, all tangible fixed assets of the same class must be revalued.

(vi) FRS 15, which effective for periods ending on or after 23 March 2000 requires companies revaluing assets to use the following bases for unimpaired tangible fixed assets:

   (a) Non-specialised properties–existing use value, with the addition of notional directly attributable acquisition costs, where material;
   (b) Specialised properties—depreciated replacement cost;
   (c) Properties surplus to an entity's requirements—open market value, after deducting expected directly attributable selling costs where material; and
   (d) Tangible fixed assets other than properties—market value or depreciated replacement cost where market value is not available.

(vii) Surpluses arising from upward revaluation are credited directly to a revaluation reserves and shown in the statement of total recognised gains and losses. Deficits are taken to the profit and loss account to the extent that they do not represented a reversal of a previous upwards revaluation.

(viii) Generally revaluation losses which reverse previously recognised revaluation gains related to the same asset or recognised in the statement of total recognised gains and losses to the extend of the previous recognised gain.

(ix) Revalued asset should be carried at current value of the balance sheet date. Specific guidance exists on how this can be achieved using a five-year valuation cycle.

(x) However, if the revaluation loss is clearly caused by the consumption of economic benefits, it is considered to be similar to depreciation and recognised in the profit and loss account.

(xi) FRS 15 requires, where fixed assets are revalued, depreciation is charged to the profit and loss account based on the revalued amount.

(xii) FRS 3 requires that recognition of profit and loss on disposal of an asset which has been revalued be based on its net carrying value at the date of disposal. Any past valuation surpluses or deficits in the revaluation reserve relating to the asset are shown as a reserve transfer. The gain or loss calculated on a historical cost basis shown in a note.

(xiii) Generally, UK GAAP requires depreciation of all assets with finite useful economic life to be recognised in the current period unless neither current year charge or accumulated amount of such recognised depreciation is material.

(xiv) UK GAAP allows the use of both straight line method and reducing balance method as well as any other method that result in depreciation charge being allocated on a systematic basis over useful economic life. However, ASB has made certain change which disallowed (with a limited exception) back-end loading methods of depreciation such as the annuity based method.

(xv) There is no specific requirement as to how depreciation is charged in the year of acquisition of an asset.

(xvi) Where the depreciation method is changed, the unamortised cost of the asset should be written off over the remaining useful life using the new method. The change in method of depreciation is treated as change in accounting estimates.

(xvii) Where estimates of useful economic lives of tangible fixed assets are changed, the undepreciated cost should be depreciated over the revised estimates of remaining lives (FRS 15).

(xviii) Interest on capital specifically borrow to finance the production of an asset may be included in the cost of the asset to the extend it accrues in the period of production (Companies Act 1985, Schedule 4). Although capitalisation of borrowing costs for a class of assets is optional (FRS 15).

## Germany

The German accounting system is based on law and tax codes and is extremely conservative. In other word the Germany is guided by the heavily codified law with its comprehensive legal provisions. As a result accounting in Germany has been basically governed by detailed legal regulations. Germany requirements are mainly based on the Commercial Code (HGB). In addition, standards prepared by the German Accounting Standard Committee (GASC) and thereafter published by the Federal Ministry of Justice supplement the HGB with respect to the consolidated financial statements of listed companies. Once the standard (GASs) has been published by the Federal Ministry of Justice, they are presumed to represent proper accounting principles for group financial reporting. So consolidated financial statements are based on the accounting and valuation principles of the German Commercial Code and the German Stock Corporation Act as well as the accounting standards of the German Accounting Standard Committee, collectively called German GAAP. However, when the GASs conflicts with the current provisions of the HGB, it is unclear whether the GASs are mandatory before they are actually incorporated into the HGB.[17]

In the past Germany industry was dominated by the *Mittelsland*—private companies (many of which are effectively family business) whose capital has traditionally been provided by the banking sector. Consequently, the major developments in German accounting has been driven by the needs of the creditors (the so called *Glaubigerschutzprinzip*) rather than those of the shareholder. Indeed it is possible to argue that the financial security (the balance sheet) has traditionally been of greatest significance to the German user rather than profitability (the profit and loss account). There is, however, a clear trend in Germany towards wider share ownership and the attractiveness of the legal form of public companies is coming to bear.[18]

Financial statements of all business entities in Germany are required to be drawn up in accordance with generally accepted accounting principles (GoB, Section 243(1) *Handelsgesetzbuch* or HGB). Traditionally, German accounting practice is a result of detailed codification. The main accounting rules are governed by the Commercial Code (HGB). For example, requirements on classification of balance sheet and profit and loss account items, special valuation rules, notes to the accounts, management report, group accounting, audit and disclosure are stated in HGB from section 264 to 335. Furthermore, special regulation applicable to specific legal forms are included in the Stock Corporation Law (*Aktiengesetz* or AKtG) dealing with public companies and in the law on Limited

Liability Companies (*GmbH—Gesetz* or GmbHG). Additionally, all other large business entities must comply with the regulation under the Publicity Law (*Publizitatsgesetz* or PublG).[19]

Since 1998 four new laws have came into force which have significantly changed the HGB and contributed towards convergence of German accounting principles with international accounting practice. Written legal regulations have been complemented by the GoB which apply to all matters not otherwise covered in the law or in all cases where specific legal regulations require on interpretation. The GoB are the generally accepted rules of maintaining commercial books of account (documentation) as well as preparing the annual financial statements (accounting) of entities. A large number of the GoB which were originally not fixed in writing have over the years been included in the HGB (e.g. completeness is included in the section 243(2) of HGB). In 1998 the German Accounting Standard Committee (*Deutsches, Rechnungslegungs Standard Committee* or DRSC) was set up by the Government with a task of development, monitoring and compliance of accounting standard.[20]

The requirements regarding property, plant and equipment and depreciation for preparing the annual financial statements are as follows.[21]

(i) An item of property, plant and equipment is initially shown at historic purchase (Section 255(1) of HGB) or manufacturing cost (Section 255(2) of HGB). Cost includes all direct cost, the cost of conversion of internally manufactured asset.

(ii) Estimated cost of dismantling, removing and restoration should not be capitalised.

(iii) Major inspection and overhaul cost are included in the cost of asset and at the same time recognised as provision.

(iv) German GAAP does not permit revaluation of an item of

property, plant and equipment in excess of original cost as reduced by depreciation.

(v) Assets costing not more than DM 800 (excluding VAT) referred to as '*geringwertige wirtschaftsguter*' or GWGs are usually treated as expense when purchased. This treatment is based on German tax law.

(vi) Interest on capital specifically borrowed to finance the production of an asset may be included in the cost of an asset to the extend that the interest is incurred during the period of production (Section 255 (3) of HGB). In practice, however, only few companies opt for capitalisation.

(vii) Due to the principle of '*umgekehrte Massgeblichkeit*' (due to many tax incentives, same treatment is adopted between tax and financial accounts) depreciation rates tend to be tax driven. Although new depreciation tables have recently been issued by the tax authorities with generally longer useful lives than in the past, the tax driven nature of the rules has traditionally resulted in fixed assets being stated at a lower value and total depreciation charge for the year not necessarily reflecting economic use of the assets (Section 273 of HGB). Example of tax allowed depreciation include:

(a) special accelerated depreciation;
(b) reducing balance depreciation;
(c) written off movable assets costing less than DM 800; and
(d) half year simplification rule.

(viii) Companies are required to justify and disclose the amount of depreciation recognised in the income statement that was based solely on tax regulation (Section 281(2) of HGB).

(ix) Both the straight line and reducing balance methods may be used. However, the reducing balance method is only permitted to be used for movable fixed assets. Due to these restrictions, building is always depreciated using straight line method. Other depreciation method are allowed if they reflect the actual usage of assets.

(x) Movable assets acquired during the first half of the accounting year quality for 100 per cent of the normal depreciation rates and those acquired during the second half only 50 per cent of normal depreciation rates based on German tax law are considered.

(xi) An enterprise is permitted to switch over from reducing balance to straight line depreciation method at any time but the reverse change is not permitted. Where the method is changed, net book value of an asset is amortised over the remaining useful life.

(xii) Where estimates useful economic lives of fixed assets are changed, the undepreciated cost should be depreciated over the revised estimates of remaining lives.

(xiii) For gain or loss on disposal of an item of property, plant and equipment, net proceeds from disposal is charged to the income statement under other operating income and other operating expenses.

## France

French requirements are based on the *Code de Commerce,* company law and decrees, rules established by *Comite de la Regelmentation comptable* (Committee of Accounting Regulation) including *Plan Comptable General* (General Accounting Plan) and interpretations of the *Comite d' Urgency* (Urgent Issues Committee).[22]

France is a leading economically advanced nation in the world. The country has a mixed economy with is controlled and regulated by the central government. Many key industries in the country are owned and operated by the public sector. French private-sector enterprises assume a variety of forms of organisation. The most important of which being family holdings, limited partnerships, private companies and public companies. Most French enterprises, especially those belonging to the private sector, are of medium and small categories. French companies depend heavily on banks in the matter of procurement of their long-term capital. The government also has a very important role to play in providing long-term capital to companies.[23]

French financial statements are highly standardised, companies are required to prepare their financial statements in strict conformity with statutory requirements. The formats to be used by French companies are clearly specified in the statute and these formats cannot be violated under any circumstances. The standardised accounts are used by governmental agencies as a basis for compilation of national income statistics. The principles and procedures used by French companies in computing their accounting profit are almost similar to that form the basis of computation of their taxable profits. That means, the French have a very elaborate system based on tax law. Because of this system the French do not have two sets of books nor do they have a provision for deferred taxes. The shareholder are not taxed on dividends and the problem of double taxation does not exist in France.[24]

In France, accounting standards are part of the basic business law and consequently every business entity is required to comply with them when publishing its accounts. There are a number of different sources of law, which are hierarchically structured as follows:[25]

- *European Directives* (Forth directive applicable to Statutory Accounts)
- *Code de Commerce* (including general accounting obligations for all commercial entities and general rules for consolidated accounts)

- Regulatory texts such as decrees and regulations (regulations are now issued by the CRC)
- *Jurisprudence*
- Guidance, interpretations and recommendations (issued by CNCC and OEC for all companies and by the COB for listed companies)

French *Code de Commerce* (first issued in 1807) was completely and recently revised and recodified in September 2000 and now includes fundamental texts such as the French law applicable to commercial entities. Article L123-12 to L123-24 and Article L233-16 to L233-28 of the *Code de Commerce* applicable to statutory accounts. For example, Article L123-12 of *Code de Commerce* defines the contents of the financial statements which include the balance sheet (*bilan*), the profit and loss account (*Compte de resultat*) and the notes (*annexe*). They are required to be presented with comparative figures.[26]

In April 1998, an official accounting body was created, the *Comite de la Reglementation Computable* (CRC) which is responsible for approving new accounting standards. This body was created to address the following issues:

- French accounting standards were often general and could be interpreted in several ways. The CRC's standards are designed to be more specific and therefore make the financial statements more transparent.
- French accounting standards had previously been set by several sources. The creation of the CRC was designed to provide more consistency to the standard-setting process.

Accounting standard are proposed by the *Conseil National de La Comptabilite* (CNC) and reviewed by the CRC before issuance. In addition, the *Comite d' Urgence du* CNC (Urgent issues committee), comprised of a limited number of CNC members, issues interpretation of and guidance on existing standards. The *Plan Comptable General* provides companies obligatory definitions and accounting principles.

The requirements regarding tangible fixed assets and depreciation for the purpose of preparation and presentation of annual financial statements are as follows:[27]

(i) Tangible fixed assets are initially recorded at cost.

(ii) Under French GAAP major maintenance and overhaul costs are recognised as provisions [CRC Regulation 2000-06].

(iii) In the French GAAP financial statement, under CRC regulation 2000-06, a provision is recognised when infrastructure is commissioned for the present value of the estimated dismantling cost and an equivalent amount is added to the carrying value of the facility.

(iv) Assets with a value below FF 2500 are generally treated as expense when incurred.

(v) Revaluation of tangible fixed assets is permitted. (although rare in practice). Where a company adopts a policy of revaluation it must revalue all relevant asset categories.

(vi) Revaluation rules for an individual company's accounts are derived from the tax rules. In case of voluntary revaluation, (from 1984 onwards) surpluses arising from any upward revaluation are immediately taxable at the corporation tax rate and therefore, such revaluation are very rare. The surpluses are credited to a revaluation reserve account, *ceart de re-evaluation libber.*

(vii) Depreciation is based on the revalued amount and the excess depreciation charge resulting from the revaluation is tax allowable.

(viii) The calculation of profit or loss on disposal of a revalued asset is based on its net carrying value at the date of disposal. The revaluation reserve is part of equity and is not part of the profit or loss on disposal. The revaluation reserve may not be distributed or used to reduce accumulated losses.

(ix) In addition to paying corporation tax on revaluation gains, companies revaluating their fixed assets will also face increased tax payable in respect of *taxes professionally* which is partly based on the value of fixed assets (Due to unfavourable tax treatment, revaluations in France are rare in found).

(x) When a group decides to revalue its fixed assets, the same method must be consistently applied for each company in a group.

(xi) Surpluses arising from upward revaluation are credited directly to a revaluation reserve. Deficits are taken to the profit and loss account.

(xii) Depreciation is based on the revalued amount and the profit or loss on disposal is calculated on the net carrying value of the date of disposal (CRC Regulation n° 99-03).

(xiii) Interest on capital may be capitalised to the extent that it is incurred the period of production of an asset and that the expenditure is financed by external borrowing. However, this practice is uncommon.

(xiv) The depreciation method used should result in a depreciation charge that reflects the economic depreciation. Straight line method is normally used. Other methods are often used in statutory accounts where the depreciation charge is based on advantageous tax rules and options (e.g. reducing balance method or accelerated tax depreciation method).

(xv) To qualify for tax deduction in the individual company's accounts depreciation must be charge using the standard rates accepted by tax authorities.

(xvi) The rates most often used under the straight line method are rigid and tax rules based. Tax authorities will not normally challenge the rates used as long as they do not deviate from the specific rates by more than 20 per cent.

(xvii) The reducing balance method can be used only for a very limited list of new items of machinery and equipment with useful lives of at least three years. The reducing balance method may be used for tax purposes even where it is established that the straight line method better reflects economic depreciation of the asset. When this is the case the difference between depreciation calculated using these two methods is credited to a specific provision account, *provision pour amortisement derogatoire.* Reducing balance rates are calculated by multiplying appropriate straight line rates by some rigid co-efficient based on asset's useful life.

(xviii) Where special accelerated depreciation rates are introduced by the authorities to encourage certain investments (e.g. in specific energy-saving and anti-pollution equipment, software etc) the difference between the normal depreciation charge and tax driven accelerated depreciation is shown in *provision paur amortisement derogatoire.* The provision is subsequently reserved when the normal depreciation charge exceeds the accelerated depreciation charge.

(xix) Where the estimate of the useful economic life of a fixed asset is changed, the remaining undepreciated cost is depreciated over the revised estimates of remaining lives (PCG art 331-8).

## The Netherlands

Dutch accounting requirements can be found in the civil code as amended by EU Directives and in Guidelines of the Council for Annual Reporting. Although the guidelines are not mandatory, they should not be departed from without good reasons. However, departure is required if application of the requirements does not provide a true and fair view of the state of affairs and results of the enterprise.[28]

The Netherlands happens to be the country which gave birth to the world's first limited liability company.[29] The Netherlands has a highly developed corporate financial accounting and reporting system and in this respect, the country has a good international reputation. The Dutch financial statements are highly informative, they provide enough information to enable users to make proper judgement regarding the financial position and performance of the company. One of the important features of the Dutch accounting system is that it is heavily influenced by the principles of business economics. Another important feature of the Dutch system of accounting is that size is an important determinant of the form and content of published accounting reports of companies.

The term 'generally accepted accounting principles' and 'generally accepted accounting practices' (or GAAP) are not defined formally in the Netherlands. Instead the term 'Netherlands accounting rules' is used to denote the body of practices forming the basis for determining what constitutes a true and fair view.[30] In the Netherlands the accounting practice is based on accounting rules that are set at two levels:

*The Dutch Civil Code*: The law incorporated in volume 2 of the Netherlands Civil Code (CC) forms the first level. The Dutch Civil Code provides for most of the country's legal requirements relating to corporate financial accounting and reporting. The civil code also includes provisions of the 1970 Act on Annual Accounts. The basic accounting principles stipulated in the Civil Code are going concern, consistence, accruals, prudence, realisation and valuation. In addition at the same level, jurisprudence is constituted by the verdicts of the

Enterprise Chamber, a special Chamber of the Court of Justice in Amsterdam. One of the main tasks of the court is to rule on charges of failure to comply with the legal requirements for financial statements on the basis of complaints from interested parties (Primarily shareholders)[31].

*Council for Annual Reporting*: The second level involves the Netherlands Council for Annual Reporting (*Road Voor de Jaarverslaggeving*—RJ) (CAR) which was founded in 1982. The Council Guidelines on Annual Reporting (*Richtlijnen Voor de Jaarverslaggeving*) (GAR) have a lower status than the law, but since the council is made up of representatives of employers, users (such as trade union and financial analysist) and auditors, the Guidelines are applied broadly throughout the Netherlands. Although formally the Guidelines are recommendations, even in the case of bold-faced pronouncements, the Guidelines are referred to as being part of GAAP in the Netherlands. Moreover the CAR is responsible for setting accounting standards in the Netherlands. Again, the accounting standards formulated by the CAR are not mandatory for companies but it is expected that departures from standards will be duly disclosed. In the past, the CAR focused its guidelines on large (listed) entities. Given the EU Regulation in respect of adoption of IFRS issued by IASB, the CAR has shifted part of its attention to small and medium-sized entities. This has resulted in new exceptions for medium sized entities and a separate publication for small entities that includes significant exemption compared to the requirements for large entities. The exemptions mainly relate to the presentation and disclosure requirements.

It is important to mention here that the Dutch tax system has a marginal influence on the financial accounting and reporting practices of companies and stock market legislations have no significant role to play in shaping the form and content of company accounts in the Netherlands.

The requirements regarding tangible fixed assets and depreciation for the purpose of preparation and presentation of financial statements are as follows:[32]

(i) Tangible fixed assets are initially recognised at historical cost. Cost comprises the costs directly attributable to bringing the asset to the location and working condition necessary for it to be capable of operating in the way management intends, including cost of testing whether the asset is functioning properly. In addition a reasonable part of the indirect costs could be capitalised.

(ii) Cost of dismantling and removing the asset and restoring the site do not need to be included in the initial valuation of asset. Instead they may be accrued over the useful life of the asset.

(iii) For the cost of major inspection or overhaul occurring at regular intervals, a provision can be formed under Dutch GAAP during a period up to the next major inspection or overhaul, or under certain requirements the major inspection or overhaul costs could be expensed directly in the income statement.

(iv) *Dutch GAAP Allows Two Measurement Method*: cost method (bench mark) and a fair-value revaluation method. Regular valuation of entire classes of assets are required when revaluation option is chosen i.e. revaluation need not be made on a regular basis.

(v) Under Dutch GAAP, there is no specific requirements regarding frequency of revaluation of tangible fixed assets. However, there are disclosure requirements in relation to the estimated use to determine the revaluation and in addition disclosures are required in relation to the ageing of the determination of the revaluations.

(vi) According to Dutch Civil Code tangible fixed assets can be valued at current value.

(vii) Increase or decrease due to revaluation of tangible assets be recognised directly in equity as part of a revaluation reserve.

(viii) Downward revaluation (an impairment loss) may be written off from revaluation reserve and may be done on a collective basis. Any uncovered deficit must be accounted for in the income statement. [Dutch Civil Code Title 9 Book 2, GAR 120, 121, 212, Asset Valuation decrease]

(ix) A retired asset may be revalued on a once-off basis if its net realisable value is significantly higher than its carrying amount.

(x) Dutch GAAP has no specific measurement criteria for valuing exchanges of assets. In practice the principles used for barter transactions for revenue recognition are applied.

(xi) The depreciable amount of an item of tangible assets must be allocated on a systematic basis over its useful life, reflecting the pattern in which the entity consumes the assets' benefits. That means Dutch GAAP virtually allows any method for charging depreciation on tangible fixed assets.

(xii) A change in depreciable method is considered to be a change in accounting estimates reflected in the depreciation charge for the current and prospective period.

(xiii) There is no strict requirement within Dutch GAAP to review the residual value and useful life of an asset at each financial year-end.

(xiv) An impaired assets should depreciated over its remaining useful life.

(xv) In relation to tangible fixed assets not in use any longer, there are specific measurement requirements. The tangible fixed assets should be measured of the lower of its carrying amount and fair value less cost to sell. When the fair value less costs to sell is significant higher than the carrying amount, this difference should be disclosed or incidentally revalued to fair value less costs. This revaluation reserve will be released to the income statement when the asset is sold. [Dutch Civil Code Title 9 Book 2, GAR 212, 345]

(xvi) Interest cost should be expensed unless it is capitalised in accordance with the allowed at alternative treatment.

(xvii) An entity can choose to capitalise borrowing costs where they are directly attributable to the acquisition, construction or production of a qualifying asset. The choice should be applied consistently (A qualifying asset is one that necessarily takes a substantial period of time to get ready for its intended use or sale). Capitalisation of interest must cease once the asset is ready for its intended use or sale. (GAR 120)

## Brazil

Brazilian legal requirements are based on the corporation law of 1976 complemented by regulations from the Securities Commission for listed companies. There are two accounting framework is Brazil: one stated by Corporation Law and one stated by the *Conselho Federal de Contabilidade* (Federal Council of Accountants) [The CFC rules]. The main difference between them relates to inflation accounting. Under the CFC rules the financial statements are required to be adjusted for inflation through to the current date if inflation effect is material. No specific definition on how to measure this materiality exists. The Corporation Law accounting principles do not allow the recognition of inflation effect after January 1, 1996. All companies are required to prepare financial statements in accordance with the Corporation Law accounting framework. Financial statements prepared in accordance with the framework of the CFC rules are optional.[33]

Brazil is one of those countries in the world that have been experiencing very high rates of inflation for a long time. But the country has shown a very remarkable ability to live with such high inflation. The Brazilion accounting system has also been able to learn the technique of responding effectively to the problems that are caused by persistent inflation. Accounting practices in Brazil are regulated from a number of sources, the most important of which being the Brazilian Commercial Code, the Corporation Act of 1976, tax laws securities commission and the accounting profession body. The accounting and auditing standards being used in Brazil are simply the adopted version of US standards.[34]

*Commercial Code*: The Brazilion Commercial Code provides for the maintenance of proper accounting records by all enterprises conducting business operation in the country. The nature of the accounting records to be maintained by an enterprise is determined greatly by the nature of the transactions with which the enterprise is concerned.

*Corporation Law*: Companies in Brazil, called *Anonnymous Societies*, are governed by the Corporation Act of 1976. The Act has provisions according to which it is obligatory for companies to prepared financial statements. Companies having subsidiaries are required under the Act to prepare consolidated financial statements.

*Tax Laws*: Companies in Brazil are required to pay income tax based on their trading profits as reported in their financial statements. There is, however, a distinction between accounting profit and taxable profit.

*Securities Commission*: The Securities Commission in Brazil is empowered to promote measures for increasing the efficiency and effectiveness of securities market in the country. It has the authority to prescribe the information to the disclosed by public owned companies. The requirements specified by the Commission have to be followed by all companies falling within its jurisdiction. It is also obligatory for publicly held companies to file with the commission certain quarterly information.

The Brazilian Institute of Accountants (IBRACON) issues accounting standards. All companies listed on the Rio de Janeiro stock exchange and Sao Paulo Stock Exchange submit financial statements that follow Brazilian GAAP.[35]

The requirements regarding property, plant and equipment and depreciation for the purpose of preparation and presentation of annual financial statements are as follows:[36]

(i) Property, plant and equipment should be recorded at historical cost.

(ii) The initial estimate of the costs of dismantling and removing the asset and restoring the site on which it is located should be included in the cost of an item of property, plant and equipment.

(iii) The cost of major inspection and overhaul occurring at regular intervals is capitalised.

(iv) Financing costs directly attributable to the construction of the fixed assets are capitalised.

(v) Revaluation above historical cost is permitted.

(vi) Revaluation surpluses arising from such revaluations are to be treated as taxable revenue in the year in which the revaluations are carried out. Alternatively, the surpluses can also be transferred to the revaluation reserve account in which case portions of the surpluses are taxed annually in succeeding year.

(vii) Where an external valuation reveals that the value of a fixed asset is below its book value, the value of property, plant and equipment should be reduced to the extent of the revaluation reserve surplus included in equity, corresponding to the same asset. The corresponding deferred tax balance should also be adjusted for this negative revaluation. A provision for losses should be established for any excess amount, through a charge to non-operational expenses. This provision should only be recorded if the loss is considered unrecoverable.

(viii) A revaluation below historical cost may not be recorded if it is the first time that an asset is being subject to external valuation. The company should however consider whether the net book value of the asset is recoverable from future operations. If the recoverable value of the asset is below its net book value, and if this difference is not considered recoverable, a provision for losses should be recorded and charged to non-operational expenses.

(ix) On sale or disposal of a discontinued revalued asset, the revaluation must be reversed.

(x) Depreciation should be allocated on a systematic basis each fical period during the useful lives of the assets.

(xi) No specific depreciation method is recommended although the method chosen should be applied consistently.

(xii) The useful lives of the assets should be revised periodically and the depreciation rates should be adjusted.

(xiii) Depreciation of assets is to be calculated in accordance with the rates prescribed by tax authorities.

(xiv) Even though it is not clearly stated in the accounting rules the change in depreciation method are usually considered as a change in accounting estimate and recorded prospectively.

(xv) Capitalisation of interest is not permitted hence it is treated as expenses when incurred.

(xvi) Gains and loss from sale or disposal of assets are recorded as non-operating expense.

## South Africa

South African reporting are based on statements of Generally Accepted

Accounting Practice (GAAP) issued by the Accounting Practices Board (APB) of the South African Institute of Chartered Accounts (SAICA), the disclosure requirements of Schedule 4 to the Companies Act and, where applicable, the JSE Securities Exchange South Africa (the JSE) Listing Requirements. The Companies Act requires fair presentation and conformity with generally accepted accounting practice (though the latter term is not defined). This lack of definition has resulted in a body of accounting practices which are uncodified but are generally followed by companies. Disclosure of any departure from statement of GAAP is required; however it is considered unlikely that fair presentation would be achieved without compliance with statements of GAAP.[37]

The South African Institute of Chartered Accountants (SAICA) is the pre-eminent accounting body in South Africa. It has established itself as one of the leading Institute in the world playing its part in a highly dynamic business sector. Statements of GAAP are drafted by the SAICA and after a period of publication for comments approved by the Accounting Practices Board (APB). South African's GAAP statements can be broadly categorised as introductory statements, general statements, statements on field work and statements on reporting. Statement of GAAP must be followed in the preparation of the financial statements of companies subject to the Companies Act.[38] In addition to the Companies Act requirement, GAAP requires the disclosure of information concerning the company's details accounting policies.

The Board considers that statements of Generally Accepted Accounting Practices (GAAP), codified by the Accounting Practices Board (APB) and issued by the South African Institute of Chartered Accountants are Generally Recognised Accounting Practice (GRAP).[39] The Accounting Standard Board (ASB) set standards and guidelines for Financial Statement as required by Section 216(a) by the Constitution of South Africa. The Public Finance Management Act (PEMA) gave effect to this requirement by providing for the establishment of the ASB and requiring mainly to set standards of

GRAP for the annual financial statements; and prepare and publish direction and guidelines concerning the standards, PFMA also addresses this requirement, by requiring public sector entities to comply with GRAP to be prescribed by Accounting Standard Board (ASB)[40].

The Accounting Standard Board (ASB) is required in terms of the Public Finance Management Act, Act No. 1 of 1999 as amended (PFMA) to determine generally recognised accounting practice referred to as Standards of Generally Recognised Accounting Practices (GRAP). Section 55(1)(b) of PFMA requires public entities to prepare financial statements in accordance with GAAP, unless the ASB approves the application of GRAP for that public entity. In terms of a resolution taken by SAICA in 2004 all new South African standards will be exactly in line with IFRS standards issued by IASB.[41]

The JSE Securities Exchange South Africa (JSE) has approved substantial amendments to its listing rules that will require all companies listed on the exchange to comply with International Financial Reporting Standards (IFRS) issued by International Accounting Standard Board for years commencing on or after 1 January, 2005. Previously, a company whose primary listing is on the JSE could elect to comply with either South African Statement of Generally Accepted Accounting Practices (SA GAAP) or IFRS. Under the amended JSE rules, a JSE GAAP Monitoring Panel will have the authority to sanction listed companies for non-compliance with either SA GAAP or IFRS.[42]

The South African Institute of Chartered Accountants and the JSE Securities Exchange South Africa (JSE) have established a panel of specialists to ensure that listed companies comply with South African Statements of Generally Accepted Accounted Practice (GAAP) accords with International Financial Reporting Standard.

At present, GAAP does not have legal backing within legislation Government in response to SAICA's request to provide legal backing, has drafted legislation in the form of the Financial Services Bill.

Currently all listed companies are obliged by the listings requirements of the JSE to comply with SA GAAP or IFRS. As the JSE lacks the resources to solely monitor compliance with accounting standard, it has partnered with SAICA to ensure that listed companies do comply. SAICA and the JSE will both be vigilant for non-compliance.[43]

The requirements regarding property, plant and equipment and depreciation for the preparation and presentation of financial statements are as follows.[44]

(i) The initial recognition of an item of properly, plant and equipment shall be measured at its cost. It includes any costs directly attributable to bringing the asset to the location and condition necessary for it to be capable of operating in the manner intended by management.

(ii) Major repairs and maintenance cost and non-recurring replacement cost are recognised in cost of property, plant and equipment i.e. capitalised. Major inspection cost are also capitalised.

(iii) The initial estimated cost of the dismantling and removing the asset and restoring the site on which it is located are capitalised.

(iv) Where an asset is acquired at no cost or for a nominal cost, its cost is its fair value as at the date acquisition.

(v) The cost of a self-constructed asset is determined using the same principles as for an acquired cost. The cost of abnormal item of wasted material, labour and other cost are not included in the cost of the asset.

(vi) Minor items (no specific amount) of purchase property, plant and equipment are also recognised in the income statement as incurred.

(vii) For exchange of asset for another asset, the cost of such item of property, plant and equipment is measured at fair value. If the acquired asset is not measured at fair value, its cost is measured at the carrying amount of the asset given up.

(viii) Revaluation of asset is permitted. However, if an item of property, plant and equipment is revalued, the entire class of property, plant and equipment to which that asset belongs shall be revalued.

(ix) An entity shall choose either cost model, where after recognition as an asset, an item of property, plant and equipment shall be carried at its cost less accumulated depreciation and any accumulated impairment losses; or the Revaluation Model, where after recognition as an asset, an item of property, plant and equipment whose fair value can be measured reliably shall be carried at a revalued amount, being its fair value at the date of the revaluation less subsequent accumulated depreciation and subsequent accumulated impairment losses.

(x) The frequency of revaluation depends upon the changes in the fair value of the item of property, plant and equipment revalued at the reporting date. When the fair value of a revalued asset differs materially from its carrying amount, a further revaluation is required. Sometimes frequent revaluation are necessary for an item may be necessary to revalue the item of property, plant and equipment only every three or five years.

(xi) It an assets' carrying amount is increased as a result of revaluation, the increase shall be credited directly to a revaluation surplus. However, the increase shall be recognised in surplus or deficit to the extent that it reverse a revaluation decrease of the same asset previously recognised in surplus or deficit. The revaluation surplus is credited directly to a revaluation reverse in equity.

(xii) If an asset's carrying amount is decreased as a result of a revaluation, the decrease shall be recognised in surplus or deficit. However, the decrease shall be debited directly to a revaluation surplus to the extent of any credit balance existing in the revaluation surplus in respect of that asset.

(xiii) The revaluation surplus included in net asset in respect of an item of property, plant and equipment may be transferred directly to accumulated surplus or deficit when the asset is derecognised in the process of retirement or disposed off.

(xiv) The depreciable amount of an asset shall be allocated on a systematic basis over its useful life. A variety of depreciation method can be used to allocate the depreciable amount of an asset on a systematic basis over its useful life. These methods include the straight line method, diminishing balance method and the unit of production method. Once the method is selected, that method is applied consistently from period to period unless there is a change in the expected pattern of consumption of these future economic benefits or service potential.

(xv) The depreciation method applied to an asset shall be reviewed at least of each reporting date and if there has been a significant change in the expected pattern of consumption of the future economic benefits or service potential embodied in the asset, the method shall be changed to reflect the changed pattern. Such a change shall be accounted for as change in an accounting estimate.

(xvi) The residual value and the useful life of an asset shall be reviewed at least at each reporting date and if expectations differ from previous estimates, the change shall be accounted for as a change in an accounting estimate.

(xvii) The gain or less arising from the derecognition of an item of property, plant and equipment shall be included in surplus or deficit when the item is derecognized. Gains shall not be classified as revenue.

(xviii) Borrowing costs incurred in respect of assets requiring a substantial period of time to prepare for their intended future use are capitalised to the date that the assets are substantially completed.

## Australia

Australia requirements are mainly based on the Corporation Act 2001 and the standards of the Australian Accounting Standards Board and Abstracts of the Urgent Issues Group.[45] Australian GAAP comprises:[46]

(i) *Accounting Standards* (*AASBs/AASs*): Historically, AASBs were applicable only to entities required to comply with the Corporation Act 2001 and its predecessors, generally companies, disclosing entities and registered schemes. AASs are applied to all other entities such as public sectors and trusts. The Australian Accounting Standards Board (AASB) has announced that there will be no further issue of AASs since August 2000 AASBs are applicable to Corporation Act entities and any other entities preparing general purpose financial reports. Existing AASs will continue to apply to non-corporation Act entities until they are replaced by AASBs.

(ii) *Other Authoritative Pronouncements of the AASB*: Currently the only other authoritative pronouncements of the AASB are Accounting Interpretations (AIs). They are meant to provide timely guidance on the applications of accounting standards. Accounting Bulletins (ABs) and Accounting Guidance Releases (AAGs) were issued by predecessors of the current AASB and are not considered authoritative pronouncements. However, in the absence of contradictory pronouncements since their issue, they generally are considered relevant guidance.

(iii) *Abstracts Issued by the Urgent Issues Group* (*UIG*): The Corporate Law Economic Reform Programme Act 1999 establishes the basis for new standard setting arrangements as part of the Government's Corporation Law Economic Reform Programme. Consequently, accounting standard setting arrangements were restructured in 2000 following amendments to the Corporation Law. As a result of these amendments, a Financial Reporting Council (FRC) was created and the Australian Accounting Standard Board (AASB) was reconstituted. As part of these arrangements the Urgent Issues Group was re-established as a committee of the AASB.

The FRC is the peak body responsible for the broad oversight of the accounting standard setting process for the private and public sectors. It comprises key stakeholders from the business community the professional accounting bodies, governments and regulatory agencies. Key functions of the FRC are to advice the Government on the accounting standard setting process and the development of international accounting standards and to determine the broad strategic direction of the AASB. The FRC may give the AASB directions, advice and feedback on matters of general policy and will be responsible for approving its priorities, business plan, budget and staffing arrangements.

The UIG was originally established by the Board of Management of the Australian Accounting Research Foundation, in consultation with the Australian Accounting Standards Board and the Public Sector Accounting Standards Board. The role of the UIG is to provide timely guidance on urgent financial reporting issues. In providing such guidance, the UIG will seeking to avoid the development of divergent or unsatisfactory financial reporting practices in areas not dealt with, or not dealt with specifically, in Accounting Standards. This role includes considering the application in Australia of Interpretations proposed or issued by the International Financial Reporting Interpretations Committee (IFRIC) of the International Accounting Standards Board (IASB). UIG consensus views are given authority by the AASB as pronouncements to be used in selecting and applying accounting policies. This is achieved by listing all current UIG Interpretations, which incorporate the consensus views, in Accounting

Standard and are first applicable for a reporting period beginning prior to 1 January, 2005.[47]

The Australian Accounting Standards Board recently issued 40 new or revised Accounting Standards referred to as Australian equivalents to International Financial Reporting Standards (AIFRS) applicable for all financial year beginning on or after 1 January, 2005. These standards reflect the 'stable platform' created by the International Accounting Standards Board (IASB) as at 31 March, 2004 and early adoption of the standards will not be permissible either on a piecemeal basis or in their entirely.

*AASB 116 Property, Plant and Equipment* is the accounting standard issued by Australian Accounting Standards Board to deal with tangible fixed assets.

The requirements regarding property, plant and equipment and depreciation for the purpose of preparation and presentation of financial statements are as follows:[48]

(i) An item of property. Plant and equipment are initially be measured at its cost. Cost of an asset includes the cost of dismantling and removing an asset and restoring the site on which the asset was created.

(ii) The cost of a major inspection and overhaul occurring at regular intervals is capitalised where recognition criteria are satisfied.

(iii) An item of property, plant and equipment, subsequently, can be measured either at cost or at fair value after initial measurement.

(iv) ACTPS policy specifies a default recording threshold of $2000. Assets up to this level may be treated as expenses and written off in the period of purchase.

(v) A threshold up to $5000 may be applied following approval by the Department of Treasury. An entity that requires a variation from the $2000 threshold should apply to the Department of the treasury.

(vi) Revaluation of assets are required to be performed at the same time for all property, plant and equipment in the same class. An entity may have some asset classes valued at cost and some asset classes valued at fair value.

(vii) It an entity chooses to apply fair value to an asset class, revaluation must be undertaken with sufficient regularity to ensure that the carrying amount of each asset in the class does not differ materially from its fair value at the date of reporting. The asset class must be revalued at least every 3 years, with agencies having the option of initiating more frequent revaluations if required. If a class of assets is valued at cost, revaluations will not be applicable.

(viii) Revaluation increments or decrements relating to property, plant and equipment held by a for-profit entity must be offset against the revaluation reserve of same class of assets.

(ix) Where a revaluation gives rise to a value uplift, it should be credited to the revaluation reserve unless it represents the reversal of a revaluation decrease of the same asset previously recognised as an expense, in which case it should be recognised as income.

(x) A decrease arising as a result of a revaluation should be recognised as an expense in so far as it exceeds the amount that can be charged to the revaluation surplus (i.e. the amount held in the revaluation surplus relating the same asset).

(xi) On revaluation, any accumulated depreciation is either: (a) restated proportionately with the change in the gross carrying amount of the asset so that the carrying amount after revaluation equals its revalued amount; or (ii) eliminated against carrying amount of the asset and the net amount restated to the revalued amount of the asset.

(xii) A gain or loss on disposal of a revalued non-current asset is to be recognised in the Statement of Financial Performance for the reporting period in which disposal of asset occurs. The standard requires that a gain or loss on disposal be measured as the difference between the carrying amount of the revalued non-current asset as at the time of disposal and the net proceeds, if any from disposal.

(xiii) The standard stated that the revenue and any related expenses occurring while property, plant and equipment is being constructed or developed is to be recognised in the profit or loss/result for the period.

(xiv) All non-current assets having limited lives are systematically depreciated over their useful lives in a manner that reflects the consumption of their service potential. Three most common methods used for calculating depreciation expenses are the straight line, reducing balance and units of output methods.

(xv) Effect of charges to depreciation rates or methods must be accumulated for as a change in the estimated useful life of the asset. The effects must be recognised only in current and/or future periods. No retrospective adjustments are allowed.

(xvi) Depreciation rates must be reviewed annually to determine whether initial assessment of their useful life was inappropriate and in case where there has been a change in the expected pattern of consumption of future economic benefits, the depreciation method must be charged to reflect the changed pattern. In such case the remaining written down value of the asset must be depreciated over the revised remaining useful life of the asset. Change in depreciation method treated as change in accounting estimates.

(xvii) It may also become apparent that the estimated residual value of an asset is no longer realistic. Increases to the estimated residual value of an asset, that are due to change in price, must only be made when the asset is revalued.

(xviii) Interest on borrowing should be capitalised as a part of the cost of asset.

## Japan

Japanese requirements are based on the Commercial Code, the standard of the Business Accounting Deliberation Council (BADC), statements of the Japanese Institute of Certified Public Accountants (JICPA) and the provisions of Japanese Securities and Exchange Law.[49]

Japan in one of the wonders of the modern economic and business world. The most dominant form of business in Japan is *Kabushikhi Kaisha* which is very much similar to the public limited company in the western country. The liability of the shareholder of the *Kabushikhi Kaisha* is limited to the nominal subscribed capital. Most Japanese companies have a very highly geared structure. It is the commercial bank which is the principal source of the borrowed capital of Japanese company. In most cases, the bank credit takes the form of short-term promissory notes that are continually rolled over. Another noticeable feature of the business environment in Japan is the cross-shareholding between banks and companies.[50]

In Japan, business accounting principles were established in 1949. Since then, Japan's business accounting system has grown from individual financial statements, under a triangular system in which the Securities and Exchange Law, Commercial Code and Corporate Income Tax Law play complementary roles.[51]

The Generally Accepted Accounting Principles (GAAP) in Japan consist of several sources. Major sources of GAAP are set forth by the Business Accounting Deliberation Council (BADC). The BADC is a advisory body to the Ministry of Finance. The BADC was established in 1949 and since then it has issued numerous statements opinion and interpretation of financial accounting standards.

The Accounting Standard Committee of the Japanese Institute of CAPs (JICPA), which is a private, self regulatory accounting organisation, issues Accounting Standard Committee Reports. The Committee Report which provides implementation guidance for the Commercial Law, MOF ordinances and regulations, BADC statements and other authorised documents are also important source of the GAAP.

*MOF Ordinances and Regulations*: As securities regulator, the Ministry of Finance (MOF) provide disclosure ordinances and regulations. They provide very detailed guidance on how financial statements should be displayed and what kind of information should be disclosed.

The MOF has been providing disclosures about segme information, earning per share and financial instruments. These disclosures issues are not addressed in detail of the BADC and recently the MOF looks very aggressive to improve disclosure.[52]

The MOF also issues its interpretation that states that a specific BADC statement is a source of the GAAP and should be enforced for the purpose of the Securities and Transaction Law.

*Corporate Income Tax Law*: Tax Laws and its implementation guidelines are important source of GAAP in Japan. The tax law provided very detailed guidance originally for tax purposes. If accounting standards are silent in some specific issues and the tax laws provide some tax guidelines, accountants tend to use tax guidelines in preparing financial statements.

*Commercial Code*: It contains a number of provisions relating to financial accounting and reporting and perhaps the most important part of Japanese accounting is that the commercial law provides some limited number of accounting requirements certainly overrule the GAAP, any BADC statements and JICPA Accounting Committee Reports should be consisted with the Commercial Law's accounting requirements. Even when the issues addressed by BADC or the JIPCA are not directly covered by the commercial law, the accounting standard-setters take very careful consideration for not being inconsistent with the law.[53]

*The Securities and Exchange Law*: The objective of the Securities Exchange Law is to protect investors, requires the use of business accounting standards that are recognised to be generally fair and appropriate (Japan GAAP) as the basis for disclosure of securities reports etc. It is basically concerned with prescribing the form and content of the financial statements of those companies that are listed on the stock exchange.

*Accounting Standard Board of Japan*: In February 2001, Accounting Standard Board of Japan, a private-sector organisation, established Financial Accounting Standard Foundation (FASF), along with Accounting Standard Board (ASB). The ASB is a body expected to have responsibility for the development of accounting standards in Japan. The FASF is expected to assume an oversight role regarding ASB activities. The organisations named above have worked together with the working committee and are now pleased to announce the establishment of the FASF, based on the necessary of the competent authorities. The objectives of the FASF are to promote progress of corporate finance and soundness of the capital markets in Japan by developing generally accepted accounting standards. The FASF will also contribute to the development of a high quality set of internationally accepted accounting standards.[54]

The requirements regarding property, plant and equipment and depreciation for the purpose of preparation and presentation of annual financial statements are as follows: [55]

(i) Purchased assets through transactions with other parties should be recognised at cost paid at acquisition. Cost paid at acquisition include the transacted costs and other accompanying expenses.

(ii) Assets acquired through self-construction, the costs of the assets should be determined by using cost accounting formula.

(iii) Assets acquired in exchange of other assets, the book value of the disposed assets should be carried over as a new cost of acquired assets. If an entity obtained assets without expense, fair value should be used as the cost of such assets.

(iv) Maintenance and repairs including minor renewals and improvement are treated as expenses when incurred and charged to income.

(v) Major renewals and betterments are capitalised at cost.

(vi) Estimated cost of dismantling, removing the asset and restoring the site are not capitalised.

(vii) Revaluation of assets is strictly prohibited i.e. Japan adhere strictly to historical cost valuation.

(viii) Small amount of depreciable assets of which the acquisition price is 1,00,000 yen or more and less than 2,00,000 yen are depreciated evenly over three years based on the provision of the Corporate Income Tax Law. Assets valued less than 100,000 yen treated as expense when incurred.

(ix) The methods of depreciation include straight line method, the declining balance method, the sum-of-the-years'-digits method and the unit-of-production method. Generally those methods can be applied alternatively, except for unit-of-production method. The unit-of-production method can be applied only to the assets whose value will decline is proportion to the use of the assets and whose total units of production are predictable.

(x) Depreciation rates for financial reporting must be the same as those for income tax purpose i.e. depreciation rates are guided by the Corporate Income Tax Laws.

(xi) There is no requirements to review the method of depreciation periodically. A change in depreciable method is considered to be a change in accounting policy. However in certain cases where the useful lives are deemed to be inadequate, useful lives should be changed.

(xii) The capital gain on disposal of assets is not recognised as income and it is adjusted with the depreciable cost of that class of assets.

(xiii) Interest capitalisation is not permitted hence it is treated as expense when incurred.

(xiv) Financing costs (e.g. interest expense) relating to the construction of property, plant and equipment is not capitalised.

## China

The financial reporting requirements of the People's Republic of China (PRC) are mainly based on the Accounting Law and on standards and regulations issued by the Ministry of Finance.[56]

In the process of transforming itself from a centrally planned economy to the market oriented economy, China has realised the importance of a sound financial accounting infrastructure. The old accounting systems and regulations were designed to meet the needs of a planned economy, and therefore focused on whether the production of state-owned enterprises and their financial and cost plan were being met. Accordingly, the objectives of accounting performance measurement some 20 years ago were significantly different from the financial reporting objectives in a modern market oriented economy.[57]

China's rapid economic growth in the last two decades has amazed the rest of the world. With China's accession to the World Trade Organisation (WTO) in December 2001, business activities with and within China have been expanding at enormous speed. China fully understand that a sound financial reporting system plays a key role in the process of economic development. The Chinese Ministry of Finance (MOF), who has the responsibility for regulating accounting matters in China, has set itself the objective of foreign investors' confidence in financial information, increase transparency of financial reporting and harmonize with IFRS. The development of the Chinese accounting standard in an important element in meeting this objective and an area where MOF has made significant progress.[58]

There are a number at laws and regulations covering accounting and financial reporting in China. The Accounting Law of the PRC, which as enacted by the National People's Congress in 1985 and was last revised as on 1 July 2000, the highest authority on accounting in China. It sets out general principles of accounting for all enterprises, including a definition of the nature and role of accounting and basic principles. It empowers the MOF to administer accounting affairs and to establish uniform accounting regulations and system. Such regulations and systems have the force of law. Development since the enactment of Accounting Law have shifted from traditional accounting practice which being comparatively more rule oriented was concerned with measuring progress by reference to the state plan and with monitoring the legitimacy of the application of state funds.[59]

In 1993 with finding from the world Bank, the MOF began a project to develop about 30 accounting standards which would be appropriate to China's development socialist market economy and in harmonization progress, Deloittee Touche Tohmatsu has been engaged as consultants to help the MOF develop a body of Chinese Accounting Standards in line with accounting and financial reporting practice used internationally. To date 16 standards have been issued as final standard and other remain under development.

Beside the development of accounting standards, the MOF announced a new *Accounting System for Business Enterprises* (the ASBE) at the end 2000. Starting from 1 January 2001, all joint stock limited enterprises were required to follow the ASBE. The implementation of the ASBE improved significantly the comparability between China and international accounting practice. With effect from 1 January, 2002 foreign investment enterprises in the PRC were required to apply the ASBE. In March 2003, the MOF further extended the applicability of the ASBE to all enterprise (other than small enterprises and financial institution—who have their separate Accounting System) newly established on or after 1 January 2003. In the long term, the MOF intends to apply the ASBE to all large and medium size enterprises, including state-owned enterprises and to unify the different accounting treatments adopted by different industries and different enterprises in order to improve the comparability of financial information.

For enterprises other than small enterprises and financial institutions, the Accounting Standards, the ASBE and other related accounting pronouncements such as Circulars issued by the MOF (known as *Caikuai*) from the fundamental regulations of PRC GAAP. When there are conflicts between pronouncements, the rules in the most recent pronouncement should be followed, unless otherwise specified. Although the general principles for accounting treatments addressed in individual specific Accounting Standards are also included in the ASBE, these are more detailed interpretations and guidance in the individual specific Accounting Standards.[60]

The requirements regarding fixed assets and depreciation for the purpose of preparation and presentation of annual financial statements are as follows:[61]

(i) Fixed asset should initially be recorded at its cost. The cost comprises the purchase price, import duties, transport and insurance cost and any directly attributable expenditure for bringing the asset to working condition for its intended use.

(ii) Estimated cost of disposal of asset including the cost of dismantling and removing of the asset are capitalised.

(iii) An enterprise should carry out major overhauls to fixed assets regularly. Major overhaul costs can be accrued in advance or deferred. If an enterprise uses the accrual method to account for major overhaul costs such costs should be accrued evenly over the period between two major overhauls are carried out and included as relevant costs or expense. If an enterprise use deferral method to account the major overhaul costs, such costs should be amortised evenly over the period up to next major overhaul and charged to relevant cost or expenses.

(iv) A self constructed fixed asset should be recorded at the total amount of all expenditure for bringing the asset to working condition for its intended use.

(v) Any fixed asset valued RMB 2000 or less should be treated as expense when incurred.

(vi) A fixed asset that undergoes modification and enhancement should be recorded at the original carrying amount of the fixed asset plus any expenditure necessary incurred for bringing the fixed asset to working condition for its intended use less any incidental income arising in the course of the modification and enhancement.

(vii) Revaluation of fixed asset is not permitted.

(viii) Fixed assets should be recorded at the lower of carrying amount and recoverable amount at the end of each period. If the recoverable amount of a fixed asset is lower than its carrying amount, the enterprise should make a provision for impairment in value of the fixed asset at an amount equal to the difference between the asset's recoverable amount and its carrying amount. The impairment loss should be recognised in the income statement for the current period.

(ix) When a provision for impairment loss has been made for a fixed asset, the depreciation rate and depreciation charge for the fixed asset should be recalculated based on the asset's carrying amount and its remaining life.

(x) An enterprise should select the depreciation method for a fixed asset according to the consumption pattern of economic benefits embodied in the fixed asset and the available methods include the straight line method, the unit-of-production method, the double declining balance method and the sum-of-the-years'-digits method. Once the depreciation method is selected, it should not be changed without reason.

(xi) Depreciation charges of fixed assets should be provided and recognised as cost of related assets or expense for the period according to the purpose for which the fixed assets are used.

(xii) An enterprise should normally provide depreciation on a monthly basis. No depreciation should be provided for fixed assets newly acquired in the month of addition, instead, they are depreciated starting from the following month. Depreciation should continue to be provided for fixed assets disposed off in the month of disposal; depreciation should cease from the following month.

(xiii) An enterprise should periodically review the useful life of a fixed asset and if expectations are significantly different from the previous estimates, the useful life should be revised in accordance with the appropriate approval and filing procedures and should be stated in the notes to the accounting statements.

(xiv) An enterprise should periodically review the depreciation method applied to fixed assets and if there has been a significant change in the expected realisation pattern of economic benefits from those assets, the method should be changed in accordance with the appropriate approval and filing procedures and should be stated in the notes to the accounting statements. In accordance with *Caikuai* (2004)

No. 3 issued by the MOF, a change of depreciation method is accounted for as a change in accounting estimates.

(xv) If the recorded amount of a fixed asset is adjusted because of reasons such as renovation and improvement, depreciation should be provided based on the adjusted recorded amount, expected remaining useful life and net residual value of the asset according to the selected depreciation method.

(xvi) When an enterprise's fixed assets have been sold, transferred, retired or destroyed, the enterprise should recognise the difference between the disposal proceeds and the carrying amount of the asset, as reduced by any related taxes and expenses, in the income statement for the current period.

(xvii) Borrowing costs incurred in connection with specific borrowings for the purchase or construction of fixed assets should be capitalised when the conditions for capitalisation are met and up to date, the assets are ready for their intended use.

## *International Accounting Standard (IAS-16)*

The International Accounting Standards Board (IASB) was established in January 2001 to replace its predecessor international standard setter, the International Accounting Standards Committee (IASC). The IASC has so far issued forty one accounting standards of which large number of standards have been revised and seven accounting standards are suspended. So the effective number of international accounting standards are thirty four only.[62]

The Board of the International Accounting Standards Committee formed The Standing Interpretations Committee (SIC) in January 1997. The SIC's objective is to enhance the rigorous application and worldwide comparability of Financial statements that are prepared using International Accounting Standards by interpreting potentially contentious accounting issues.

Creation of The IASB arose from the recommendations of the

IASC's Strategy Working Party and charged with reviewing the IASC's structure and process and proposing changes to better prepare that organisation for the future of international accounting standard setting. IASB publishes its standards in a series of pronouncements called International Financial Reporting Standards (IFRS). It has also adopted the body of standards issued by the Board of the International Accounting Standards Committee. Those pronouncements continue to be designated 'International Accounting Standards (IAS)'.

IASB has also approved all existing SIC Interpretation. The SIC has been reconstituted in December 2001 and renamed as the International Financial Reporting Interpretations Committee (IFRIC). IFRIC is charged with development of a series of Interpretations of International Accounting Standards under the approval of IASB.

International Accounting Standard (IAS)-16 deals with Property, Plant and Equipment. This standard should be applied in accounting for tangible fixed and depreciation. This standard is adopted by many countries who do not have their own accounting standard in this area.

The main requirements of IAS-16 are as follows:[63]

(i) An item of property, plant and equipment is initially recognised at cost. The cost includes an amount of cash or cash equivalents paid or fair value of the other consideration given to acquire an asset at the time of its acquisition or construction.

(ii) The initial estimate of the costs of dismantling and removing the item and restoring the site on which it is located are capitalised.

(iii) The cost of a major inspection or overhaul occurring at regular intervals is capitalised where the recognition criteria are satisfied.

(iv) Subsequent to initial recognition, an item of property, plant and equipment is carried either at:

(a) Cost less accumulated depreciation and any accumulated impairment losses; or

(b) Revalued amount less subsequent accumulated depreciation and any accumulated impairment losses. The revalued amount is fair value of the date of revaluation.

The choice of measurement is applied consistently to an entire class of property, plant and equipment.

(v) Revaluation should be made with sufficient regularity such that the carrying amount does not differ materially from that which would be determined using fair value at the reporting date.

(vi) When an item of property, plant and equipment is revalued, the entire class of property, plant and equipment to which the asset belongs should be revalued.

(vii) When an asset's carrying amount is increased as a result of a revaluation, the increase is credited to equity under the heading of revaluation surplus. However, a revaluation increase is recognised as income to the extend that it reverses a revaluation decrease of the same assets previously recognised as an expense.

(viii) A revaluation decrease as a result of revaluation, is recognised as an expense i.e. recognised in profit and loss statement. However, a revaluation decrease is charged directly against any related revaluation surplus to the extent that the decrease does not exceed the amount held in the revaluation surplus in respect of that same asset.

(ix) The depreciable amount of an item of property, plant and equipment should be allocated on a systematic basis over its useful life. The depreciation method used should reflect the pattern in which the assets economic benefits are consumed by the enterprise. That means, it virtually allows all available methods for charging depreciation.

(x) The useful life of an item of property, plant and equipment should be reviewed periodically and, it expectations are significantly different from previous estimates. The depreciation charge for the current and future periods should be adjusted.

(xi) The depreciation method applied to property, plant and equipment should be reviewed periodically and, if there has been a significant change in the expected pattern of economic benefits from those assets, the method should be changed to reflects the changed pattern. When such a change in depreciation method is necessary the change should be accounted for as a change in accounting estimates.

(xii) For recovery of carrying amount, the carrying amount of an item or a group of identical items of property, plant and equipment should be reviewed periodically in order to assess whether the recoverable amount has declined below the carrying amount. When such a decline has occurred, the carrying amount should be reduced to the recoverable amount and termed as impairment loss. The amount of the reduction should be recognised as an expense immediately, unless it reverses a previous revaluation in which case it should be charged to equity.

(xiii) Gains or losses arising from the retirement or disposal of an item of property, plant and equipment should be determined as the different between the estimated net disposal proceeds and the carrying amount of the asset and should be recognised as income or expenses in the income statement.

(xiv) Borrowing costs that are directly attributable to the acquisition, construction or production of a qualifying asset are capitalised as a part of the cost of that asset. Alternatively expensed all borrowing costs when incurred.

In order to present the difference among the different countries and International Accounting Standard relating to depreciation accounting and tangible fixed asset in a concise and easy-to-understand manner, we included in the comparison table only a limited number of significant items and provided only brief explanation. It is important to mention here that the accounting pronouncement regarding depreciation and tangible fixed assets of different countries and IAS as they stood at the end of 31 December 2004 were investigated and summarised into the comparison table so that it can be used as a ready reckoner.

The differences what ever exist among the different countries will disappear sooner or later. Evidences are clear that in near future accounting standards will sharply divided into two poles: IASB and FASB. There is a tendency throughout the world to adopt IAS/IFRS issued by IASB i.e. IAS/IFRS are gradually gaining popularity. Actually the IASB is a private-sector organisation and as such it has no authority of its own to enforce the standards formulated by it. It must depend on others for ensuring compliance with its standard. There are many third world countries that have adopted IAS as their own national standards (e.g. Zimbabwe, Kuwait etc.) and many third world countries use the standards formulated by the IASB as a starting point in formulating their domestic accounting requirements (e.g. India, Singapore etc.). On the other hand, in some countries IASs are commended in those cases where there are no corresponding domestic requirements (e.g. Nigeria).[64] Again, a key moment in the more to IAS/IFRS came on 6 June, 2002 when the European Council of Ministers approved the regulation that would require all EU Companies listed on a regulated market to prepare amounts in accordance with International Accounting Standards for accounting periods beginning on or after 1 January 2005.[65] Moreover in recent

**Table 5.1:** I Showing the Accounting Pronouncements Relating to Depreciation and Tangible Fixed Assets

| *Country* | *Initial Recognition* | *Subsequent Measurement* | *Major Inspection and Overhaul cost* | *Dismantling and Removing cost* | *Revaluation of Asset* | *Treatment of Revaluation surplus* | *Frequency of Revaluation* | *Depreciation Method Used* | *Depreciation Rate* | *Change is Method of Depreciation* | *Change in Life of Asset* | *Fully Depreciated Asset* | *Borrowing Cost* | *Gain or Loss on Disposal of Asset* |
|---|---|---|---|---|---|---|---|---|---|---|---|---|---|---|
| The United States | Historical Cost | Cost less depreciation | Generally expensed | Expensed | Not permitted | Not applicable | Not applicable | Any methods except annuity method | Separate rate for tax accounting and financial accounting | Allowed and treated as change in accounting policy | Not allowed | Not available, apply GAAP | Capitalised | Adjusted with accumulated depreciation |
| Canada | Historical Cost | Cost less depreciation | Capitalised | Capitalised | Not permitted | Not applicable | Not applicable | Any methods | Separate rate for tax accounting and financial accounting | Allowe, Treated as Change in accounting policy | Allowe, Treated as change in accounting policy | Not available, apply GAAP | Capitalised | Transfer to income statement |

*(Contd.)*

| Country | Initial Recognition | Subsequent Measurement | Major Inspection and Overhaul cost | Dismantling and Removing cost | Revaluation of Asset | Treatment of Revaluation surplus | Frequency of Revaluation | Depreciation Method Used | Depreciation Rate | Change is Method of Depreciation | Change in Life of Asset | Fully Depreciated Asset | Borrowing Cost | Gain or Loss on Disposal of Asset |
|---|---|---|---|---|---|---|---|---|---|---|---|---|---|---|
| The United Kingdom | Historical Cost | Cost or market value / depreciated replacement cost | Capitalised | Capitalised | Permitted | Credited to revaluation reserve | Every 5 years | Any methods except annuity based method | Separate rate for tax accounting and financial accounting | Allowe, Treated as Change in accounting estimates | Allowe, Treated as Change in accounting estimates | No specific minimum value, follow GAAP | Generally capitalised | Trans-for to reserve |
| Germany | Historical Cost | Cost less depreciation | Capitalised | Not Capitalised | Not Permitted | Not Applicable | Not Applicable | Generally straight line and reducing balance method | Same for tax accounting and financial accounting | Permitted, only Reducing Balance method to S.L.M. | Allowed | Less than DM 800 | Generally Capitalised | Transfer to income statement |
| France | Historical Cost | Cost or Revalued amount | Not Capitalised | Not Capitalised | Permitted | Credited to revaluation reserve | Optional | S.L.M, R.B.M. and accelerated tax depreciation | Same for tax accounting and financial accounting | Allowed | Allowed | Below FF 2500 | Generally Capitalised | Transfer to Profit and Loss Account |

(Contd.)

| *Country* | *Initial Recognition* | *Subsequent Measurement* | *Major Inspection and Overhaul cost* | *Dismantling and Removing cost* | *Revaluation of Asset* | *Treatment of Revaluation surplus* | *Frequency of Revaluation* | *Depreciation Method Used* | *Depreciation Rate* | *Change is Method of Depreciation* | *Change in Life of Asset* | *Fully Depreciated Asset* | *Borrowing Cost* | *Gain or Loss on Disposal of Asset* |
|---|---|---|---|---|---|---|---|---|---|---|---|---|---|---|
| The Netherlands | Historical Cost | Cost or fair value | Expensed | Not Capitalised | Permitted | Credited to revaluation reserve | Not on regular basis | Any methods | Separate for tax accounting and financial accounting | Allowe, Treated as change in accounting estimates | No strict requirement | Not available, apply GAAP | Generally Capitalised | Transfer to income statement |
| Brazil | Historical Cost | Cost or Revalued amount | Capitalised | Capitalised | Permitted | Generally transfer to income statement & taxable | Optional | Any Methods | Same for tax accounting and financial account ing | Allowe, Treated as change in account ing estimat es | Allowed | Not available, apply GAAP | Expensed | Non-operating expense |
| South Africa | Historical Cost | Cost or fair value | Capitalised | Capitalised | Permitted | Credited to revaluation reserve | Every 3 or 5 years | Any methods | Separate for tax accounting and financial accounting | Allowe, Treated as change in accounting estimates | Allowe, Treated as change in accounting estimates | Minor items (no specific value) | Capitalised | Transfer to accumulated surplus or deficit |

(*Contd.*)

| *Country* | *Initial Recognition* | *Subsequent Measurement* | *Major Inspection and Overhaul cost* | *Dismantling and Removing cost* | *Revaluation of Asset* | *Treatment of Revaluation surplus* | *Frequency of Revaluation* | *Depreciation Method Used* | *Depreciation Rate* | *Change is Method of Depreciation* | *Change in Life of Asset* | *Fully Depreciated Asset* | *Borrowing Cost* | *Gain or Loss on Disposal of Asset* |
|---|---|---|---|---|---|---|---|---|---|---|---|---|---|---|
| Australia | Historical Cost | Cost or fair value | Capitalised | Capitalised | Permitted | Credited to revaluation reserve | At least every 3 years | Common methods S.L.M., R.B.M. and Output Methods | Separate for tax accounting and financial accounting | Allowe, Treated as change in accounting estimates | Allowed | Up to $2000, up to $5000 with prior approval | Capitalised | Transfer to Statement of Financial performance |
| Japan | Historical Cost | Depreciated Cost | Capitalised | Not Capitalised | Not Permitted | Not applicable | Not applicable | S.L.M., D.B.M. sun-of-the-years' digits method unit-of-production method | Same for tax accounting and financial accounting | Allowe, Treated as change in accounting policy | Allowed | Less than 100,000 Yen | Not Capitalised | Adjusted with depreciable cost (Not recognised as income) |
| China | Historical Cost | Cost less depreciation | Not Capitalised | Capitalised | Not Permitted | Not applicable | Not applicable | Any methods | Separate for tax accounting and financial accounting | Allowed Treated as change in accounting estimates | Allowed | Up to RMB 2000 | Capitalised | Transfer to income statement |

(*Contd.*)

| *Country* | *Initial Recognition* | *Subsequent Measurement* | *Major Inspection and Overhaul cost* | *Dismantling and Removing cost* | *Revaluation of Asset* | *Treatment of Revaluation surplus* | *Frequency of Revaluation* | *Depreciation Method Used* | *Depreciation Rate* | *Change is Method of Depreciation* | *Change in Life of Asset* | *Fully Depreciated Asset* | *Borrowing Cost* | *Gain or Loss on Disposal of Asset* |
|---|---|---|---|---|---|---|---|---|---|---|---|---|---|---|
| India | Historical Cost | Depreciated cost or fair value | Generally Capitalised | No general guidance for capitalisation | Permitted | Credited to revaluation reserve | No requirement for regular intervals | Permitted method – S.L.M. & W.D.V. | Separate for tax accounting and financial accounting | Allowe, Treated as change in accounting policy | Allowed | Below Rs. 5000 | Generally Capitalised | Transfer to Profit and Loss Account (income statement) |
| International Accounting Standard (IAS)-16 | Historical Cost | Cost less accumulated depreciation or fair value | Capitalised | Capitalised | Permitted | Credited to revaluation reserve | Carrying cost differ materially from fair value | Any methods | Not applicable | Allowe, Treated as change in accounting estimates | Allowed, Treated as change in accounting estimates | Not available | Generally capitalised | Transfer to income statement |

**DM** – Deutsche Mark  **$** - Australian Dollar  **S.L.M.** – Straight line method  **W.D.V.** – Written down value method

**FF** – Franc  **RMB** – Yuan  **R.B.M.** – Reducing balance method  **D.B.M** – Diminishing balance method

times many countries outside EU are already moving towards IAS/ IFRS. In addition to the EU member states, over 70 countries currently permit or require the use of IFRS by some or all of their domestic listed companies or have announced plans to do so. Australia and New Zealand have already re-modelled almost all of their standards on IAS. Singapore is now adopting them. When Europe moves to IAS/IFRS, it will be more difficult for others to abstain.[66]

There is a lot of meetings between IASB and FASB to resolve the differences between them. Now the new structure of IASB has characteristics similar to that of the FASB's structure. One of the roles of the IASB is to promote the convergence of accounting standard around the world. Seven national accounting standard setters have on IASB Member resident in their jurisdiction. The IASB constitution envisages a 'partnership' between IASB and their national bodies as they work together to achieve the convergence of accounting standard world wide. The biggest issue that haunts the corporates and investors across the world whether international accounting standards can be used for the purpose of preparation and presentation of financial statements without recognition with the US GAAP. On the contrary, The FASB in the USA accepts the idea of increasing international comparability while maintaining the highest quality accounting standards in the United States.

In October 2002 the FASB reached a historic agreement with the IASB to use best-efforts to align over agendas and very importantly to undertake a specific project (with the help and support of the SEC staff) aimed to accelerating the convergence process by trying to eliminate or narrow some of the areas of difference between current US and international standards. Because there are literally hundreds differences between US and international standards, realistically, this effort will still be ongoing, will beyond 2005, when Europe adopts international accounting standards for annual financial reporting purpose. The overall objective of international convergence is not convergence just for the sake of convergence, but rather to arrive to high-quality accounting solutions that improve the transparency of financial reporting in the US and abroad.[67] Untill and unless the IASB and FASB resolve their differences amicably the real global convergence will not be possible.

## REFERNECES

1. www.iasplus.com/country/canada.htm
2. www.iasplus.com/au/0509differences.pdf
3. A.K. Basu, *International Accounting Hormonisation,* DSA in Commerce, University of Calcutta, 1995, pp. 175-177.
4. www.iasplus.com/resource/gaap2001.pdf
5. Patrick R. Delancy, Ralph Nach, Barry J. Epstein and Susan Weiss Budak, *Wiley GAAP-2003- Interpretation and Application of Generally Accepted Accounting Principles,* New Jersey, John Wiley & Sons. Inc., 2003, p. 5.
6. *Ibid.*, p. 6.
7. *Ibid.*, p.7.
8. *Ibid.*, pp. 326-60.
9. www.iasplus.com/dttpubs/2005ifrsus.pdf
10. www.iasplus.com/resource/gaap2001.pdf
11. www.camagazine.com
12. T.P. Ghosh, *Accounting Standards and Corporate Accounting Practices,* New Delhi, Taxmann Allied Services (Pvt.) Ltd., 2003, p. 1737.
13. *Ibid.*, pp. 1737-38.
14. *CICA Handbook* Section 3061, 3063
15. www.iasplus.com/dttpubs/uk_ger.pdf
16. FRS 15, www.iasplus.com/dttpubs/pubs.htm#ce, www.kpmg.co.uk/pubs/ias_comp_ukusgaap.pdf
17. www.iasplus.com/recource/gaap2001.pdf
18. www.iasplus.com/dttpubs uk_ger.pdf
19. *Ibid.*
20. *Ibid.*
21. www.kpmg.co.uk/pubs/ias_gaap_german.pdf. www.iasplus.com/dttpubs/uk_ger.pdf
22. www.iasplus.com/resource/gaap2001.pdf
23. A.K. Basu, *op. cit.*, p. 67.
24. Roger K. Doost and Karen M. Ligon, reprinted in a website with permission of the Institute of Management Accountants from *Management Accounting,* October, 1986.

25. www.iasplus.com/dttpubs/uk_fra.pdf
26. *Ibid.*
27. *Ibid.*
28. www.iasplus.com/resource/gaap2001.pdf.
29. A.K. Basu, *op. cit.*, p. 78.
30. www.kpmg.co.uk/pubs/ias_dutch_gaap.pdf
31. *Ibid.*
32. www.iasplus.com/dttpubs/iasnlus.pdf, www.gweglobal.com/gx/eng/about/svcs/corporatereporting/Dutchand D04.pdf, www.kpmg.co.uk/pubs/ias_dutch_gaap.pdf.
33. www.iasplus/com/resource/gaap2001.pdf
34. A.K. Basu, *op. cit.*, p. 88.
35. T.P. Ghosh, *op. cit.*, p. 1745.
36. www.pwcglobal.com/gx/eng/about/svcs/corporatereporting/BrazilSandD.pdf; KPMG Brazil, *Accounting Practices Comparison,* DPP Brazil, Second Edition, May 2001.
37. www.iasplus.com/resource/gaap 2001.pdf
38. www.werksmans.co.za
39. www.asb.co.za/template.asp?Menu ID = 11
40. www.saiga.co.za
41. www.ey.com/global
42. www.iasplus.com/dttpubs/pubs.htm#ce
43. *Ibid.*
44. www.asp.co.za/back office/content does/grap_17_ppe.pdf
45. www.iasplus.com/resource/gaap2001.pdf
46. www.kpmg.co.uk/pubs/Extract_IFRS_Australia_GAAP.pdf
47. www.aasb.com.au
48. www.aasb.com.au; www.treasury.act.gov.au/accounting
49. www.iasplus.com/resource/gaap 2001.pdf
50 A.K. Basu, *op. cit.*, p. 84.
51. www.iasplus.com/dttpubs/pubs.htm#ce
52. www2g.biglabe.ne.jp/~ykawamer/gaap 010.htm
53. *Ibid.*
54. www.asb.or.jp
55. www.asb.or.jp/e_asbj/begriff/ConceptualFramework.pdf; www.net-ir.ne.jp; www2g.biglobe.ne.jp/~ykawamer/gaap050 htm; www.mof.go.jp/english/tax/taxes2004e_c.pdf; www.kpmg.co.uk/pubs/Extract_IFRS_Japanese.pdf
56. www.iasplus.com/resource/gaap2001.pdf
57. www.iasplus.com/china/asbe.pdf
58. www.icaew.co.uk/librarylinks/index.cfm ? AUB = TB21_27450-41K

59. www.iasplus.com/china/asbe.pdf
60. www.icaew.co.uk/librarylinks/index.cfm ? AUB = TB21_27450-41K
61. www.iasplus.com/china/asbe.pdf
62. T.P. Ghosh, *op. cit.*, p. 25.
63. Sanjiv Agarwal, *A Manual of Accounting Standards*, New Delhi, Snow White Publications (P) Ltd., 2002, pp. 786-790; Dolphy D'Souza, *Indian Accounting Standards & GAAP,* India, Snow White Publications (P) Ltd., 2005, pp. 1453-1457.
64. A.K. Basu, *op. cit.*, pp. 175-77.
65. A.L. Saini, *International Financial Reporting Standards (IFRS), US-GAAP, UK-GAAP and Indian GAAP*, India, Snow White Publishers (P) Ltd., 2005, p. 3.
66. *Ibid.*, p. 7.
67. T.P. Ghosh, *op. cit.*, pp. 1736-37.

# 6

# Depreciation Accounting Practices in Indian Corporate Sector

This chapter presents data relating to depreciation accounting practices of 100 Indian companies covered in the sample. We are forced to take a sample of 100 companies out of first 200 companies of the 'ET 500' December 2004 edition published by Economic Times Intelligence Group because some of the companies are kept outside the purview of out study for example, Banking and Insurance companies (Companies having insignificant amount of fixed assets particularly plant and machinery) and annual reports of some of the companies are not available for example, Nestle India Limited. Another criteria we have fixed that the net turnover of this 100 companies must be Rs. 100 crores or more for the financial year 2003-04. Obviously the period of our study is only for one year i.e. 2003-04 and to examine how companies in India account for depreciation in their published annual accounts. The sample has been drawn in a way as to cover all the major segments or divisions of India industries. It also covers cross section wise of Indian industry. Here, focus has been given on the fixed assets turnover ratio to judge the degree of managerial efficiency in utilisation of fixed assets deployed in the company. A high fixed assets turnover ratio indicates company's ability to generate larger volume of sales with respect to a given amount of fixed assets. On the other hand, a low ratio indicates inefficiency in utilisation of fixed assets. However, a very high fixed assets turnover ratio may also be the result of over trading by the company and it is not a healthy practice as it may likely disrupt the normal operation. So to evaluate the fixed assets turnover ratio it would be logical to compare with industry average ratio. The corporate depreciation practices of selected 100 companies are described briefly in the following sections.

## Oil and Natural Gas Corporation Ltd.

The fixed assets turnover ratio of the company is 5.66. During the period of study the company provides depreciations on fixed assets under the written down value (WDV) method in accordance with the rates specified in Schedule XIV of the Companies Act 1956 except on fixed assets with 100 per cent rate of depreciation which are fully depreciated in the year of addition. Leasehold land is amortised over the lease period. The company provides depreciation on adjustments to fixed assets on account of foreign exchange differences and price variation over the remaining useful life of such assets. Depreciation on fixed assets (including support equipment and facilities) used for exploration and drilling activities on facilities is initially capitalised as part of exploration or development costs.

## Reliance Industries Ltd.

The fixed assets turnover ratio of the company is 1.63. The company has provided depreciation on fixed assets on written down value method at the rates and in the manner prescribed in Schedule XIV of the Companies Act 1956 except on fixed assets pertaining to crude oil refining and marketing infrastructure for petroleum products, depreciation has been charged over its residual life on straight line method (SLM). Incremental cost arising on account of translation of foreign currency liabilities for acquisition of fixed assets is forming a part of plants and depreciation has been provided as aforesaid over the residual life of the respective plants. Premium on leasehold land is amortised over the period of lease. Depreciation on revalued assets has been charged over the residual life of the assets.

## Indian Oil Corporation Ltd.

In case of this company, depreciation on fixed assets including LPG cylinders and pressure regulators is provided in accordance with the rates as specified in Schedule XIV of the Companies Act, 1956, on straight line method up to 95 per cent of the cost of the asset. Depreciation is charged pro rata on quarterly basis on assets, from/ up to the quarter of capitalisation/sale, disposal and dismantled during the year 2003-04. Assets other than LPG cylinders and pressure regulators costing up to Rs. 5000 are depreciated fully in the year of capitalisation. Cost of leasehold land for 99 years or less is amortised during the lease period. The fixed asset turnover ratio of the company is 6.08.

## Infosys Technologies Ltd.

The fixed assets turnover ratio of the company is 6.21. During the period of study, the company has adopted straight line method for charging depreciation on fixed assets over the useful lives of assets as estimated by the management. Depreciation for assets purchased/ sold during a period is proportionately charged. Individual low cost assets (acquired for less than Rs. 5000) are entirely depreciated in the year of acquisition. The company also mentioned the fact in respect of 100 per cent depreciation on assets under the heading of 'Management Discussion and Analysis.'

## Wipro Ltd.

The fixed assets turnover ratio of the company is 7.84. The company provides depreciation on straight line method at rates specified in Schedule XIV of the Companies Act 1956, except on data processing equipment and software, furniture and fixture, office equipment, electrical installations (other than those of factories) and vehicles for which commercial rates are applied.

## ITC Ltd.

The company calculates depreciation on fixed assets in a manner that amortises the cost of assets after commissioning over their estimated useful lives or where specified, lives based on the rates specified in Schedule XIV of the Companies Act 1956 which ever is lower, by equal annual installments. Leasehold properties are amortised over the period of lease. Incremental depreciation on revalued assets is charged to Revaluation Reserve Account. The fixed asset turnover ratio of the company is 1.96.

## Steel Authority of India Ltd.

During the period of study, the fixed asset turnover ratio of the company is 1.62. The company charges depreciation on straight line method at the rates specified is Schedule XIV of the companies Act 1956, However, where the historical cost of depreciable assets under goes a change the depreciation on the revised unamortised depreciable amount is provided prospectively over the residual useful life of the asset based on the rates specified in Schedule XIV of Companies Act 1956. The company also charges depreciation on asset installed/ disposed off during the year on pro rata basis. Leasehold land and mining rights are amortised over the lease period.

## Gas Authority of India Ltd.

The fixed asset turnover ratio of the company for the financial year 2003-04 is 1.52. During the period of study the company is adopting straight line method for the purpose of calculating depreciation on fixed asset in accordance with the rates as specified in Schedule XIV of the Companies Act 1956 on pro rata basis (monthly pro rata for bought out assets) excepting certain assets where depreciation rates are higher than Schedule XIV rates. Asset costing up to Rs. 5000 are depreciated fully in the year of capitalisation. Leasehold land is amortised over the lease period. Depreciation due to price adjustment on account of foreign exchange rate variations or otherwise in the original cost of fixed assets is charged prospectively.

## Tata Iron and Steel Company Ltd.

The company provides depreciation on a straight line basis applying rates specified in Schedule XIV of the Companies Act 1956 as under:

In respect of plant and machinery, railway siding, buildings and vehicles acquired before 1.4.1993 the specified period has been recalculated by applying the revised rates in force in terms of the notification dated 16.12.1993 and unamortised value of the asset has been allocated equally over the remaining part of the specified period and on assets acquired after 31.3.1993 at the revised rates. Plant and machinery has been identified as continuous process plants. Extra shift depreciation is calculated on actual shift basis in respect of each mill/shop/unit. In respect of furniture, fixtures and office equipment acquired before 1.4.1993 at the rates in force prior to the above mentioned notification and at the revised rates for assets acquired thereafter. Leasehold land is not amortised. Foreign change differences are adjusted to the carrying value of respective assets and the fixed assets turnover ration of the company is 1.36.

## Bharat Heavy Electricals Ltd.

During the period of study, the fixed asset turnover ratio of the company is 8.10. The company charges depreciation on straight line method as per the rates prescribed in Schedule XIV of the Companies Act 1956, except for certain assets where single shift, double shift and triple shift depreciation rates are adopted. In respect of addition/ deduction of fixed assets depreciation is charged on pro rata monthly basis. Fixed assets costing Rs. 10,000 or less and those whose written down value as at the beginning of the year Rs. 10,000 or less are depreciated fully. Leasehold land is amortised over the lease period. Foreign exchange gain or lose is adjusted with fixed assets and is spread over the residual useful life of the asset.

## Tata Motor Ltd.

During the period of study the company has adopted straight line method of depreciation at the rates and in the manner prescribed in Schedule XIV of the Companies Act 1956 except assets acquired prior to April 1, 1975. In case of assets acquired prior to April 1, 1975, depreciation is charged on written down value method at rates specified in Schedule XIV. For certain assets, the company charges depreciation at a rate which is higher than the rates mentioned under Schedule XIV rates. Leasehold land is amortised over the lease period. The company has changed the useful life of certain assets. Exchange rate variation is attributable to respective fixed assets. The fixed asset turnover ratio of the company for the financial year 2003-04 is 5.12.

## Hindalco Industries Ltd.

The company provides depreciation on fixed assets on straight line method at the rates and manner prescribed under Schedule XIV of the Companies Act as amended. Leasehold land and mining right are amortised over the period of lease. The fixed asset turnover ratio of the company is 1.38.

## HCL Technologies Ltd.

The fixed asset turnover ratio of the company during the period of study is 5.49. The company is adopting straight line method at a rates equal to or higher than the rates specified by Schedule XIV for the Companies Act 1956. The depreciation is based on estimated useful lives as determined by the management except leasehold land which is amortised over the lease period. The depreciation is charged on a pro rata basis for asset purchased/sold during the year. Assets costing less than Rs. 5000 are fully depreciated in the year of purchase.

## National Aluminium Company Ltd.

During the period of study, the fixed asset turnover ratio of the company is 0.86. Depreciation on fixed assets is provided by the company on straight line method at the rates and in the manner prescribed under Schedule XIV of the Companies Act 1956 as amended except for certain assets where depreciation at higher rates is provided based on their estimated useful life. Assets costing Rs. 5000 or less individually are depreciated fully in the year in which they are put to use. Exchange variation loss/gain adjusted to cost of plant and machinery is fully depreciated over the residual life of assets. Leasehold land is amortised over the lease period.

## Hindustan Petroleum Corporation Ltd.

In case of this company, the fixed asset turnover ratio for the financial year 2003-04 is 8.79. The company is providing depreciation on fixed assets on straight line method, in the manner and at rates prescribed under Schedule XIV of the Companies Act 1956 and depreciation is charged pro rata on monthly basis on assets from/up to and inclusive of the month of capitalisation/sale, disposal or deletion during the year. Leasehold land is amortised over the lease period. Foreign exchange gain/loss adjusted in the cost of assets.

## Bharat Petroleum Corporation Ltd.

The company amortises its leasehold land over the lease period. LPG cylinders and pressure regulators and other fixed assets costing not more than Rs. 5000 each are depreciated @ 100 per cent in the year of capitalisation. Depreciation on other fixed assets is provided under straight line method, at rates prescribed under Schedule XIV of the Companies Act 1956. The fixed asset turnover ratio of the company during the period of study is 8.84.

## Maruti Udyog Ltd.

In case this company, the fixed asset turnover ratio is 5.12. The company follows straight line method for charging depreciation on fixed assets except leasehold land which is amortised over the lease period, on a pro rata basis from the month in which the asset is put to use. In respect of assets which have been capitalised before 02.04.1987, depreciation has been provided according to section 205(2)(b) of the Companies Act 1956 in terms of Circular No. 1/86 dated 21.05.86. For assets which have been capitalised on or after 02.04.1987, depreciation has been provided of the rates prescribed in Schedule XIV of the Companies Act 1956 except for certain assets where higher depreciation has been provided base on management's estimate of the useful life of assets. The company also uses extra shift depreciation on plant and machinery. Plant and machinery, the written down value of which at the beginning of the year is Rs. 5000 or less and other assets, the written down value of which at the beginning of the year is Rs. 1,000 or less are depreciated at the rate of 100 per cent. Foreign exchange fluctuation is adjusted with assets and is amortised prospectively over the residual useful life of the asset.

## Grasim Industries Ltd.

During the period of study, the fixed asset turnover ratio of the company is 1.67. The company is adopting written down value method on fixed assets (other than revalued asset) in some divisions and straight line method in other division at the rates prescribed in Schedule XIV of the Companies Act 1956 on pro rata basis with reference to month of addition/deduction. Continuous process plant as defined in Schedule XIV has been taken on technical assessment. The company is providing straight line method on revalued fixed assets based on revised life of assets as ascertained by the valuers. Amount capitalised due to foreign exchange fluctuation is provided prospectively over the residual life of the assets. Leasehold land is amortised over the period of lease.

## Larsen & Toubro Ltd.

The company provides depreciation on assets acquired up to March 31, 1968 on written down value method at the rates prescribed under Schedule XIV to the Companies Act 1956 except depreciation on revalued assets on which depreciation is calculated on straight line basis. Depreciation on assets acquired up to September 30,1987 is provided on straight line basis at the rates prevailing at the time of acquisition and at the rates prescribed under Schedule XIV on assets acquired after that date. Depreciation on additions/deductions is calculated pro rata from/to the month of additions/deductions. Extra shift depreciation is provided on a location basis. Leasehold assets are depreciated over the lease period. It is significant that during the period of study the company maintains a high fixed assets turnover ratio of 9.99.

## Bajaj Auto Ltd.

The company amortise the leasehold land over the lease period. Depreciation on all assets is provided on straight line method in accordance with the provision of section 205(2)(b) of the Companies Act 1956, in the manner and at the rates specified in Schedule XIV on pro rata basis from the month of addition/deduction. Higher than the rates of Schedule XIV is provided at straight line method on plant and machinery given on lease. Foreign exchange variation is adjusted with the cost of assets and are spread over the useful life of the relevant asset. During the period of study the fixed asset turnover ratio of the company is 3.94.

## Hero Honda Motors Ltd.

The fixed asset turnover ratio of the company is 10.21. The company charges depreciation on a pro rata basis under straight line method and as per the rates prescribed in Schedule XIV of the Companies Act 1956. The depreciation on the revised unamortised depreciable amount due to foreign exchange fluctuation is provided prospectively over the residual useful life of the asset. Assets costing less than Rs. 5000 are fully depreciated in the year of purchase.

## Cipla Ltd.

During the period of study, the fixed asset turnover ratio of the company is 3.61. The company is providing depreciation on plant and machinery (other than office machinery) purchased from 1.11.1986 to 31.3.1993 on the straight line method at rates prescribed under Schedule XIV of the Companies Act 1956. Depreciation on all other assets added up to 31.3.93 and on amount added on revaluation of building are provided on the written down value method at rates prescribed under Schedule XIV. Depreciation on all other assets added from the year 1993-94 are provided on the straight line method at rated prescribed under Schedule XIV of the Companies Act 1956. 100 per cent depreciation is charged on assets value less than Rs. 5000 each. Leasehold land is amortised over the lease period. Foreign exchange differences relating to fixed assets are adjusted in the cost of the asset.

## Sun Pharmaceuticals Industries Ltd.

The company is providing depreciation on tangible assets on straight line method at the rates specified in Schedule XIV of the Companies Act 1956. Leasehold land is amortised over the period of lease. During the period of study the fixed asset turnover ratio of the company is 3.11.

## National Mineral Development Corporation Ltd.

The fixed asset turnover ratio of the company is 2.53. The company is providing depreciation on straight line method based on the life of the assets determined by technical assessment at the rates equal to or higher than those prescribed in Schedule XIV of the Companies Act, 1956 on pro rata monthly basis. In respect of assets acquired before 01.04.1987, depreciation is provided at the rates based on the lives adopted earlier. Leasehold land is amortised over the period of lease.

## Zee Telefilms Ltd.

During the period of study, the fixed assets turnover ratio of the company is 3.69. The company adopts straight line method for charging depreciation on fixed assets at the rate specified in Schedule XIV of the Companies Act 1956. Leasehold land is amortised over the period of lease.

## Gujarat Ambuja Cement

The company provides depreciation on all assets other than vehicles on the straight line method in accordance with the provision of section 205(2)(b) of the Companies Act, 1956. In case of vehicles the company follows written down value method in accordance with the provisions of section 205(2)(a) of the Companies Act 1956. The company charges depreciation on pro rata monthly basis and at the rates specified in Schedule XIV of the Companies Act 1956. On the basis of technical assessment, the company defines its plants as continuous process plant and depreciates as per Schedule XIV. Leasehold land is amortised over the period of lease. During the period of study, the fixed asset turnover ratio is 0.83.

## Sterilite Industries (India) Ltd.

In this company, the fixed asset turnover ratio for the financial year 2003-04 is 2.01. The company provides depreciation on fixed assets on straight line method at the rates and in the manner specified in Schedule XIV of the Companies Act, 1956. Leasehold land is amortised over the lease period. Depreciation is provided over the residual life of the respective fixed assets for additions arising on account of translation of foreign currency.

## Dr. Reddy's Laboratories Ltd.

During the period of study the fixed asset turnover ratio of the company is 3.64. The company is adopting straight line method for charging depreciation on fixed assets based on the useful life of the assets as estimated by management. Depreciation is calculated on a pro rata basis from the date of installation till the date the assets are sold or disposed. Individual assets costing less than Rs. 5000 are depreciated in full in the year of acquisition. The cost of fixed assets includes the foreign exchange differences.

## Motor Industries Company Ltd.

Depreciation on fixed assets is provided by the company using the written down value base on the useful life as estimated by the management. Low value assets not exceeding Rs. 15000 per unit is depreciated @ 100 per cent in the year of addition. Full year's depreciation is provided in the year of addition of assets and no depreciation is provided in the year of disposal. Leased assets are depreciated over the estimated useful life or the lease term which ever is lower. The fixed asset turnover ratio of the company during the period of study is 11.96.

## BIOCON Ltd.

During the period of study, the company charges depreciation on fixed assets other than freehold land but including revalued building on pro rata basis to the period of use, on the straight line method at the annual rates based on the estimated useful lives. The depreciation charge over and above the depreciation calculation on original cost of the revalued assets is transferred from the revaluation reserve to the profit and loss account. Assets individually costing less than Rs. 5000 are fully depreciated in the year of purchase. The company also mentioned some facts regarding depreciation and fixed asset under the heading 'Management Discussion and Analysis'. The fixed asset turnover ratio of the company is 3.48.

### Mahindra and Mahindra Ltd.

The Company amortises that leasehold over the period of lease. Depreciation on assets is calculated on straight line method at the rates and in the manner prescribed in Schedule XIV of the Companies Act 1956, except certain assets. It mentions indirectly regarding fully depreciated assets value up to Rs. 5000. The depreciation on the increase due to revaluation of land and building is transferred from revaluation reserve. Exchange difference are adjusted to the cost of respective assets. During the period of study the fixed asset turnover ratio is 4.31.

### Glaxo Smithkline Pharmaceuticals Ltd.

The company is providing depreciation on the straight line method over the useful life of assets as determined by the management. Depreciation on sale/disposal of assets is provided on pro rata basis up to the end of the month of sale/disposal. In case of an asset which is purchased on or after 1.4.93 and whose actual cost does not exceed Rs. 5000, depreciation is charged at the rate of 100 per cent. Leasehold land is not amortised during the period of study and the fixed asset turnover ratio of the company is 15.82.

## Indian Petrochemicals Corporation Ltd.

During the year 2003-04 fixed asset turnover ratio of the company is 1.67. Depreciation on fixed assets is provided on straight line method at the rates and in the manner prescribed in Schedule XIV of the Companies Act, 1956 except, in respect of plant and machinery and furniture and fixtures at Vadodara Complex where depreciation is provided on written down value method. In respect of assets acquired prior to 1.4.93 depreciation is provided on straight line method as prescribed under section 205(2)(b) of the Companies Act, 1956. Incremental cost arising on account of translation of foreign currency is added with the respective assets and is charged over the residual life of respective asset. Leasehold land is amortised over the lease period.

## Videsh Sanchar Nigam Ltd.

The company adopted written down value method for charging depreciation on assets acquired during the period 1.4.1986 to 31.3.1994. It charged depreciation according to the rates as specified in Schedule XIV of the Companies Act 1956. In case of assets acquired after 31.3.1994 depreciation is provided on a straight line method at the rates prescribed in Schedule XIV of Companies Act, 1956. Since 1st January 2004, the company has revised the estimated useful lives of plant and equipment and as a result the rates of depreciation are higher than the rates of Schedule XIV. Exchange differences are adjusted in the carrying cost of the fixed assets. Leasehold lands are amortised over the period of lease. During the period of study the fixed asset turnover ratio of the company is 1.80.

## Hindustan Zinc Ltd.

The company provides depreciation on fixed assets using straight line method at rates prescribed under Schedule XIV of the Companies Act 1956. Addition and disposal are reckoned on the first day and the last day of the quarter respectively. Individual item of plant and machinery and vehicles costing up to Rs. 25,000 are wholly depreciated. For the financial year 2003-04, the fixed asset turnover ratio of the company is 2.88.

## Shipping Corporation of India Ltd.

During the period of study the fixed asset turnover ratio of the company is 1.04. Depreciation on ships is charged on straight line method at the rates prescribed in Schedule XIV to the Companies Act 1956 except in case of offshore vessels, which are written off over a period of 12 years and second hand vessels which are written off over their respective useful lives as determined by technical evaluation. On assets other than ships, depreciation is charged on the written down value method as per the rates prescribed in Schedule XIV. Full year depreciation is charged irrespective of the dates of additions and no depreciation is charged on assets sold/discarded during the year. Assets costing individually Rs. 5000 and below are fully depreciated in the year of addition. Foreign exchange rate fluctuation is added with ships and is depreciated over the useful life of the ships.

## Associated Cement Companies Ltd.

In case of this company, the fixed asset turnover ratio for the financial year 2003-04 is 1.64. The company is providing depreciation on assets acquired up to July 31,1968 on the written down value method at the rates prescribed in Schedule XIV of the Companies Act 1956. In respect of assets acquired during the period August 1, 1968 to July 31, 1986, depreciation is provided on the straight line method at the rates in force at the time of acquisition in accordance with Circular No. 1/86 dated May 1, 1986 issued by the Department of Company Affairs. In respect of assets acquired on or after August 1, 1986 on the straight line method at the rates prescribed in Schedule XIV of the Companies Act, 1956, on a pro rata basis. Cost of leasehold land is amortised over the period of the lease.

## I-Flex Solutions Ltd.

During the period of study, the company is adopting straight line method for charging depreciation on fixed assets at the rates specified in Schedule XIV of the Companies Act 1956 or based on the estimated useful life of assets, whichever is higher. Vehicles under financial lease are amortised over the useful life or lease term which ever is lower. The fixed asset turnover ratio of the company is 7.45, in case of the financial year 2003-04.

## Container Corporation of India Ltd.

The fixed assets turnover ratio of the company during the period of study is 1.83. Depreciation on fixed assets including assets created on leasehold land is provided on straight line method at the rates and in the manner prescribed in Schedule XIV of the Companies Act 1956 except for some assets. Leasehold land is amortised over the period of lease.

## Bharat Electronics Ltd.

Tangible depreciable fixed assets are generally depreciated on straight line method at the rates (or higher rates as disclosed) and in the manner prescribed in Schedule XIV of the Companies Act 1956 except in cases where the machine utilisation hour basis is adopted. Special instruments are amortised over production. Pro rata depreciation is charged from/to the month in which the assets are ready to be put to use/are deleted or discarded. Leasehold land is amortised over the period of lease. The fixed asset turnover ratio of the company is 9.72.

## Nicholas Piramal India Ltd.

During the period of study, the fixed asset turnover ratio of the company is 2.60. The company provides depreciation on fixed assets under straight line method at the rates specified in Schedule XIV of the Companies Act 1956. Diagnostic equipments placed with customers are amortised over a period of 60 months. Depreciation on additions/deletions of assets during the year is provided on a pro rata basis the company also mentions some information regarding depreciation under the heading of 'Management Discussion and Analysis'.

## Siemens Ltd.

The company charges depreciation on straight line method at the rates based on the estimated useful economic lives of the fixed assets as determine by the management which are greater than or equal to the rates prescribed in Schedule XIV on pro rata basis. Asset costing less than Rs. 5000 are fully depreciated in the year of acquisition. Leasehold land is amortised over the lease period. During the period of study the fixed asset turnover ratio of the company is 10.18.

## Wockhardt Ltd.

The fixed asset turnover ratio of the company during the period of study is 2.73. The company is providing depreciation using the straight line method, pro rata to the period of use of assets, at the rates specified in Schedule XIV of the Companies Act 1956 or based on the estimated useful life of the assets, which is higher. Fixed assets whose aggregate cost is Rs. 5000 or less are depreciated fully in the year of acquisition. Leasehold land is amortise over the lease period. Exchange differences relating to the acquisition of fixed assets are adjusted in the cost of the assets.

## Chennai Petroleum Corporation Ltd.

The company charges depreciation on fixed assets in accordance with the rates as specified in Schedule XIV of the Companies Act, 1956 on straight line method, up to 95 per cent of the cost of the asset. Depreciation is charged pro rata on quarterly basis on assets from/ up to the quarter of capitalisation/sale, disposal and dismantled during the year. Assets costing not more than Rs. 5000 each are depreciated in full in the year of addition. Cost of leasehold land is amortised over the period of lease. During the period of study the fixed asset turnover ratio of the company is 3.38.

## Great Eastern Shipping Company Ltd.

For the financial year 2003-04, the fixed asset turnover ratio of the company is 0.58. The company charges depreciation on flats and office premises on the written down value method at the rates prescribed in Schedule XIV of the Companies Act 1956. Depreciation on all other assets including ships, rigs and barges are being charged on straight line method at the rates prescribed in Schedule XIV or on the useful life as estimated by the management which ever is higher. Depreciation on assets other than fleet, rigs and barges acquired and/ or sold during the year is provided for the full year on additions and no depreciation is provided in the year of disposal. Leasehold land is amortised over the lease period. Gain or loss on account of foreign exchange variation is adjusted to the carrying cost of such fixed assets.

## Asian Paints (India) Ltd.

During the period of study the fixed asset turnover ratio of the company is 6.19. The company is providing depreciation on fixed assets under straight line method and at the rates specified under Schedule XIV of the Companies Act, 1956 except tinting systems. Leasehold land is amortised over the period of lease.

## Tata Chemicals Ltd.

The company is adopting straight line method for charging depreciation on assets acquired prior to 31.3.87 in accordance with Circular No. 1/86 dt. 21.5.86 of the Department of Company Affairs and in respect of assets acquired on or after 1.4.87 at the rates and in the manner prescribed in Schedule XIV of the Companies Act 1956, except for certain assets which is depreciated on the basis of useful life as technically assessed. Leasehold land is amortised over the period of lease. The fixed asset turnover ratio of the company is 1.45.

## Jaiprakash Associated Ltd.

The fixed asset turnover ratio of the company during the period of study is 1.65. Depreciation on fixed assets is provided on straight line method as per the classification and in the manner as specified in Schedule XIV of the Companies Act, 1956.

## Tata Teleservices (Maharashtra) Ltd.

The company charges depreciation on fixed assets on straight line method based on the estimated useful economic lives by management. Leasehold land is amortised over the period of lease. The company also mentions some facts regarding depreciation in 'Management Discussion and Analysis'. The fixed asset turnover ratio of the company for the financial year 2003-04 is 0.33. Depreciation on additions and deletions to assets during the year is charged on pro rata basis to the period of their use.

## Nirma Ltd.

During the period of study the fixed asset turnover ratio of the company is 1.27. The company is charging depreciation on fixed assets on written down value method except for certain division where depreciation is charged on fixed assets on straight line method at the rates specified in Schedule XIV of the Companies Act 1956. The company adopts pro rata monthly basis for charging depreciation. It also provides some information regarding depreciation under 'Management Discussion and Analysis.'

## Lupin Ltd.

Leasehold land is amortised over the lease period. The company is providing depreciation on fixed assets on straight line method in the manner and at the rates prescribed in Schedule XIV of the Companies Act 1956. The fixed asset turnover ratio of the company is 2.28 during the period of study.

## Cummins India Ltd.

The fixed asset turnover ratio of the company is 5.24. The company is providing depreciation using straight line method in the manner specified in Schedule XIV of the Companies Act 1956 and at the rates prescribed therein or based on the useful life of assets, which ever is higher. Leasehold land is amortised over the lease period.

## Tata Tea Ltd.

During the period of study the fixed asset turnover ratio of the company is 2.49. Depreciation on fixed assets including assets created on land under lease is provided on straight line method in accordance with Schedule XIV to the Companies Act, 1956.

## Moser Baer (India) Ltd.

The company is charging depreciation on tangible fixed assets using straight line method on pro rata basis at the rates specified in Schedule XIV of the Companies Act, 1956, other than certain plant and machinery at the magnetic and optical media manufacturing units which is depreciated at the rate which is based on the management's estimate of useful life of the assets and is higher than the rates specified in Schedule XIV. Leasehold land and improvement to the leased premises are amortised over the period of lease. During the period of study the fixed asset turnover ratio of the company is 0.66. The company also mentions similar information in respect of depreciation in 'Management Discussion and Analysis'.

## Ashok Leyland Ltd.

The company is charging depreciation on assets on straight line method at the rates specified in Schedule XIV to the Companies Act, 1956 except certain assets. Assets costing Rs. 10,000 or less is treated as expense. During the period of study the company revalue some of its assets and is depreciated over the balance useful life. Leasehold land is amortised over the period of lease. Depreciation is charged for the full year on the addition made during the first half of the year and for six months on the additions made during the second half of the year. No depreciation is provided for in respect of assets disposed of during the year. Foreign exchange fluctuations is adjusted with the cost of respective assets and depreciation is charged accordingly. The fixed asset turnover ratio of the company during the period of study is 4.55.

## Mphasis BFL Ltd.

In case of this company, the fixed asset turnover ratio is 29.34. Depreciation on fixed assets is provided using straight line method over the estimated useful useful lives of assets. Depreciation is charged on a proportionate basis for all assets purchased and sold during the period. Individual asset costing less than Rs. 5000 are depreciated in full in the period of purchase. Leasehold land in amortised over the period of lease. Cost of fixed assets also includes exchange differences. The company also mentions some facts regarding depreciation standard in 'Management Discussion and Analysis'.

## Dabur India Ltd.

The company is charging depreciation on fixed assets on written down value method at rates specified in Schedule XIV of the Companies Act except for certain division/units where depreciation is charged on straight line method at the rates specified in the aforesaid Schedule. During the period of study the fixed asset turnover ratio is 7.41.

## Indian Hotels Company Ltd.

The fixed asset turnover ratio of the company during the period of study is 1.11. The company is providing depreciation on assets using straight line method at the rates as specified in Schedule XIV of the Companies Act 1956 except certain assets. Leasehold land is amortised over the period of lease. Foreign exchange difference is capitalised with the respective asset.

## Aventis Pharma Ltd.

The company is adopting straight line method for charging depreciation on all assets at a rates not lower than those prescribed in Schedule XIV of the Companies Act 1956. The company has revalued some assets during the period of study. The incremental depreciation on enhanced cost is adjusted against revaluation reserve. Leasehold land is amortised over the lease period. The fixed asset turnover ratio of the company is 4.85.

## Colgate Palmolive (India) Ltd.

During the period of study the fixed asset turnover ratio of the company is 10.46. The company amortises the leasehold over the period of lease. Depreciation is provided pro rata to the period of use on straight line method based on the estimated useful life as determined by the management. During the year, the company has revised the estimated useful lives of factory building and residential and office building and the effect is given in the accounts. Assets individual costing less than Rs. 5000 are fully depreciated in the year of acquisition.

## United Phosphorus Ltd.

With respect to certain units, the company is charging depreciation on fixed assets which is capitalised up to 1st April, 1987 at the straight line rates corresponding to the rates applicable under the Income tax Rules in force at the time of acquisition/installation, in accordance with Circular No. 1/86 dated 21st May 1986 issued by the Department of Company Affairs. In respect of additions to that unit's fixed assets on or after 2nd April 1987, depreciation is charged at the straight line rates specified in Schedule XIV of the Companies Act 1956. In respect of addition to plant and machinery after 1st October, 2001 at the straight line rates which is higher than the rates specified in Schedule XIV. In respect of all other fixed assets, depreciation is charged on written down value basis in accordance with section 205(2)(a) of the Companies Act 1956 at the rates specified in Schedule XIV to the Companies Act. Assets costing Rs. 5000 or less is depreciated at the rate of 100 per cent. Depreciation is charged on pro rata basis with reference to the month of addition/deletion of the Assets. During the period of study the fixed asset turnover ratio is 1.67. Leasehold land is not amortised.

## Bongaigaon Refinery & Petrochemical Ltd.

In case of this company, the fixed asset turnover ratio during the period of study is 7.08. Depreciation on fixed assets is provided in accordance with the rates as specified in Schedule XIV of the Companies Act 1956, on straight line method up to 95 per cent of the cost of the assets. Depreciation is charged pro rata on quarterly basis on assets from/up to the quarter of capitalisation/sale, disposal and/or dismantled. Assets costing up to Rs. 5000 are depreciated fully in the year of capitalisation. The company provides some information regarding depreciation under 'Management Discussion and Analysis.'

## TVS Motor Company Ltd.

The company is charging depreciation on fixed assets under straight line method at the rates prescribed under Schedule XIV of the Companies Act 1956 with the applicable shift allowance. In respect of assets added/asset sold during the year pro rata depreciation is provided. Depreciation in respect of computers and vehicles is provided at a higher rates than the rates prescribed under Schedule XIV. Assets whose value does not exceed Rs. 5000 are depreciated at the rate of 100 per cent. The Fixed assets turnover ratio of the company is 4.06.

## Jubilant Organosys Ltd.

During the period of study the fixed asset turnover ratio of the company is 2.71. The company charges depreciation on plant and machinery of Nira and Savli plants under written down value method at the rates specified in Schedule XIV of the Companies Act, 1956. Depreciation is provided on straight line method in respect of assets added/installed up to 15th December, 1993 at the rates applicable at the time of addition/installations of the assets as per Schedule XIV to the Companies Act 1956. Depreciation, in respect of assets added/installed during the subsequent period, is provided using straight line method at the rates mentioned in Schedule XIV of the Companies Act 1956 read with Notification dated 16th December, 1993 issued by Department of Company Affairs. Depreciation on assets added/disposed off during the year is charged on pro rata basis with reference to the month of addition/ disposal. During the period of study the company revalued some of its assets. Certain plants were classified as continuous process plant. Leasehold land is not amortised.

## National Fertilizer Ltd.

The company provides depreciation on fixed assets using straight line method at the rates specified in Schedule XIV of the Companies Act 1956. Assets costing up to Rs. 5000 is depreciated at the rate of 100 per cent when installed. Leasehold land is amortised over the lease period. The fixed assets turnover ratio of the company is 2.95.

## Britannia Industries Ltd.

For the financial year 2003-04, the fixed assets turnover ratio of the company is 11.54. Depreciation in respect of all assets acquired up to 30th June 1984 is provided on written down value method. For additions on or after 1st July 1984, depreciation is provided on straight line method at the rates specified in the amended Schedule XIV of the Companies Act 1956. Assets costing less than Rs. 5000 are fully depreciated in the year of addition.

## Engineers India Ltd.

The company charges depreciation on fixed assets under straight line method either on the basis of rates arrived at with reference to the useful life of the assets evaluated by the management or the minimum rates prescribed under Schedule XIV of the Companies Act 1956, whichever is higher. Leasehold land is amortised over the period of lease. Assets individually costing less than Rs. 5000 and library books are fully depreciated in the year of acquisition. During the period of study the fixed assets turnover ratio of the company is 27.83.

## Arvind Mills Ltd.

The company adopts straight line method for charging depreciation on fixed assets added after 1.4.2000 at the rates specified in Schedule XIV of the companies Act 1956. Depreciation on revalued (dt. 1.4.2000) fixed assets is calculated on the residual life of the assets or as per rates specified in Schedule XIV whichever is higher. The fixed assets turnover ratio of the company is 0.99.

## Ispat Industries Ltd.

The company provides depreciation on fixed assets using straight line method at the rates and in the manner prescribed in Schedule XIV of the Companies Act 1956. The classification of plant and machinery into continuous and non-continuous process is done as per technical certification and depreciation thereon is provided accordingly. During the period of study the fixed assets turnover ratio of the company is 0.56. Foreign exchange rates variation is adjusted with the cost of assets and depreciation is provided prospectively over the residual life of the assets. Depreciation on revalued assets is provided at the rates specified in section 205(2)(b) of the Companies Act 1956. However, in case of fixed assets whose life is determined by the valuer to be less than their useful life under section 205, depreciation is provided at the higher rates. Leasehold land is being amortised over the period of lease.

## P & G Hygiene & Health Care Ltd.

The company charges depreciation on assets using straight line method based on the useful lives of the assets as estimated by the management or the rates specified in accordance with the provisions of Schedule XIV of the Companies Act 1956, which ever is higher. Depreciation is charged on a pro rata basis for assets purchased/sold during the year. The fixed asset turnover ratio of the company for the financial year 2003-04 is 7.20. Individual fixed assets costing less than Rs. 5000 are depreciated in full, in the year of purchase. Cost of leasehold land is amortised over the period of the lease.

## Indian Rayon & Industries Ltd.

During the period of study, the fixed asset turnover ratio of the company is 2.21. The company provides depreciation on fixed assets on straight line method at the rates and in the manner specified in the Schedule XIV of the Companies Act 1956 except certain assets where estimated useful life is than Schedule XIV. Depreciation on fixed assets added/disposed off/discarded during the year has been provided on pro rata basis with reference to the month of addition/ disposal/discarding. Continuous process plant have been classified on technical assessment and depreciation is charged accordingly. Depreciation on the amounts capitalised on account of foreign exchange fluctuation is provided prospectively over residual life of the assets. Leasehold land is amortised over the period of lease.

## Pfizer Ltd.

The company adopts straight line method for charging

depreciation on assets at the higher of the rates determined by the company or the rates specified in Schedule XIV of the Companies Act 1956. Depreciation on addition of assets is charged on a pro rata basis. Depreciation on deletions during the year is provided up to the quarter in which the asset is sold/discarded. Assets costing up to Rs. 5000 are written off and those costing more than Rs. 5000 but up to US $1000 are fully depreciated in the year of purchase. Leasehold land is amortised over the period of lease. The fixed asset turnover ratio of the company for the financial year 2003-04 is 7.78.

## Monsanto India Ltd.

The fixed asset turnover ratio of the company for the financial year 2003-04 is 5.67. The company provides depreciation on fixed assets acquired prior to 1st April 2000 (other than Silvassa) on written down value method at the rates specified in Schedule XIV of the Companies Act 1956. Depreciation is charged on fixed assets acquired after 1st April 2000 on straight line basis at the rates specified in Schedule XIV of the Companies Act except certain assets where higher rate is applied. Leasehold improvements are amortised over the period of lease.

## Raymod Ltd.

The company charges depreciation on certain assets acquired up to 31.3.87 using straight line method at the rates prevalent that time in pursuance of Circular No 1 of 1986 and in accordance with the provision of section 205(2)(b) of the Companies Act 1956. Depreciation on addition of fixed assets acquired after 1.4.87 is charged at the relevant rates of depreciation in respect of straight line method and written down value method as specified in Schedule XIV of the Companies Act 1956. Land and Live stock is not depreciated. The company used separate method for separate assets but the different depreciation rate for same assets. Depreciation on addition to assets or on sale/discardment of assets is calculated on pro rata monthly basis. Cost of leasehold land is amortised over the period of lease. For the financial year 2003-04, the fixed asset turnover ratio of the company is 2.45.

## Hindustan Copper Ltd.

During the period of study the fixed assets turnover ratio of the company is 2. Depreciation on fixed assets is provided under straight line method at the rates prescribed in Schedule XIV of the Companies Act 1956. Depreciation on assets acquired prior to 01.04.93 is charged on derived rates by allocating the unamortised value over the remaining life arrived at on the basis of rates prescribed under the Schedule XIV of the Companies Act 1956.

## Essar Steel Ltd.

The company is charging depreciation on plant and machinery and railway siding on straight line method and on other assets on written down value method at the rates specified in Schedule XIV of the Companies Act 1956. Depreciation in respect of revalued assets is recouped from revaluation reserve. Depreciation on additions to/ deletions from fixed assets is provided on pro rata basis. Depreciation on addition to assets due to exchange variation is provided over the remaining useful life of the assets. For the financial year 2003-04, the fixed assets turnover ratio of the company is 1.15.

## Sesa Goa Ltd.

The fixed asset turnover ratio of the company, during the period of study is 3.52. The company provides depreciation on assets acquired on or after 1st April 1981 using straight line method except leasehold mine of Karnataka. In case of assets acquired prior to 1st April 1981, depreciation is charged under written down value method of the rates specified in the Companies Act 1956. Depreciation is charged on assets on pro rata monthly basis. Foreign exchange rate differences is capitalised with the respective assets.

## EIH Ltd.

The company charges depreciation on fixed assets using straight line method at the rates which are conformity with the requirements of the Companies Act 1956. Leasehold land is not amortised. Other lease assets are amortised over the period of lease. Some assets are revalued and the incremental depreciation on revalued amount of fixed assets is adjusted with revaluation reserve. The fixed assets turnover ratio of the company is 0.39.

## Ballarpur Industries Ltd.

During the period of study the fixed asset turnover ratio of the company is 1.14. The company adopts straight line method for charging depreciation on certain fixed assets and written down value method on other assets in accordance with Schedule XIV of the Companies Act, 1956. Certain assets are revalued during the year and depreciation on revalued assets are adjusted with revaluation reserve.

## Crompton Greaves Ltd.

The company provides depreciation on fixed assets at the rates and in the manner specified in Schedule XIV of the Companies Act 1956, on written down value method other than on building and plant and equipment which are depreciated on a straight line method. Leasehold land is amortised over the lease period. Certain assets are revalued and incremental depreciation on revalued assets is recouped out of revaluation reserve. The fixed assets turnover ratio of the company during the period of study is 4.79.

## IBP Company Ltd.

In case of the company, the fixed assets turnover ratio is 12.50 during 2003-04. Depreciation on fixed assets is provided in accordance with the rates specified in Schedule XIV of the Companies Act 1956 on straight line method up to 95 per cent of the cost of fixed assets. Depreciation is charged pro rata on quarterly basis from/up to the quarter of capitalisation/sales, disposal and dismantled during the year. Assets costing up to Rs. 5000 are depreciated @ 100 per cent in the year of capitalisation. Cost of leasehold land for 99 years or less is amortised during the period of lease.

## Amtek Auto Ltd.

The company adopts straight line method for charging depreciation on fixed assets in the manner and at the rates as specified in Schedule XIV of the Companies Act 1956. Depreciation on additions/deductions to fixed assets is provided on pro rata basis from the date of actual installation or up to the month of such sale/disposal. The fixed assets turnover ratio of the company during the period of study is 1.73.

## Jindal Iron & Steel Company Ltd.

In case of this company, the fixed asset turnover ratio for the financial year 2003-04 is 2.24. Depreciation on assets is provided on straight line basis at the rates and in the manner as specified in Schedule XIV of the companies Act 1956. Certain assets are revalued and depreciation on revalued assets is charged prospectively over the residual life of the assets. Cost of leasehold land is amortised over the period of lease. Depreciation on the amount capitalised during the year on account of foreign exchange fluctuation is provided prospectively over residual life of the assets. Depreciation on fixed assets added/disposed off/discarded during the year is provided on a pro rata basis with reference to the month of addition/disposal/

discarding. Continuous process plants as defined in Schedule XIV of the Companies Act 1956, is considered on technical assessment and depreciation is provided accordingly.

## Punjab Tractors Ltd.

The company charges depreciation on all fixed assets on straight line method, pro rata with monthly rests, at the rates prescribed in Schedule XIV of the Companies Act 1956 except for certain assets where the rates of depreciation are higher than the rates prescribed in Schedule XIV of the Companies Act 1956. Assets individually costing up to Rs. 5000 are depreciated at the rate of 100 per cent in the year of purchase. During the period of study, the fixed assets turnover ratio of the company is 5.50.

## Hindustan Machine Tools Ltd.

The fixed assets turnover ratio of the company for the financial year 2003-04 is 5.10. Depreciated on fixed assets is provided on straight line method, at the rates prescribed in Schedule XIV of the Companies Act, 1956 with reference to the date of addition or deletion except assets costing less than Rs. 5000 per assets which is written off to Rs. 1 in the year of purchase. Depreciation on fixed assets is calculated on a pro rata basis from the date of such addition or as the case may be up to the date on which such asset is sold, discarded or destroyed. Premium for leasehold land is amortised equally over the period of lease.

## Exide Industries Ltd.

The company classifies its plant and machinery into continuous and non continuous process as per technical certification and depreciation is provided accordingly. Depreciation is provided on straight line method at the rates and in the manner specified in Schedule XIV of the Companies

Act 1956 except certain assets where depreciation is provided at the adjusted higher rates and cost of assets is written off over the economic life determined by the valuer. Depreciation includes amount written off in respect of leasehold land properties, over the respective lease period. Foreign exchange fluctuation is capitalised and depreciation is provided prospectively over the residual life of respective asset. Depreciation on fixed assets added/disposed off during the year is provided on pro rata basis with reference to the month of addition/disposal. During the period of study the fixed assets turnover ratio is 2.56.

## Thermax Ltd.

The fixed assets turnover ratio of the company during the period of study is 6.98. The company charges depreciation on all fixed assets using straight line method at the rates and in the manner by Schedule XIV of the Companies Act 1956 except certain assets where depreciation is provided at a higher rates than Schedule XIV. No depreciation is charged on assets sold during the year. Depreciation on the entire plant and machinery of chemical division is charged considering the chemical plant as a continuous process plant. Leasehold land is amortised over the period of lease. Exchange difference on liability relating to fixed assets is adjusted in the carrying cost of the respective fixed assets.

## Birla Corporation Ltd.

In case of this company the fixed assets turnover ratio is 3.86 during 2003-04. The company adopts straight live method for charging depreciation on assets of cement division on the specified period basis as per the rates as prescribed in Schedule XIV of the Companies Act 1956. On the assets of other divisions, depreciation is provided at the rates prescribed in Schedule XIV of the Companies Act 1956. Certain assets are revalued and depreciation is provided as per requirements. Leasehold land is amortised over the period of lease.

## Sundaram Clayton Ltd.

The company is providing depreciation under straight line method at the rates prescribed under Schedule XIV of the Companies Act 1956. In respect of the assets added/sold during the year pro rata depreciation is provided. Depreciation in respect of computers and vehicles is provided at a higher rate than Schedule XIV. Asset whose value does not exceed Rs. 5000 is provided at 100 per cent. The fixed assets turnover ratio of the company during the year of study is 1.47.

## Asahi India Glass Ltd.

During the period of study the fixed assets turnover ratio of the company is 1.71. The company follows straight line method and written down value method for separate division/unit at the rates and in the manner provided in Schedule XIV of the Companies Act 1956 except certain assets where the rate of depreciation is higher than the rate mentioned in Schedule XIV. Leasehold land is amortised over the period of lease. Assets costing less than Rs. 5000 each are depreciated fully in the year of purchase.

## Indo Rama Synthetics (India) Ltd.

Depreciation on fixed assets is provided on straight line method at the rates prescribed in Schedule XIV of Companies Act 1956. Leasehold land is amortised over the period of lease. Depreciation on the amount of additions made to fixed assets on account of foreign exchange fluctuations is provided for over the remaining useful lives of the respective assets. Incremental depreciation on revalued assets is recouped from revaluation reserve. The fixed assets turnover ratio of the company during the period of study is 1.27.

## Bharat Earth Movers Ltd.

The fixed assets turnover ratio of the company for the financial year 2003-04 is 13.18. The company charges depreciation on fixed assets using straight line method at the rates prescribed in Schedule XIV of the Companies Act 1956. Leasehold land is amortised over the period of lease.

## Chambal Fertiliser & Chemicals Ltd.

During the period of study, the fixed assets turnover ratio of the company is 1.10. The company adopts straight line method for charging depreciation on fixed assets at the rates prescribed in Schedule XIV of the Companies Act 1956 except certain assets where rates of depreciation are higher than the rates of Schedule XIV. Leasehold land and improvements are amortised over the period of lease. Increase or decrease in value of fixed assets due to foreign exchange fluctuation is spread over the remaining useful life of asset.

## Apollo Tyres Ltd.

The company provides depreciation on fixed assets using straight line basis at the rates specified in Schedule XIV of the Companies Act, 1956. The company is classifying certain plant and machinery as continuous process plant on technical evaluation. Certain vehicles are depreciated at a rate higher than Schedule XIV. Incremental depreciation on revalued assets is adjusted from revaluation reserve. Leasehold land is amortised over the period of lease. Foreign exchange fluctuation is adjusted with respective asset. For the financial year the fixed assets turnover ratio of the company is 3.57.

## ICI India Ltd.

The company charges depreciation on fixed assets using straight line basis as per the rates prescribed in Schedule XIV of the Companies Act 1956. Leasehold land and improvements are amortised over the period of lease. During the period of study the fixed assets turnover ratio of the company is 4.14.

## Marico Industries Ltd.

During 2003-04, the fixed assets turnover ratio of the company is 10.38. The company provides depreciation on fixed assets using straight line basis at higher of the rates than Schedule XIV of Companies Act 1956 based on useful lives of the assets as estimated by the management or those stipulated in Schedule XIV. Assets individually costing Rs. 5000 or less are depreciated fully in the year of acquisition. Leasehold land is amortised over the period of lease. Extra shift depreciation is provided on plant basis.

## Balarampur Chini Mills Ltd.

During the period of study the fixed assets turnover ratio of the company is 1.36. The company charges depreciation on fixed assets using straight line method in accordance with the rates as specified in Schedule XIV of the Companies Act 1956. Leasehold land is not depreciated. The effect of exchange rate fluctuations in respect of fixed assets is adjusted with the cost of the respective asset.

## Finolex Industries Ltd.

The company provides depreciation on fixed assets on straight line method at the rates and in the manner specified in Schedule XIV of the Companies Act 1956. Amortisation of leasehold land is provided over the period of lease. Exchange difference relating to fixed assets is adjusted in the carrying amount of respective asset. The fixed asset turnover ratio of the company is 1.69.

## Gujarat Mineral Development Corporation Ltd.

In case of this company, the fixed asset turnover ratio is 3.87 during the period of study. The company charges depreciation on assets purchased up to March 31, 1987 on straight line method as per 205(2)(b) of Companies Act 1956, pursuant to the Circular dated 21.05.1986 issued by the Department of Company Affairs at the rates applicable under Income Tax Act. In respect of the assets purchase after 31st March, 1987 depreciation is charged under written down value method at the rates prescribed in Schedule XIV of the Companies Act, 1956. On the assets disposed off/discarded during the year, depreciation is charged on pro rata basis up to the date of their disposal/discarding. Foreign exchange rate variation is adjusted with fixed assets and depreciation is spread prospectively over the period of the residual life of the respective assets. Leasehold land is written off over the period of lease.

## Pidilite Industries Ltd.

The fixed asset turnover ratio of the company during the period of study is 3.72. The company provides depreciation under straight line basis for assets acquired up to 30.6.1987 except certain assets for which written down value basis is adopted at rates equivalent to the rates specified in Income Tax Act, 1961. Depreciation is provided for assets acquired after 30.06.1987 and before 31.3.1993, on straight line method at rates specified in Schedule XIV of the Companies Act 1956. For assets acquired after 31.3.1993, depreciation is changed under straight line method as per new rates prescribed in Schedule XIV. The company provides pro rata depreciation on additions made during the year except for certain assets less than Rs. 5000, for which depreciation is provided at 100 per cent.

The depreciation accounting practices of different sample companies during the period of study can be depicted in a summarised form with the help of the following table.

Table 6.1: Showing Depreciation Accounting Disclosure Practices of Sample Companies (2003-04)

| SL. No. | Name of the Company | Fixed Assets Less Depre-ciation Rs' Crores | Net Sales Rs' crores | Depreciation Method used | Different Method for different Assets | Different Method for same Assets | Change in Method of Depreciation | Change in Life of Asset | Any reference to Income Tax | Pro rata Depreciation | 100% Depreciation | Amortisation of Intangible Asset in Depreciation | Depreciation higher than Schedule XIV Rates | Extra Shift Depreciation | Continuous Process plant | Revaluation of Assets | Assets disposed off substantial | Foreign exchange gain / loss Adjusted | Amortisation of lease-hold land |
|---|---|---|---|---|---|---|---|---|---|---|---|---|---|---|---|---|---|---|---|
| (1) | (2) | (3) | (4) | (5) | (6) | (7) | (8) | (9) | (10) | (11) | (12) | (13) | (14) | (15) | (16) | (17) | (18) | (19) | (20) |
| 1. | Oil and Natural Gas Corporat-ion Ltd. | 41007.62<br>35339.16<br>5668.46 | 32076.02 | WDV | | | | | | | Yes | | | | | | | Yes | Yes |
| 2. | Reliance Industries Ltd. | 53502.91<br>21713.74<br>31789.17 | 51801.53 | WDV<br>SLM | Yes | | | | | | | Yes | | | | Yes | | Yes | Yes |
| 3. | Indian Oil Corpora-tion Ltd. | 36388.3<br>14339.6<br>22048.7 | 134084 | SLM | | | | | | Yes | FA?<br>Rs.5000 | | | | | | | | Yes |
| 4. | Infosys Technol-ogies Ltd. | 1570.23<br>803.41<br>766.82 | 4760.89 | SLM | | | | | | Yes | FA<<br>Rs.5000 | Yes | Yes | | | | | | |
| 5. | Wipro Ltd | 1333.67<br>678.60<br>655.01 | 5132.68 | SLM | | | | | | | | Yes | Yes | | | | | | |

(Contd.)

| (1) | (2) | (3) | (4) | (5) | (6) | (7) | (8) | (9) | (10) | (11) | (12) | (13) | (14) | (15) | (16) | (17) | (18) | (19) | (20) |
|---|---|---|---|---|---|---|---|---|---|---|---|---|---|---|---|---|---|---|---|
| 6. | ITC Ltd. | 4740.94<br>1442<br>3298.31 | 6470.44 | SLM | | | | | | | | Yes | | | | Yes | | | Yes |
| 7. | Steel Authority of India Ltd | 27712.71<br>14558.86<br>13153.85 | 21296.82 | SLM | | | | | | Yes | | | | | | | | | Yes |
| 8. | Gas Authority of India Ltd. | 13584.73<br>5441.85<br>8142.88 | 12414.36 | SLM | | | | | | Yes | FA? Rs.5000 | | Yes | | | | | Yes | Yes |
| 9. | Tata Iron & Steel Company Ltd. | 13269.47<br>5411.62<br>7857.85 | 10702.39 | SLM | | | | | | | | | Yes | Yes | Yes | | | Yes | No |
| 10. | Bharat Heavy Electricals Ltd. | 3459.61<br>2365.47<br>1094.14 | 8866.13 | SLM | | | | | | Yes | FA? Rs.5000 | Yes | Yes | Yes | | | | Yes | Yes |
| 11. | Tata Motors Ltd. | 5985.40<br>3023.69<br>2961.71 | 15165.85 | SLM<br>WDV | | Yes | | Yes | | | | Yes | Yes | | | | | Yes | Yes |
| 12. | Hindalco Industries Ltd. | 6658.49<br>1918.28<br>4740.21 | 6563.88 | SLM | | | | | | | | Yes | | | | | | | Yes |
| 13. | HCL Technologies Ltd. | 412.32<br>206.04<br>205.28 | 1127.98 | SLM | | | | | | Yes | FA< Rs.5000 | Yes | Yes | | | | | | Yes |
| 14. | National Aluminium Company Ltd. | 8092.87<br>4189.39<br>3903.48 | 3344.84 | SLM | | | | | | | FA ? Rs.5000 | Yes | Yes | | | | | Yes | Yes |

(Contd.)

| (1) | (2) | (3) | (4) | (5) | (6) | (7) | (8) | (9) | (10) | (11) | (12) | (13) | (14) | (15) | (16) | (17) | (18) | (19) | (20) |
|---|---|---|---|---|---|---|---|---|---|---|---|---|---|---|---|---|---|---|---|
| 15. | Hindust-an Petro-leum Corpora-tion Ltd. | 11387.43<br>4809.32<br>6578.11 | 57827.07 | SLM | | | | | | Yes | | | | | | | | Yes | Yes |
| 16. | Bharat Petroleum Corporation Ltd. | 11157.80<br>5111.97<br>6045.83 | 53448.36 | SLM | | | | | | | FA< Rs.5000 | | | | | | | | Yes |
| 17. | Maruti Udyog Ltd. | 4566.7<br>2735.9<br>1830.8 | 9373.40 | SLM | | | | | | Yes | FA< Rs.5000 | | Yes | Yes | | | | Yes | Yes |
| 18. | Grasim Industries Ltd. | 5705.53<br>2588.92<br>3116.61 | 5213.21 | WDV<br>SLM | | Yes | | Yes | | Yes | | | | | Yes | Yes | | Yes | Yes |
| 19. | Larsen & Toubro Ltd. | 2005.42<br>1015.24<br>990.18 | 9895.44 | SLM<br>WDV | | Yes | | | | Yes | | Yes | | Yes | | | Yes | | Yes |
| 20. | Bajaj Auto Ltd. | 2702.99<br>1496.68<br>1206.31 | 4755.17 | SLM | | | | | | Yes | | No | Yes | | | | | Yes | Yes |
| 21. | Hero Honda Motors Ltd. | 916.91<br>345.79<br>571.12 | 5832.43 | SLM | | | | | | Yes | FA< Rs.5000 | Yes | | | | | | Yes | |
| 22. | Cipla Ltd | 740.79<br>193.23<br>547.56 | 1974.63 | SLM<br>WDV | | Yes | | | | | FA? Rs.5000 | | | | | | | Yes | Yes |
| 23. | Sun Pharmaceutical Industries Ltd. | 465.86<br>131.04<br>334.82 | 1042.17 | SLM | | | | | | | | Yes | | | | | | | Yes |

(Contd.)

| (1) | (2) | (3) | (4) | (5) | (6) | (7) | (8) | (9) | (10) | (11) | (12) | (13) | (14) | (15) | (16) | (17) | (18) | (19) | (20) |
|---|---|---|---|---|---|---|---|---|---|---|---|---|---|---|---|---|---|---|---|
| 24. | National Mineral Development Corporat-ion Ltd. | 1148.15<br>573.88<br>574.27 | 1453.69 | SLM | | | | | | Yes | | | Yes | | | | | | Yes |
| 25. | Zee Telefilms Ltd. | 176.67<br>31.01<br>145.66 | 537.11 | SLM | | | | | | | | | | | | | | | Yes |
| 26. | Gujarat Ambuja Cement Ltd. | 3658.07<br>1284.14<br>2373.93 | 1968.11 | SLM<br>WDV | Yes | | | | | Yes | | Yes | | | Yes | | | | Yes |
| 27. | Sterlite Industries (India) Ltd. | 2127.45<br>599.07<br>1528.38 | 3069.81 | SLM | | | | | | | | | | | | | | Yes | Yes |
| 28. | Dr. Reddy's Laborato-ries Ltd. | 810.95<br>352.85<br>458.10 | 1666.63 | SLM | | | | | | Yes | FA<<br>Rs.5000 | Yes | Yes | | | | | Yes | |
| 29. | Motor Industries Company Ltd. | 1489.37<br>1294.68<br>194.69 | 2327.91 | WDV | | | | | | Yes | FA<Rs.<br>15000 | Yes | Yes | | | | | | Yes |
| 30. | BIOCON Ltd | 191.23<br>47.12<br>144.11 | 501.88 | SLM | | | | | | Yes | FA<<br>Rs.5000 | Yes | Yes | | | | | | |
| 31. | Mahindra & Mahindra Ltd. | 2519.02<br>1165.83<br>1353.19 | 5828.46 | SLM | | | | | | | Yes | Yes | Yes | | | | | Yes | Yes |
| 32. | Glaxo Smithk-line pharmac-euticals Ltd. | 252.64<br>165.66<br>86.98 | 1375.89 | SLM | | | | | | Yes | FA<<br>Rs.5000 | Yes | Yes | | | | | | No |

(Contd.)

| (1) | (2) | (3) | (4) | (5) | (6) | (7) | (8) | (9) | (10) | (11) | (12) | (13) | (14) | (15) | (16) | (17) | (18) | (19) | (20) |
|---|---|---|---|---|---|---|---|---|---|---|---|---|---|---|---|---|---|---|---|
| 33. | Indian Petro Chemicals Corporat-ion Ltd. | 9646.89<br>4260.96<br>5385.93 | 9019.14 | SLM<br>WDV | | Yes | | | | | | | | | | | | Yes | Yes |
| 34. | Videsh Sanchar Nigam Ltd. | 2348.54<br>590.80<br>1757.74 | 3163.54 | SLM<br>WDV | | Yes | | Yes | | | | Yes | Yes | | | | | Yes | Yes |
| 35. | Hindus-tan Zinc Ltd. | 1599.74<br>959.71<br>640.03 | 1841.49 | SLM | | | | | | Yes | FA? Rs. 25000 | Yes | | | | | | | |
| 36. | Shipping Corpora-tion of India Ltd. | 6073.85<br>3092.04<br>2981.81 | 3100.34 | SLM<br>WDV | Yes | | | | | Yes | FA? Rs.5000 | | Yes | | | | | Yes | |
| 37. | Associa-ted Cement Compan-ies Ltd. | 3789.75<br>1414.14<br>2375.61 | 3888.30 | WDV<br>SLM | | Yes | | | | Yes | | Yes | | | | | | | Yes |
| 38. | I-Flex Solutions Ltd. | 157.96<br>66.13<br>91.83 | 684.46 | SLM | | | | | | | Yes | | Yes | | | | | | |
| 39. | Contai-ner Corpora-tion of India Ltd | 1198.79<br>235.59<br>963.20 | 1764.43 | SLM | | | | | | | | Yes | | | | | | | Yes |
| 40. | Bharat Electro-nics Ltd | 1040.96<br>752.98<br>287.98 | 2798.59 | SLM<br>Unit Basis | Yes | | | | | Yes | | | Yes | | | | | | Yes |
| 41. | Nicholas Piramal India Ltd. | 617.29<br>130.09<br>487.20 | 1269.05 | SLM | | | | | | Yes | | Yes | | | | | | | |

(Contd.)

| (1) | (2) | (3) | (4) | (5) | (6) | (7) | (8) | (9) | (10) | (11) | (12) | (13) | (14) | (15) | (16) | (17) | (18) | (19) | (20) |
|---|---|---|---|---|---|---|---|---|---|---|---|---|---|---|---|---|---|---|---|
| 42. | Simens Ltd | 546.14<br>359.46<br>186.68 | 1901.30 | SLM | | | | | | Yes | FA<<br>Rs. 5000 | | Yes | | | | | | Yes |
| 43. | Wockha-rdt Ltd. | 408.35<br>98.10<br>310.25 | 846.74 | SLM | | | | | | Yes | FA?<br>Rs. 5000 | Yes | Yes | | | | | Yes | Yes |
| 44. | Chennai Petrol-eum Corporat-ion Ltd. | 3759.93<br>1189.20<br>2570.73 | 8693.51 | SLM | | | | | | Yes | FA?<br>Rs. 5000 | Yes | | | | | | | Yes |
| 45. | Great Eastern Shipping Company Ltd. | 3698.91<br>1370.39<br>2328.52 | 1360.54 | SLM<br>WDV | Yes | | | | | Yes | | Yes | Yes | | | | | Yes | Yes |
| 46. | Asian Paints (India) Ltd | 651.19<br>310.65<br>340.54 | 2108.41 | SLM | | | | | | | | Yes | | | | | | | Yes |
| 47. | Tata Chemicals Ltd. | 3042.48<br>1328.80<br>1713.68 | 2484.49 | SLM | | | | | | | | | Yes | | | | | | Yes |
| 48. | Jaiprakash Associa-tes Ltd. | 2517.04<br>931.24<br>1585.80 | 2615.73 | SLM | | | | | | | | | | | | | | | |
| 49. | Tata Teleserv-ices (Mahara-shtra) Ltd | 2494.91<br>694.76<br>1800.15 | 597.50 | SLM | | | | | | Yes | | Yes | Yes | | | | | | Yes |
| 50. | Nirma Ltd | 2710.92<br>672.67<br>2038.25 | 2583.57 | WDV<br>SLM | | Yes | | | | Yes | | Yes | | | | | | | |

(Contd.)

| (1) | (2) | (3) | (4) | (5) | (6) | (7) | (8) | (9) | (10) | (11) | (12) | (13) | (14) | (15) | (16) | (17) | (18) | (19) | (20) |
|---|---|---|---|---|---|---|---|---|---|---|---|---|---|---|---|---|---|---|---|
| 51. | Lupin Ltd | 640.41<br>123.20<br>517.21 | 1179.56 | SLM | | | | | | | | Yes | | | | | | | Yes |
| 52. | Cummins India Ltd. | 473.24<br>295.40<br>177.84 | 932.42 | SLM | | | | | | | | Yes | Yes | | | | | | Yes |
| 53. | Tata Tea Ltd. | 517.09<br>205.86<br>311.23 | 775.83 | SLM | | | | | | | | | | | | | | | |
| 54. | Moser Baer (India) Ltd. | 2731.51<br>462.85<br>2268.66 | 1502.17 | SLM | | | | | | Yes | | Yes | Yes | | | | Yes | | Yes |
| 55. | Ashok Leyland Ltd. | 1875.64<br>1000.81<br>874.83 | 3979.57 | SLM | | | | | | Yes | FA?<br>Rs.<br>10000 | Yes | | | | Yes | | Yes | Yes |
| 56. | Mphasis BFL Ltd. | 68.80<br>59.94<br>8.86 | 259.97 | SLM | | | | | | Yes | FA<<br>Rs. 5000 | Yes | Yes | | | | | Yes | Yes |
| 57. | Dabur India Ltd. | 274.50<br>119.56<br>154.94 | 1147.98 | WDV<br>SLM | | Yes | | | | | | Yes | | | | | Yes | | |
| 58. | Indian Hotels Company Ltd. | 944.77<br>346.56<br>598.21 | 665.23 | SLM | | | | | | | | Yes | Yes | | | | | Yes | Yes |
| 59. | Aventis Pharma Ltd. | 274.19<br>122.53<br>151.66 | 734.99 | SLM | | | | | | | | Yes | Yes | | | Yes | | | Yes |

(Contd.)

| (1) | (2) | (2) | (3) | (4) | (5) | (6) | (7) | (8) | (8) | (10) | (11) | (12) | (13) | (14) | (15) | (16) | (17) | (18) | (19) |
|---|---|---|---|---|---|---|---|---|---|---|---|---|---|---|---|---|---|---|---|
| 60. | Colgate Palmolive (India) Ltd. | 321.23<br>231.44<br>89.79 | 939.19 | SLM | | | | Yes | | Yes | FA<<br>Rs. 5000 | Yes | Yes | | | | | | Yes |
| 61. | United Phosphorus Ltd. | 808.91<br>315.13<br>493.78 | 823.60 | SLM<br>WDV | Yes | | | | Yes | Yes | FA?<br>Rs. 5000 | | Yes | | | | | | No |
| 62. | Bongaigaon Refinery & Petroche-mical Ltd. | 927.49<br>525.90<br>401.59 | 2841.42 | SLM | | | | | | Yes | FA?<br>Rs. 5000 | Yes | | | | | | | |
| 63. | TVS Motor Company Ltd. | 1132.57<br>437.91<br>694.66 | 2820.21 | SLM | | | | | | Yes | FA<<br>Rs. 5000 | | Yes | Yes | | | | | |
| 64. | Jubilant Organo-sys Ltd. | 716.15<br>282.52<br>433.63 | 1175.71 | SLM<br>WDV | | Yes | | | | Yes | Yes | Yes | | | Yes | Yes | | | No. |
| 65. | National Fertilizers Ltd. | 2846.29<br>1693.31<br>1152.98 | 3405.73 | SLM | | | | | | | FA?<br>Rs. 5000 | Yes | | | | | | | Yes |
| 66. | Britannia Industries Ltd. | 273.51<br>146.07<br>127.44 | 1470.53 | WDV<br>SLM | | Yes | | | | | FA<<br>Rs. 5000 | Yes | | | | | | | |
| 67. | Engineers India Ltd. | 127.52<br>80.62<br>46.90 | 1281.63 | SLM | | | | | | | FA<<br>Rs. 5000 | | Yes | | | | | | Yes |
| 68. | Arvind Mills Ltd. | 2035.21<br>583.72<br>1451.49 | 1435.28 | SLM | | | | | | | | | | | | | | | |

(Contd.)

| (1) | (2) | (3) | (4) | (5) | (6) | (7) | (8) | (9) | (10) | (11) | (12) | (13) | (14) | (15) | (16) | (17) | (18) | (19) | (20) |
|---|---|---|---|---|---|---|---|---|---|---|---|---|---|---|---|---|---|---|---|
| 69. | Ispat Industries Ltd. | 8047.52<br>1398.26<br>6649.26 | 3734.30 | SLM | | | | Yes | | | | | Yes | | Yes | Yes | | Yes | Yes |
| 70. | P & G Hygiene & Health Care Ltd. | 170.88<br>90.68<br>80.20 | 577.29 | SLM | | | | | | Yes | F.A< Rs. 5000 | | Yes | | | | | | Yes |
| 71. | Indian Rayon & Industries Ltd. | 1301.31<br>588.53<br>712.78 | 1573.84 | SLM | | | | | | Yes | | Yes | Yes | | Yes | | | Yes | Yes |
| 72. | Pfizer Ltd. | 158.77<br>87.06<br>71.71 | 557.78 | SLM | | | | | | Yes | F.A< U.S $ 1000 | Yes | Yes | | | | Yes | | Yes |
| 73. | Mosanto India Ltd. | 82.24<br>23.49<br>58.75 | 333.30 | WDV<br>SLM | | Yes | | | | | | | Yes | | | | | | Yes |
| 74. | Raymond Ltd. | 979.53<br>573.09<br>406.44 | 994.32 | SLM<br>WDV | Yes | | | | | Yes | | Yes | | | | | | | Yes |
| 75. | Hindustan Copper Ltd. | 694.75<br>478.45<br>216.30 | 432.49 | SLM | | | | | | | | | | | | | | | |
| 76. | Essar Steel Ltd. | 6802.54<br>3317.01<br>3485.53 | 4024.60 | SLM<br>WDV | Yes | | | | | Yes | | | | | | Yes | | Yes | |
| 77. | Sesa Goa Ltd. | 291.92<br>107.49<br>184.43 | 650.03 | SLM<br>WDV | | Yes | | | | Yes | | | | | | | | Yes | |

(Contd.)

| (1) | (2) | (3) | (4) | (5) | (6) | (7) | (8) | (9) | (10) | (11) | (12) | (13) | (14) | (15) | (16) | (17) | (18) | (19) | (20) |
|---|---|---|---|---|---|---|---|---|---|---|---|---|---|---|---|---|---|---|---|
| 78. | EIH Ltd. | 1427.02<br>294.01<br>1133.01 | 445.03 | SLM | | | | | | | | Yes | | | | Yes | | | No |
| 79. | Ballarpur Industries Ltd. | 3086.64<br>1092.60<br>1994.04 | 2274.88 | SLM<br>WDV | Yes | | | | | | | | | | | Yes | | | |
| 80. | Crompton Greaves Ltd. | 790.35<br>432.76<br>357.59 | 1711.32 | WDV<br>SLM | Yes | | | | | | | No | | | | Yes | | | Yes |
| 81. | IBP Company Ltd. | 1067.26<br>255.59<br>811.67 | 10148.19 | SLM | | | | | | Yes | FA?<br>Rs. 5000 | | | | | | | | Yes |
| 82. | Amtek Auto Ltd. | 410.82<br>119.16<br>291.66 | 505.96 | SLM | | | | | | Yes | | | | | | | | | |
| 83. | Jindal Iron & Steel Company Ltd. | 1428.08<br>452.03<br>976.05 | 2190.17 | SLM | | | | | | Yes | | Yes | | | Yes | Yes | | Yes | Yes |
| 84. | Punjab Tractors Ltd. | 285.20<br>158.31<br>126.89 | 698.06 | SLM | | | | | | Yes | FA?<br>Rs. 5000 | | Yes | | | | | | |
| 85. | Hindu-stan Machine Tools Ltd. | 211.72<br>172.86<br>38.86 | 198.21 | SLM | | | | | | Yes | FA<<br>Rs. 5000 | | | | | | | | Yes |
| 86. | Exide Industries Ltd. | 807.21<br>331.22<br>475.99 | 1219.67 | SLM | | | | | | Yes | | Yes | Yes | | Yes | Yes | | Yes | Yes |

(Contd.)

| (1) | (2) | (3) | (4) | (5) | (6) | (7) | (8) | (9) | (10) | (11) | (12) | (13) | (14) | (15) | (16) | (17) | (18) | (19) | (20) |
|---|---|---|---|---|---|---|---|---|---|---|---|---|---|---|---|---|---|---|---|
| 87. | Thermax Ltd. | 165.23<br>84.43<br>80.80 | 563.88 | SLM | | | | | | Yes | | No | Yes | | Yes | | | Yes | Yes |
| 88. | Birla Corpora-tion Ltd. | 899.49<br>577.54<br>321.95 | 1243.18 | SLM | | | | | | | | Yes | | | | Yes | | | Yes |
| 89. | Sundaram Clayton Ltd. | 239.49<br>79.22<br>160.27 | 471.35 | SLM | | | | | | Yes | FA< Rs. 5000 | Yes | Yes | | | | | | |
| 90. | Asahi India Glass Ltd. | 678.98<br>392.74<br>286.24 | 489.85 | WDV<br>SLM | | Yes | | | | | FA< Rs. 5000 | Yes | Yes | | | | | | Yes |
| 91. | Indo Rama Synthetics (India) Ltd. | 2057.82<br>752.45<br>1305.37 | 1663.61 | SLM | | | | | | | | | | | | | | Yes | Yes |
| 92. | Bharat Earth Movers Ltd. | 543.33<br>409.49<br>133.84 | 1764.33 | SLM | | | | | | | | | | | | | | | Yes |
| 93. | Chambal Fertiliser & Chemicals Ltd. | 2680.37<br>979.02<br>1701.35 | 1872.80 | SLM | | | | | | | | | Yes | | | | | Yes | Yes |
| 94 | Apollo Tyres Ltd. | 975.87<br>327.79<br>648.08 | 2314.31 | SLM | | | | | | | | Yes | Yes | | Yes | | | Yes | Yes |
| 95. | ICI India Ltd. | 351.58<br>186.24<br>165.34 | 685.12 | SLM | | | | | | | | Yes | | | | | Yes | | Yes |

(Contd.)

| (1) | (2) | (3) | (4) | (5) | (6) | (7) | (8) | (9) | (10) | (11) | (12) | (13) | (14) | (15) | (16) | (17) | (18) | (19) | (20) |
|---|---|---|---|---|---|---|---|---|---|---|---|---|---|---|---|---|---|---|---|
| 96. | Marico Industries Ltd. | 152.48<br>70.31<br>82.17 | 852.56 | SLM | | | | | | | FA?<br>Rs. 5000 | Yes | Yes | Yes | | | | | Yes |
| 97. | Balram-pur Chini Mills Ltd. | 744.28<br>200.32<br>543.96 | 738.19 | SLM | | | | | | | | | | | | | | Yes | No |
| 98. | Finolex Industr-ies Ltd. | 865.87<br>381.60<br>484.27 | 818.07 | SLM | | | | | | | | | | | | | | Yes | Yes |
| 99. | Gujarat Mineral Develop-ment Corporat-ion Ltd. | 372.49<br>301.93<br>70.56 | 272.96 | SLM<br>WDV | | Yes | | | Yes | Yes | | | Yes | | | | | Yes | Yes |
| 100. | Pidilite Industries Ltd. | 340.30<br>137.21<br>203.09 | 755.77 | SLM<br>WDV | | Yes | | | Yes | Yes | FA<<br>Rs. 5000 | Yes | Yes | | | | | | |

SLM – Straight Line Method

WDV – Written Down Value Method

FA – Fixed Assets

*Sources*: Annual Reports of 100 sample companies for the period 2003-04.

# 7

# Analysis and Interpretation

In the backdrop of the discussion so far made in the present study, let us now analyse and interpret the data presented in chapter VI in respect of depreciation accounting practices of the Indian companies Before analysing and interpreting the data under this chapter it will be logical to give an idea regarding the term disclosure.

Disclosure, simply means the release of information. Accountants tend to use the word in a slightly more restrictive sence to mean the release of financial information about company through financial report under the garb of annual report. The term is sometimes further restricted to mean the information not contained in the financial statement themselves. Questions regarding the release of information in the Balance Sheet, Profit and Loss Account and Cash Flow Statement fall under the rubrics of recognition and measurement. Disclosure in its narrowest sense covers such things as managements discussion and analysis, footnotes, schedules, and supplementary statements.

As per International Accounting Standard Committee (IASC) "Financial Statements must be clear and understandable. They are based on accounting policies which vary from enterprise to enterprise, both within a single country and among countries. Disclosure of the significant accounting policies on which the financial statements are based is therefore necessary so that they may be properly understood".

The Financial Accounting Standard Board (FASB) observed that information being disclosed in financial reports should be:

"Comprehensible to those who have a reasonable understanding of business and economic activities and are willing to study the information with reasonable diligence".

Hendriksen mentioned that the "three concepts of disclosure generally proposed are 'adequate', 'fair' and 'full' disclosure. Adequate disclosure implies a minimum amount of disclosure congruous with the negative objective of making the statements not misleading. Fair disclosure implies an ethical objective of providing equal treatment for all potential readers. Full disclosure implies the presentation of all relevant information."

In India the disclosure of some of the accounting policies followed in the preparation and presentation of the financial statement is governed by Indian GAAP. Indian GAAP comprises a set of pronouncements issued by various regulatory authorities but is predominantly controlled by the Institute of Chartered Accountants of India (ICAI). Besides accounting standards, ICAI issues Guidance Notes on area not specifically covered by Accounting Standards. The ICAI has also started issuing Accounting Standards Interpretation (ASIs) and General Clarifications (GCs) which also form part of Indian GAAP. The ICAI also makes several announcements and issues clarifications on accounting related matters. The Companies Act is the significant part of GAAP. The Companies Act provides legal requirements for maintenance of books of account by the company; requires compliance with mandatory accounting standards issued by ICAI; and lays down format of financial statements e.g., Schedule VI. Securities and Exchange Board of India (SEBI) also mandates certain disclosures in the annual reports of listed companies such as cash flow statement, corporate governance reporting etc. Moreover SEBI plays an important role in ensuring compliance with Accounting Standards in respect of listed companies, similar to the role played by the United States' Securities and Exchange Commission (SEC). Reserve Bank of India has issued various circulars dealing with income recognition, asset classification and provisioning by banks.

Accounting policies refer to specific accounting principles and the methods of applying those principles adopted by enterprise in the preparation and presentation of financial statements. Enterprises operate in diverse and complex economic environment. Transactions and events are products of such diverse and complex economic environment in which the enterprise operates. Accordingly it is believed that no unified and exhaustive list of accounting policies can be suggested which has universal application. Rather the choice of accounting policy is guided by specific circumstances and it involves considerable judgement of the management.

In the Companies Act and various Accounting Standards, Statements, Guidance Notes etc. issued by the ICAI, it has been attempted to reduce the large number of diverse accounting policies in use. Wide variation in the choice of accounting policies leads to create a set of accounting numbers which are not comparable across the enterprises. In other words, it is appropriate to say that flexibility in the choice of accounting policies affects 'comparability' of accounting data among the enterprises.

On the other hand, 'comparability' is considered as an important qualitative characteristic of financial statements (Framework for the Preparation and Presentation of Financial Statements, International Accounting standards Committee, Paras 39-42). Although, by way of accounting regulations attempts are made to reduce the number of alternative accounting policies, applicable to a particular situation, it is difficult to follow a uniform accounting policy in all the circumstances.

Para 40 of the IASC Documents, 'Framework for the Preparation and Presentation of Financial statements', explains that 'users need to be able to identify differences between the accounting policies for like transaction and other events used by the some enterprise from period to period and by different enterprises'. The said document clarifies in Para 41 that 'The need of comparability should not be confused with mere uniformity and should not be allowed to become an impediment to the introduction of improved accounting standards. It is not appropriate for an enterprise to continue accounting in the same manner for a transaction and other event if the policy adopted is not in keeping with the qualitative characteristics of relevance and reliability. It is also inappropriate for an enterprise to leave its accounting policies uncharged when more relevant and reliable alternatives exist.'

This means, it is not proper to follow an accounting policy without any change only to maintain comparability when more and more relevant and appropriate accounting policy emerges. The quality of comparability should be understood with reference to relevance and reliability of accounting data.

An inappropriate choice of accounting policy may misguide and also affect the true and fair view of the financial statements which is a legally required qualitative characteristic of financial statements. It may be mentioned that section 211 (3c) of the Companies Act, 1956 requires that every balance sheet of a company shall give a true and fair view of the state of affairs of the company as at the end of the financial year and every profit and loss account of a company shall give a true and fair view of the profit and loss of the company for the financial year and in case of the cash flow statement, it shall give a true and fair view of the cash flows for the financial year of a company.

Thus, choice of accounting policy and making a change thereof are important accounting policy decisions that effect the performance measurement as well as indication of financial position of the reporting entity. The choice of inappropriate accounting policy results in either overstatement or understatement of performance and financial position of the reporting entity. Therefore, accounting policy should be adopted with due care and considering its effect on the financial performance and position of the reporting entity from the angle of the various users of accounts.

The study has been conducted in the light of the aforesaid concept of disclosures of financial information so far as these relate to Depreciation Accounting.

As stated earlier we have taken a sample of 100 companies out of first 200 companies of the 'ET 500', December 2004 edition published by Economic Times Intelligence Group (ETIG). For the purpose of this ranking, the Economic Times Intelligence Group has taken into account the average market capitalisations of companies for the period October 16 to 31, 2003 and companies being traded for six days or more [Source: ETIG Database]. The data has been collected from the Annual Reports of these 100 companies for the year 2003-04 having net turnover Rs. 100 crores or more. The companies belong to the manufacturing group only i.e. the companies either manufacturing goods or producing services having huge investments in tangible fixed assets. The selected company is either a company in the public sector or in the public limited companies. The sample has been drawn in a way as to cover all the major segments or divisions of Indian industries. That is cross section wise the sample companies have been selected. The companies selected are from automobile industry, oil and gas industry, chemical industry, iron and steel industry, pharmaceutical industry, infotech industry, cement industry, aluminium industry, paper industry, agro industry, hotel industry, cotton and textiles industry, shipping industry, engineering industry, fertilizers industry etc. Thus, the coverage of the industry is as wide as possible. Therefore certain companies are obviously kept outside the purview of this study. These companies are:

(i) Investment and Financing Company

(ii) Banking and Insurance Company

(iii) Trading and Export Company

(iv) Company which generates electricity i.e. the company which follows specific rules while preparing the annual report.

The study highlights significantly into the disclosure practices of the different companies regarding depreciation accounting. Though all the selected company clearly stated in the significant accounting policies under 'Notes on Accounts' that the financial statements are prepared in accordance with generally accepted accounting principles and comply with the accounting standards specified by the Institute of Chartered Accountants of India under section 211 (3c) of the Companies Act 1956 but there is a wide spectrum of accounting procedures regarding depreciation in their published reports. The revelation from the study are:

(i) Out of the 100 sample companies, 74 per cent companies followed single method for charging depreciation. Out of these companies, 72 per cent companies adopted straight line method, while 2 per cent used written down value method for charging depreciation (e.g. Oil and Natural Gas Corporation Limited and Motor Industries Company Limited)

(ii) 25 per cent companies used straight line method and written down value method for charging depreciation on their assets. A further detailed analysis of the 25 per cent companies that used both the methods can be depicted as follows.

(a) 5 per cent companies adopted straight line method for one division or unit and written down value method for other division/unit (e.g. Grasim Industries Limited)

(b) 11 per cent companies reported that they used straight line method for charging depreciation up to certain period of time and after that period they used written down value method and vice versa (e.g., Associated Cement Companies Limited).

(c) 9 per cent companies reported that they adopted straight line method for certain class of assets and written down value method for other class of assets. (e.g. United Phosphorus Limited, Essar Steel Limited)

(iii) There had been however 1 per cent company used straight line method and use-base method for charging depreciation on different categories of assets. Bharat Electronics Ltd, for example, stated in its annual report that "tangible depreciable fixed assets are generally depreciated on straight line method of the rates (or higher rates as disclosed) and in the manner prescribed in Schedule XIV to the Companies Act, 1956 except in cases where the machine utilisation hour basis is adopted. Special instruments are amortised over production". It is clearly a deviation from Companies Act 1956. The Department of Company Affairs in General Circular No. 12/2003 dated 21.02.2003 has stated that it disapproves used of 'unit of product' based computation of depreciation for the purpose of section 205(2)(b) of the Act, as the same ignores the impact of time element in depreciation and has a potential to be manipulative. Further, if allowed, it may prolong the life of the asset beyond its specified life. But the company did not mention anything regarding the life of that category of assets.

(iv) 10 per cent companies adopted different methods of depreciation for different classes of asset. Para 12 of AS 6 approved a combination of more than one method. Para 5 of Guidance Note on Accounting for Depreciation in Companies clearly stated that 'a company may adopt more than one method of depreciation. Thus it is permissible to follow different methods for different type of assets provided the same methods are consistently adopted from year to year in accordance with section 205 (2). Also units in different geographical location can follow different methods of depreciation provided the same are consistently followed. The Department of Company Affairs in its Circular Letter No. 10(1)CL-VI dated 27.09.1961 also approved different depreciation method for different types of assets. From the above, it is clear that a company can adopt different depreciation methods for different type of fixed assets. Gujarat Ambuja Cement Limited, for example, stated in its annual report that depreciation on all assets other than vehicles is provided on the 'Straight Line Method' in accordance with the provisions of section 205(2)(b) of the Companies Act, 1956 and on vehicles on the "Written Down Value Method' in accordance with the provisions of section 205(2)(a) of the Companies Act 1956, in the manner and at the rates specified in Schedule XIV to the Companies Act. 1956.

(v) 16 per cent companies reported that they used different depreciation methods for the same class of fixed asset. Out of these companies 5 per cent companies adopted different methods of depreciation for similar types of assets simply because location of usage is different. As for instance when straight line method has been used under one division for charging depreciation on plant and machinery but written down value method was for the same class of asset under another division. Nirma Limited is a typical example of this type of practice. 11 per cent companies reported that they adopted different depreciation method for the same type of fixed assets on the basis of specific period of acquisition. This means straight line method for assets acquired after 2001 and written down value method for assets acquired upto 2001. Depreciation policy of Tata Motors Limited is an example on this point. Companies Act 1956 and AS-6 are silent in this respect. Actually this type of practice carries no logic. Therefore, normally an uniform depreciation rate and method is applied for the same class of fixed assets.

(vi) Regarding change in the method of deprecation during the financial year 2003-04, no company reported that they had changed the method of charging depreciation on certain asset.

(vii) 5 per cent companies reported that there is a change in the estimated useful life of the depreciable asset and they charged depreciation on their basis of remaining useful life of the asset as per the re-estimated useful life. Out of these companies 2 per cent companies (e.g. Ispat Industries Limited and Grasim Industries Limited) reported that the change in the estimated useful life of asset due to revaluation of assets as ascertained by the valuers. Other 3 per cent companies have revised estimated useful life. Colgate Palmolive (India) Limited disclosed that 'it has revised the useful life of factory building to 20 years and residential and office building to 40 years. The useful life of assets are based on technical estimates approved by management and are lower than the implied useful live arrived on the basis of the rates prescribed under Schedule XIV to the Companies Act, 1956 of India'. It is important to notice that the above reassessment of useful life does not result in depreciation lower than that required under Schedule XIV as that would result in contravention of section 205(2) of the Companies Act 1956.

(viii) 14 per cent companies reported that certain assets have been revalued during the year. All the companies did not mentioned the method used for revaluation of assets. But they mentioned directly or indirectly AS-6 for revaluation of fixed assets in the 'Notes to Accounts.'

(ix) Regarding any reference to Income Tax, 3 per cent companies reported that they have been used Income Tax Rules, 1961 while determining the rate to be charged on certain assets. For example, Pidilite Industries Limited stated in its annual report that 'for assets acquired up to 30.6.1987, on straight line method basis, except certain assets for which written down value basis is adapted at rates equivalent to the rates specified in Income Tax Act.' Actually a company can follow rates prescribed under the Income Tax Act/Rules only if these rates represent bona fide commercial depreciation and are higher than Schedule XIV rates.

(x) 53 per cent companies disclosed in their annual reports that pro rate depreciation has been charged on addition to and disposal of assets. These disclosure are under Note No. 4 to Schedule XIV to the Companies Act 1956 and the standard on depreciation. The study also revealed that 6 per cent companies used pro rata on quarterly basis instead of depreciation on addition/disposal during the year on pro rata basis with reference to the date of purchase/sale. IBP Company Limited, for example, reported that depreciation is charged pro rata on quarterly basis on assets from/up to the quarter of capitalisation/sale, disposal and dismantled during the year. 4 per cent companies reported that full depreciation has been charged on addition of asset irrespective of date of purchased of assets and no depreciation has been charged on disposed off assets. Great Eastern Shipping Company Limited is a typical example of this type of practices. 1 per cent company reported that the pro rata depreciation on half yearly basis but in different manner. Ashok Leyland Limited, for example, reported this fact—"Depreciation/amortisation is charged for the full year on the addition made during the first half of the year and for six month on the addition made during the second half of the year. No depreciation is provided for in respect of assets disposed off during the year". Another 1 per cent company charged depreciation on asset at fortnight pro rata basis but in different ways. Gujarat Mineral Development Corporation limited disclosed that depreciation on the assets purchased during the accounting year is charged proportionately for the period from the month of acquisition if it is acquired during the first fortnight of that month or from the subsequent month if acquired during the second fortnight of that month. But on the assets disposed off/discarded during the year, depreciation is charge on pro-rata basis upto the date of their disposal/discarding. It is important to mention here that with regard to pro rata depreciation, the Research Committee of the ICAI has expressed the view that a company may group additions and disposals in appropriate time period(s), e.g., 15 days, a month, a quarter etc. for the purpose of charging pro rata depreciation in respect of additions and disposals of its assets keeping in view the materiality of the amounts involved [Guidance Note on Accounting for Depreciation by the Companies issued by the Research Committee of the ICAI, 1989, Para 24].

(xi) Regarding 100 per cent depreciation on small items of asset or low valued asset, 41 per cent companies reported in their annual report that they have been charged 100 per cent depreciation on the low valued assets. Out of these companies 32 per cent companies disclosed in their annual report that they have charged 100 per cent depreciation on the asset whose value was less or equal to Rs. 5000. (e.g. BIOCON Limited). 5 per cent companies reported that they charged 100 per cent depreciation on asset value above Rs. 5000. Hindustan Zine Limited, for example, disclosed in its annual report that individual items of plant and machinery and vehicles costing upto Rs. 25,000 are wholly depreciated. 4 per cent companies disclosed this fact in a slightly different manner. Actually these companies made only indirect reference of this fact. Jubilant Organosys Limited reported this fact—'Depreciation, in respect of assets added/installed during the subsequent period, is provided at the rates, mentioned in Schedule XIV to the Companies Act, 1956 read with Notification dated 16th December, 1993 issued by Department of Company Affairs, Government of India'. It actually refers the assets up to value of Rs. 5000 can be written off in the first year of purchase entirely. Expert Advisory Committee (EAC) of ICAI opined that the accounting policy to charge off small items of plant and equipment costing less than Rs. 1 lakh to revenue would be in conformity with AS-6 and AS-10, provided the aforesaid amount is not considered material. Materiality has to be determined keeping in view the circumstances prevailing within the company which may be different from those prevailing in other companies (Source: The Chartered Accountant (Journal), January 2004).

(xi) Regarding, charging higher rate of depreciation than the rate as contained in Schedule XIV of Companies Act 1956, 49 per cent companies reported that they used higher rate of depreciation than Schedule XIV on certain categories of assets. Actually rates specified in the Schedule XIV indicate minimum depreciation rates. A company can charge higher depreciation based on bona fide technological estimation of the useful life and scrap value. Para 11 of AS-6 (Revised) states that quantum of depreciation to be provided in an accounting period involves judgement of the management. Para 11 of AS-6 (Revised) states that 'the statute governing an enterprise provides the basis for computation of the depreciation. For example, the Companies Act 1956 lays down the rates of depreciation in respect of various assets. Where the management's estimate of the useful life of an asset of the enterprise is shorter than the envisaged under the provisions of the relevant statute, the depreciation provision is appropriately computed by applying a higher rate'. Moreover this practice is at per with the Circular 2 of 1989 dated 07.03.1989 issued by Department of Company Affairs, under Ministry of Industry of Government of India.

(xii) 6 per cent companies in the sample reported that they use 'extra shift depreciation' (double, triple) rate of depreciation on certain plant and machinery. A further analysis reveal that 2 per cent companies (Maruti Udyog Limited and Bharat Heavy Electricals Limited) reported the double shift and triple shift rate in their annual report but not mentioned that basis, while 3 per cent companies reported the basis of charging extra shift depreciation but not disclosed the applicable double shift/triple shift rate. Tata Iron and Steel Company Limited is a typical example of this type of practices. Clause 6 to Schedule XIV to the Companies Act, 1956 prescribes: 'The calculation of extra depreciation for double shift working and for triple shift working shall be made separately in the proportion which the number of days for which the concern worked double shift or triple shift, as the case may be, bears to the normal number of working days during the year. Again paragraph 12 of the Guidance Note on Accounting for Depreciation in Companies, *inter alia*, recommends: Schedule XIV requires that where the concern has worked extra shift, the multiple or extra shift depreciation will have to be provided on the plant and machinery, wherever applicable. In this regards, various units/departments/mills/factories should be taken as separate concerns.

(xiii) 10 per cent companies disclosed that their plant is termed as 'continuous process plant' on the basis of technical assessment and the depreciation is provided on these assets as per rules in this regard. Jubilant Organosys Limited, one of the sample companies, mentioned that 'certain plants mere classified as continuous process plant from the financial year ended 31.03.2000 and such classification has been done on technical assessment, (relied upon by the auditor being a technical matter) and depreciation has been provided accordingly.' While Thermax Limited disclosed this information in different manner and reported in policies statement as 'Depreciation on entire plant and machinery of Chemical Division is charged considering the chemical plant as a 'Continuous Process Plant'. Note 7 to the Schedule XIV of Companies Act 1956, defines continues process plant as one which is required and designed to operate 24 hours a day. Guidance Note on Schedule XIV issued by ICAI further clarifies that the technical design of a continuous process plant is such that there is a requirement to run it continuously for 24 hours a day, if it is not so run, there are significant shutdown and/or start up costs.

Other important points that transpired from the study on depreciation policy in the corporate sector are:

(a) 69 per cent companies disclosed that lease assets held by them were amortised over the period of lease and many companies treated this amortised amount as a depreciation. But company to company the policy regarding amortisation of lease had been different. Sterlite Industries (India) Limited one of the sample companies mentioned that 'amortisation of lease hold land and building has been done in proportion to the period of lease.' While 6 per cent companies reported that leasehold land were not amortised. Glaxo Smith Kline Pharmaceuticals Limited is a typical example of this practice.

(b) Regarding technical know-how/intangible assets, 55 per cent companies reported that they included technical intangible/intangible assets in the fixed assets and the amortised portion of technical know-how/intangible assets was included in the amount of depreciation during the year (e.g. ITC Limited). 3 per cent companies disclosed that they did not include it as a part of fixed asset and as such amortisation of technical know-how/intangible assets did not include in depreciation. Bajaj Auto Limited, for example, was one of that categories.

(c) Regarding capitalisation of gain or loss due to foreign exchange fluctuations, 37 per cent companies reported directly or indirectly that the depreciation on the revised unamortised depreciable amount is provided prospectively over the residual useful life of the asset. This treatment is in accordance with Para 25 of the AS-6 (Revised). (e.g. Indian Petrochemical Corporation Limited)

(d) Regarding 'a substantial part of fixed assets has been disposed off during the year and whether it has affected the going concern' [a statutory requirement under Clause 4(i)c of the Companies (Auditor's Report) Order, 2003 as amended by Companies (Auditor's Report) Amended Order 2004 (together the 'Order) issued by the Central Government of India in terms of subsection (4A) of Section 227 of the Companies Act, 1956] the auditor in case of 89 per cent companies reported "in our opinion and according to the information and explanation given to us by management a substantial part of fixed assets has not been disposed by the company during the year." It means there is a sale of fixed assets but not significant hence the disposal of fixed assets has not affected the going concern status of company. The auditor in case of 5 per cent companies' reported that the company has sold a substantial part of the fixed assets but it has no affect on going concern assumption. The auditors of Larsen and Toubro for example, reported this fact—'During the year the company has disposed off the cement division by demerger into another company. Accordingly to the information and explanation given to us, we are of the opinion that the said disposal not affected the going concern status of the company.' While auditor of 6 per cent companies' reported that Clause 4(i)(c) of the Companies (Auditor's Report) Order 2003 was not applicable to the company. Aventis Pharma Limited was one of that categories.

In order to present the major findings of the study relating to the disclosure policy of depreciation accounting, we provided the following table in a concise and easy-to-understand manner.

Table 7.1: Summary of Depreciation Accounting Disclosure Practices of Sample Companies (Sample Size 100)

| *Sl. No.* | *Major Findings* | *Percentage (%) of Companies* |
|---|---|---|
| 1. | Use of Straight Line Method | 72 |
| 2. | Use of Written Down Value Method | 2 |
| 3. | Use of both Straight Line Method and Written Down Value Method | 25 |
| 4. | Use of both Straight Line Method and Use-Based Method | 1 |
| 5. | Charging different method of depreciation for different assets | 10 |
| 6. | Charging different method of depreciation for same classes of assets | 16 |
| 7. | Change in Method of deprecation | NIL |
| 8. | Change in useful life of asset | 5 |
| 9. | Revaluation of assets during the year | 14 |
| 10. | Any reference to Income Tax | 3 |
| 11. | Depreciation on addition/disposal of fixed assets on pro rata basis | 53 |
| 12. | Charging full depreciation on addition but no depreciation on disposal of assets (Included in Sl. No. 11) | 4 |
| 13. | 100% depreciation on assets not exceeding or up to Rs. 5000 | 32 |
| 14. | 100% depreciation on assets exceeding Rs. 5000 | 5 |
| 15. | Indirect reference regarding 100% depreciation on assets | 4 |
| 16. | Charging depreciation at a rate higher than Schedule XIV rates | 49 |
| 17. | Adaptation of extra shift depreciation allowance | 6 |
| 18. | Information about continuous process plant | 10 |
| 19. | Amortisation of leasehold land included in depreciation | 69 |
| 20. | Not Amortisation leasehold land | 6 |
| 21. | Amortisation of Intangible Assets included in depreciation | 55 |
| 22. | Amortisation of Intangible Assets not included in depreciation | 3 |
| 23. | Capitalisation of foreign exchange gain/loss | 37 |
| 24. | Disposal of a substantial part of fixed assets | 5 |

# 8

# Summary and Conclusions

It will be recalled that the present study is concerned with the "Corporate depreciation accounting practices in India : a critical study". The study is now over and we are to come out with our observations and conclusions on the topic of discussion. Before we proceed to make our conclusions, let us sum up the chapter wise discussions that we have made so far.

Chapter I of the study had been on the introduction. This chapter comprised of the objective of the study, review of literature, data source and methodology, limitations of the study and layout of the chapters. In the discussion it is stated that the objective of the study is to examine the prevailing depreciation accounting practices in the corporate sector in India having due regard to the legal framework of depreciation including accounting standard on depreciation and at the same time efforts will also be made to judge the effectiveness of the rules themselves with compare to standards prevailing in some selected countries. We have made a brief study of the prior research on this subject since 1903, though the prior period study was based mainly on the conceptual aspect. The review of prior period study covers the works of eminent persons and body like Ewing Matheson, P.D. Leake, G.T. Webb, Eugene L. Grant and Paul T. Norton, National Association of Accountants, Louis Goldberg, Leonard E. Morrissey, F.K. Wright, William Thomas Hogan, G.D. Roy, W.T. Baxter etc. The study is basically a descriptive one. So the test of hypothesis is beyond the scope of this study. The source of information for the study are published literature, provisions of Companies Act, provisions of Income Tax Act, ICAI accounting standards on depreciation accounting (AS-6) (Revised) and guidelines, accounting standards promulgated by the leading accounting standard setters of the world on depreciation accounting and published annual reports of the companies. The present study may be considered relevant for understanding the necessity of framing accounting standard in respect of depreciation accounting as a step towards harmonisation of accounting practices relating to depreciation.

In chapter II we have concentrated on the discussion of the conceptual aspect of depreciation dividing the whole chapter into five sections. The discussion in the first section started with the definition of depreciation as given in different dictionaries and encyclopaedias. Dictionary for Accountant edited by E.L. Kohler, the Hand Book of International Financial Terms by Peter Moles and Nicholas Terry, Encyclopaedia Britannica, the Encyclopaedia Americana etc. are important among them. The discussion in this section ended with definition given by the different recognised accounting bodies for example, the American Accounting Association (AAA), The American Institute of Certified Public Accountants (AICPA), The Institute of Chartered Accountants in England and Walse. In this section we also discussed the economist's view regarding depreciation. In economist's view, depreciation recognises as a flow of stream of services from the capital fund contributing to the cost of products or services properly chargeable against revenue earned. A brief account of eminent economist's view like Adam Smith, Alfred Marshall, R.A.D. Egerton, R.F. Fowler, R.G. Hawtrey and J.M. Keynes have also discussed in this section. Some case laws regarding depreciation also figured in discussion in this section. In the second section we have traced the causes of depreciation as given by different academicians. The causes identified for depreciation by those authority are wear and tear, efflux of time, obsolescence, inadequacy, accident etc. In third section we have discussed the effect of depreciation from the view point of balance sheet, profit and loss account, working capital and product cost determination etc. In fourth section, We have focused on the practical concept regarding depreciation as expressed by the researchers and academicians. In this exercise we have included the concept as developed by Louis Goldberg, Singer, G.D. Roy, E.S. Hendriksen etc. Their views on depreciation is that depreciation is a recognition of the physical or functional determination of a fixed asset (George A. Mac Farland, Robert D. Ayars), depreciation is a process of allocation of cost of an asset (AICPA), depreciation is a measure of the maintenance of capital (E.S. Hendriksen), depreciation is a provision for replacement of depreciable assets. (G.T. Webb), depreciation is a measure of decline in service potential (AAA), depreciation is a current cost of service consumed (Sprouse and Moonitz). In fifth section an effort has been made to examine the question whether depreciation is a source of fund or not. Here it has stated that when E.W. Walker, G.D. Roy etc. expressed their view in favour of depreciation serving as a source of fund; I.M. Pandey. Anthony, Harold Bierman, C.T. Horngren etc. expressed their view against the same.

In chapter III we have discussed the method of depreciation. Here we have stated that the periodic depreciation not only depends on the method of depreciation adopted by the firm but also on other factors that are responsible for varying amount of depreciation namely, cost of the asset, life of the asset, the scrap value at the end of the effective life of the asset though there is a lot of subjectivity in estimation. Of these influencing factors on method of depreciation it has been stated that there are five different methods of depreciation and these five different methods are constant charge method, variable charge method, declining charge method, increasing charge method and miscellaneous method. Some of the methods which are much in use for charging depreciation have been discussed in details are straight line method, diminishing balance method, sum-of-the-years'-digits method, double decline balance method, sinking fund method, annuity method, discounted cash flow method. Moreover, the merits and demerits have been analysed with every method. In course of discussion it has been pointed out that no allocation method is fully defensible. Some of the other methods of depreciation have been discussed briefly. These include output method, revaluation method, group or composition method. A brief analysis has been done at the end of this chapter regarding selection of a best depreciation method. In this regard the study of Charles W. Lamden is important and his view over the selection of method of depreciation has been discussed in brief. The analysis has whatever may be the method of depreciation chosen for amortisation of an asset it must be within the purview of generally accepted accounting principles, legal framework and also cost effective.

In Chapter IV we have discussed the regulatory requirements concerning depreciation accounting in India. It has three section. In first section, we have discussed the different provisions relating to depreciation in details under Companies Act 1956. Under Companies Act 1956 we have discussed the provision of sections 205 and 350 in respect of depreciation. We have also analysed here the Schedule XIV of Companies Act relating to rates of depreciation. In the process we have also discussed the several clarification regarding depreciation which has been given time to time by Department of Company Affairs under the Ministry of Industry of Government of India on the requirements under Schedule XIV of the Companies Act. In second section we have discussed the depreciation accounting standard in India i.e., AS-6. Here we have focused on the compliance with the accounting standards which has been made mandatory according to subsection (3A) to section 211 of Companies Amendment Act 1999. In this section, we have discussed briefly the objectives of accounting standard. Here we have also focused in brief, how and why Accounting Standard Board (ASB) has been established in India by ICAI in 1977. The main functions of ASB has also been explained in this section. In the discussion it has been stated that though accounting standard on depreciation (AS-6) has been issued in November, 1982 by ICAI but it was recommendatory in nature. As such it had not much of its effectiveness. To overcome the difficulty, with effect from 1st April, 1995 the standard has been mandatory. The history of development of accounting standard on depreciation (AS-6) also figured in the discussion. In the third section, our focus had also been on section 32 relating to depreciation under Indian Income Tax Act, 1961. Here we have discussed asset which are eligible for depreciation, condition to be satisfied to claim depreciation, assets on which depreciation are disallowed etc. We have also analysed here the way in which depreciation allowance is computed e.g., method of depreciation, rates of depreciation, block of assets, actual cost and written down value. The discussion in this chapter ended by making a comparative analysis between Companies Act and Income Tax Act on the requirements for depreciation.

In Chapter V, we have presented a comperative study of depreciation accounting rules prevailing in some selected countries to judge how far Indian depreciation accounting rules are compatible with those prevailing elsewhere. For the purpose of this study we have selected twelve countries including India and the International Accounting Standards (IAS) issued by International Accounting Standards Board (IASB) on this subject. The selected countries were the United states, Canada, the United kingdom, Germany, France, the Netherlands, Brazil, South Africa, Australia, Japan and China. The countries have been chosen in such a way as to represent all major accounting model that are currently prevailing in the world and these countries are also the leading countries in their respective continent. The selection of IAS has justified on the ground that at present more than 100 countries directly or indirectly use International Accounting Standards for their accounting practices. The depreciation accounting practices along with tangible fixed assets have been discussed with respect to different countries. We have also focused on the 'Generally Accepted Accounting Principles/ Practices' (GAAP) prevailing in the different countries with a view to understanding the subject well. The analysis revealed that though all countries used to follow 'historical cost' for initial recognition but there was practically many differences among the countries relating to depreciation accounting. In order to highlight the significant differences relating to depreciation accounting among the different countries and IAS in a brief and easy-to-understand manner, we have included a comparison table at the end of this chapter.

In Chapter VI, we have shown data relating to depreciation accounting practices in Indian companies covered in the sample. We have taken a sample of 100 companies out of first 200 companies of 'ET 500' December 2004 edition published by Economic Times Intelligence Group. Another criteria of these companies were that the turnover of selected companies must be Rs. 100 crores or above. The sample has been drawn in such a way as to cover all the major segments or divisions of Indian industries. We have discussed the accounting policy on depreciation accounting of 100 sample companies chronologically on the basis of their ranking in 'ET 500'. We have also focused on fixed assets turnover ratio of all companies to judge the degree of managerial efficiency in utilisation of fixed assets. Based on the discussion relating to depreciation accounting practices of 100 companies, we have presented a table containing the summary of disclosure practices regarding depreciation accounting at the end of this chapter.

In Chapter VII, an effort has been made to what extent the selected sample of 100 companies discussed the different regulations under the Companies Act and the Accounting Standard (AS-6) relating to the disclosure of depreciation accounting in their annual report. The analysis revealed that the companies are not so transparent in disclosing information regarding depreciation accounting. The study also disclosed that straight line method is the most popular method among the companies for charging depreciation and there was no unanimity among the companies for charging depreciation on their assets within the conceptual and legal frameworks. It has been observed that some of the sample companies have changed the rate of depreciation without providing any reason. So there is lack of transparency in respect of changing the rate of depreciation.

## Conclusions

On the basis of the discussions that we have made from Chapter I to Chapter VII of the study, we now make the following conclusions:

1. The gap between the international accounting standard and Indian accounting standard must be narrowed down for promoting harmonisation in accounting principles and procedures relating to depreciation.
2. The standard should specify the procedure that companies are to adopt in revaluating their fixed assets. The standard should also specify the condition under which revaluation are to be made.
3. If there occurs any impairment of fixed assets, the same should be recognised in the books of accounts and future depreciation charges should be adjusted accordingly.
4. The accounting standard should restrict the management of companies for choosing any method for charging depreciation. The standard should make a parity with the Companies Act in order to select a particular depreciation method for better comparability of accounting information across the different companies.
5. Accounting policy should contain detailed particulars regarding depreciation. There should not be any ambiguity.
6. If method of depreciation is changed, the reason thereof should be clearly stated in the accounting policy statement.
7. If there occurs any addition to fixed assets during the period, the depreciation applicable to the additional amount should be separately disclosed with the date of addition in the annual report. The same practice should be adopted when there occurs disposal of fixed assets during the period.

8. Depreciation charge should not include amortisation charges applicable to intangible fixed assets. Amortisation of intangible fixed assets should be shown separately.

9. If any tangible fixed asset is not depreciated the reason for this should be clearly stated in the accounting policy statement.

10. Company sometimes vary their depreciation charges in order to smooth periodic profit. This creative practice should be stopped.

11. Effort may be made to maintain a parity between financial accounting and tax accounting particularly in the sphere of depreciation.

12. If revaluation of fixed asset is made in earlier year, the incremental depreciation due to revaluation should be transferred to Revaluation Reserve Account not to any other reserve account through profit and loss account and that should be clearly stated in the accounting policy statement.

13. If the company charges depreciation at higher rate than Schedule XIV rates, the reasons thereof should be clearly stated in the annual report.

14. If the company does not charge depreciation at the rate of 100 per cent on fixed asset whose value does not exceed Rs. 5000, the reasons should be clearly stated. Similar practice should be adopted if the company charges depreciation at the rate of 100 per cent on fixed assets whose value exceed Rs. 5000.

15. If the company adopts more than one method for charging depreciation, the division of assets should be clearly stated categorically with the name of method used.

16. Adopting different methods for same class of asset because

of location of usage is different carries no logical. Therefore, the company should clarify the reason behind it.

17. If the company adopts extra depreciation for double shift or triple shift, the double shift or triple shift rates should be clearly stated in the accounting policy along with the name of assets categorically.

18. Charging double shift depreciation will not be required unless normal capacity is exceeded. Therefore, the double shift depreciation charge will carry proportionate relationship with number of days actually worked under double shift over and above the normal capacity. Same principle should apply to the technique of calculation triple shift depreciation charge.

19. Continuous process plant are subject to single shift depreciation. Therefore, disclosure policy on how a continuous process plant has been defined by a company, should be clearly stated in the accounting policy statement.

20. Depreciating same class of asset using two different depreciation rates depending on a cut off date of capitalisation should not be permitted.

21. If a company does not provide depreciation in pursuant to a Central Government order under section 205(2)(c) of the Companies Act, a fact must be adequately disclosed in the financial statement.

22. If the estimated useful life of the depreciable asset is changed, the reasons thereof should be clearly stated in the accounting policy statement and the name of the asset and re-estimated useful life should be shown separately.

23. If the company disposed off substantial part of fixed assets, the company should specify the condition under which disposal of fixed assets are to be made along with the name of fixed assets.

## Scope for Further Research

The present study had been undertaken, it would be recalled, with the sole objective of examining the corporate accounting practices with regard to depreciation having due regard to the legal framework of depreciation including accounting standard on depreciation. Depreciation impacts financial statements in a number of ways. It has wider scope in the industries. It may be related to tax aspect. It may also be related to depreciation and capital investment decisions, depreciation and the effect of inflation, analysis of trend relating to depreciation over a long period etc. The objective of the present study being very much limited, it made no attempt to examine these issues. These issues, therefore, in our opinion offer scopes for further research relating to depreciation aspect in the Indian industries.

# Bibliography

## Books


Agarwal, Sanjiv, *A Manual of Accounting standards*, India, Snow white publications Pvt. Ltd., 2002.

Agarwal, Sanjiv, *Accounting Standards and Corporate Practices*, New Delhi, Snow white publications Pvt. Ltd.,1998.

Backer, Morton, *Handbook of Modern Accounting Theory*, Prentice Hall, 1955.

Banerjee, B. *Financial Policy and Management Accounting*, Calcutta, The World Press Private Ltd., 1999.

Basu, A.K., *International Accounting Harmonisation*, Calcutta, DSA in Commerce, University of Calcutta, 1995.

Baxter, W.T. and Davidson, Sidney, *Studies in Accounting Theory*, London, Sweet & Maxwell Ltd., 1962.

Baxter, W.T., *Depreciating Assets: An Introduction*, The Institute of Chartered Accountants of Scotland, Gee & Co. Ltd., 1981.

Bierman, Harold, *Managerial Accounting—An Introduction*, New York, The Macmillan Company, 1959.

Bigg, Walter W., *Spicer & Pegler's Practical Auditing*, Indian Edition by S.V. Ghatalia, New Delhi, Allied Publishers Pvt. Ltd., 1989.

Blake, John, *Accounting Standards*, London, Longman, 1981.

Breaby, Richard and Myers, Stewart, *Principles of Corporate Finance*, Auckland, McGraw-Hill International Book Company, 1985.

Brown, E.C., Barlow, J. and Terborgh, G., *Depreciation and Taxes*, Princeton, Tax Institute Inc., 1959.

Burton, John C., Palmer, Russell E. and Koy, Robert S., *Handbook of Accounting and Auditing*, Boston, Warren, Gorham & Lamont, 1981.

Canning, J.B., *The Economics of Accountancy—A Critical Analysis of Accounting Theory*, New York, The Ronald Press Company, 1929.

Conghlan, Jeseph D. and Strand, William K., *Depreciation Accounting, Taxes and Business Decisions*, New York, Ronald Press Co., 1969.

D'Souza, Dolphy, *Indian Accounting Standards & GAAP*, India, Snow White Publication Pvt. Ltd., Volume I and II, 2005.

Dava G.L. *Emerging Dimensions in Accounting*, Jodhpur, Scientific Publishers, 1994.

Davidson, Sidney, *Handbook of Modern Accounting*, New York, McGraw-Hill Book Company.

Davidson, Sidney, Schindler, James S., and Weil, Roman L., *Fundamental of Accounting*, Illinois, The Dryden Press, Hinsdale.

Delaney, Patrick R., Nach, Ralph, Epstein, Barry J. and Budak, Susan Weiss, *Wiley GAAP 2003-Interpretation and Application of Generally Accepted Accounting Principles*, New Jersey, John Wiley & Sons Inc., 2003.

Dicksee, Lawrence R., *Auditing—A Practical Manual for Auditors*, London, Gee & Co. (Publishers) Ltd., Tenth Edition.

Edwards, James Don and Black, Homer A., *The Modern Accountant's Handbook*, Homewood, Illinois, Dow Jones-Irwin, 1976.

Ghosh, T.P., *Accounting Standards and Corporate Accounting Practices*, New Delhi, Taxmann Allied Services Pvt. Ltd., 2003.

Glautier, M.W.E. and Underdown, B., *Accounting Theory and Practice*, Pitman Publishing, 1977.

Goldberg, Louis, *Concepts of Depreciation*, Sydney, The Law Book Company of Australsia Pty. Ltd., 1960.

Grant, Eugene L. and Norton, Paul T. Jr., *Depreciation*, New York, The Ronald Press Company, 1955.

Guthmann, Harry G., *Analysis of Financial Statements*, New Delhi, Prentice Hall of India Pvt. Ltd., Fourth Edition, 1978.

Heitger, Lester E. and Matulich, Serge, *Managerial Accounting*, Dew York, McGraw-Hill Book Company, Second Edition.

Hendiksen, Eldon S., *Accounting Theory*, Homewood, Richard D. Irwin Inc., 1977.

Hogan, William Thomas, *Depreciation Policies and Resultant Problems*, New York, Fordhan University Press, 1967.

Horngren, C.T., *An Introduction to Management Accounting*, New Delhi, Prentice-Hall of India Pvt. Ltd., 1984.

ICAI, *Compendium of Statements and Standards Accounting*, New Delhi, ICAI, 1994.

Jackson, J.H., *Accounting Principles*, New York, McGraw Hill Book Company Inc, 1956.

Jinnah, M.M., *Depreciation Accounting—A Study of Practices of Indian Business*, Delhi, Himalaya Publishing House, 1989.

Kam, V., *Accounting Theory*, New York, John Wiley & Sons, 1986.

Leach, R. and Stamp, E., *British Accounting Standards—The First 10 years*, Cambridge, Woodhead-Faulkner.

Leake, P.D., *Depreciation and Wasting Assets and Their Treatment in Assessing Annual Profit and Loss*, New York, Henry Good and Sons, 1912, Reprint Edition, Arno Press, 1976.

Lele, R.K. and Lal, J., *Accounting Theory*, Allahabad, Kitab Mahal, 1989.

MacFarland George A., Ayars Robert D. and Stone, Willard E., *Accounting Fundamentals*, New York, McGrow Hill Book Company Inc., 1957.

Majumdar, A.K. and Kapoor, G.K., *Company Law and Practice*, New Delhi, Taxmann Publications (P) Ltd, 2003.

Matheson, Ewing, *The Depreciation of Factories—Mines and Industrial Undertaking and their Valuation*, London, E & F.N. Spon Ltd, Third Edition, 1903.

McCullers, Levis D. and Schroeder, Richard G., *Accounting Theory—Text and Readings*, New York, John Wiley & Sons, 1978.

Meigs, Walter B. and Meigs Robert F., *Financial Accounting*, New York, McGraw—Hill Book Company, 1986.

Meij, Jacob Louis, *Depreciation and Replacement Policy*, Amsterdam, North-Holland Publishing Co., 1961.

Morrissey, Leonard F., *The Many Sides of Depreciation*, New Hampshire, The Amos Tuck Schook of Business Administration, Dartmouth College, 1960.

Mukherji, K and Ray, G.D., *Studies in Accounting Theory*, Calcutta, The World Press Pvt. Ltd.

National Association of Accountants, *Current Practice in Accounting for Depreciation, Research Series No. 33*, New York, NAA, 1958.

Niswanger, C.R. and Fess, Philip E., *Accounting Principles* Chicago, South Western Publishing Co., Ninth Edition.

Pandey I.M., *Financial Management*, New Delhi, Vikas Publishing House Pvt. Ltd. 1998.

Paton, W.A., *Accountant Handbook*, New York, the Ronald Press Company 1953.

Pickles, William, *Accounting*, London, The English Language Book Society, 1960.

Porwal, L.S., *Accounting Theory—An Introduction*, New Delhi, Tata McGraw-Hill Publishing Co. Ltd., 1996.

Pyle, William W., White, John A., Larson Kemit D. and Zin Michael, *Fundamental Accounting, Principles*, Georgetown, Irwin-Dorsey Limited, 1980.

Ramaiya, A., *Guide to the Companies Act*, Agra, Wadhwa and Company, 1998.

Roy, G.D., *Anatomy of Depreciation*, Calcutta, The World Press Pvt. Ltd., 1977.

Roy, G.D., *A survey of Accounting Ideas*, Calcutta, Alpha Publishing Concern, 1963.

Roy, P.R., *Accounting for Cattle Depreciation and Replacement*, New Delhi, Discovery Publishing House, 1990.

Saini, A.L., *International Financial Reporting Standards (IFRS), US-GAAP, UK-GAAP and Indian GAAP*, India, Snow White Publication Pvt. Ltd., 2005.

Schmidt, L.A., and Bergston, W.N., *Fundamental Accounting*, Chicago, Richard D. Irwin Inc., 1952.

Singhania, Vinod K. and Singhania, Kapil, *Direct taxes—Law & Practice*, New Delhi, Taxmann Publications (P) Ltd, 2004.

Sinha, G., *Accounting Theory*, Calcutta, Book World, 1986.

Smith, Jack L., Keith, Robert M. and Stephens, William L., *Accounting Principles*, New York, McGraw Hill book Co., Third Edition, 1989.

Suchhal, S.C., *Financial Management—An Analytical and Conceptual Approach*, Allahabad, Chaitanya Publishing House, 1990.

Van Horne, J.C., *Financial Management and Policy*, New Delhi, Prentice-Hall of India Pvt. Ltd., 1988.

Wade, Harry H., *Fundamentals of Accounting*, New York, John Wiley and Sons, Inc.

Walker, E.W., *Essentials of Financial Management*, New Delhi, Prentice Hall of India Ltd., 1978.

Webb, G.T., *Depreciation of Fixed Assets—In Accountancy and Economics*, Australia, The Law Book Co. of Australia Pvt. Ltd., 1954.

Wild, John J., Subramanyam, K.R. and Halsey, Robert F., *Financial Statement Analysis*, Singapore, McGraw-Hill, 2003.

Wixon, Rutus, Kell, Walter G. and Bedford, Norton, *Accountants Handbook*, New York, John Wildey & Sons Inc., Fifth Edition.

Yorston, R.K., Smyth E.B. and Brown S.R., *Advanced Accounting*, Bombay, N.M. Tripathi Pvt. Ltd., 1968.

## Journals and Periodicals

Agarwal, Jai Dev, "Depreciation Accounting—A Probabilistic Approach", *The Chartered Accountant,* Vol. XXVI, No. 7, January 1978.

Aggarwal, Anil K., "Depreciation under Straight Line Method", *The Chartered Accountant,* Vol. XXXII, No. 6, December 1983.

Agrawal, Jaidev, "Depreciation Accounting—A Probabilistic Approach", *The Management Accountant*, Vol. 13, No. 6, June 1978.

Archibald, T. Ross, "Stock Market Reaction to the Depreciation Switch Back", *The Accounting Review*, Vol. XLVII, No. 1, January 1972.

Baid, Dhanraj, "Table of Depreciation Rate on Straight Line Method", *The Chartered Accountant*, Vol., XVI, Part III, September 1967.

Baid, Priti, "Amalgamation and Depreciation claim Under Income Tax Act", *The Chartered Accountant*, Vol. XLV No. 2, August 1995.

Bailey, F.A., "Depreciation and the Measurement of Profitability", *Accountancy*, Vol. LXXII, No. 928, December 1970.

Bailey, F.A., "Asset Valuation and Depreciation under Current Cost Accounting", *Accounting and Business Research*, Vol. 12, No. 46, spring 1982.

Banerjee, B. and Jaggi, B., "Accounting Standards and Standard Setting Process in India—An Appraisal", *Indian Accounting Review*, Vol. 1 No. 1, June 1997.

Banerjee, B., "Depreciation As An Internal Source of Fund: A Conceptual Problem", *Business Studies*, Vol. VI, No. 2, July, 1980.

Barefield, Russell M. and Comiskey, Engene E., "Depreciation Policy and the Behaviour of Corporate Profits", *Journal of Accounting Research*, Vol. 9, No. 2, Autumn 1971.

Barnes, Paul, "Accounting for Deferred Tax on Depreciable Assets—A Note", *Accounting and Business Research*, Vol. 12, No. 47, Summer 1982.

Bastable, C.W., "Depreciation in an inflationary environment", *The Journal of Accountacy*, Vol. 142, No. 2, August 1976.

Basu, A.K., "The International Accounting Standards Committee—A

Twenty year Perspective", *Business Studies,* Vol. XVII Nos. 1 and 2, January and July, 1994.

Basu, P.K., "Initial Depreciation Allowance—A Critical Look", *The Management Accountant,* Vol. 10, No. 6, June 1975.

Basue, P.C., "Depreciation—A Rethinking", *The Management Accountant,* Vol. 15, No. 3, March 1980.

Baxter, W.T. and Carrier, N.H., "Depreciation, Replacement Price and Cost of Capital", *Journal of Accounting Research,* Vol. 9, No. 2, Autumn 1971.

Baxter, W.T., "Play it Straight on Depreciation", *Accountancy,* Vol. 83, No. 958, June 1973.

Baxter, William, "Depreciation and interest", *Accountancy,* Vol. 126, No. 1286, October 2000.

Beaton, D.C., "Some Reflection on depreciation", *The Accountant,* Vol. CLIII, No. 4749, December 25th, 1965.

Beaton, D.C., "Replacement Value and Depreciation", *The Accountant,* Vol. CLV, No 4777, July 9th, 1966.

Beaver, W.H. and Dukes R.E., "d—Depreciation Methods: Some Analytical Results", *Journal of Accounting Research,* Vol. 12, No. 2, Autumn 1974.

Bhadada, B.M., "On Allocating Depreciation Cost—An Appraisal", *The Management Accountant,* Vol. 12, No. 8, August 1977.

Bierman, Harold Jr., "A Further Study of Depreciation", *The Accounting Review,* Vol. XLI, No. 2, April 1966.

Bierman, Harold Jr., "Accelerated Depreciation and Rate Regulation", *The Accounting Review,* Vol. XLIV, No. 1, January 1969.

Bird, Francis A., "A Note on—The Return to Straight Line Depreciation", *Journal of Accounting Research,* Vol. 7, No. 2, Autumn 1969.

Brief, Richard P., "A Late Nineteenth Century Contribution to the Theory of Depreciation", *Journal of Accounting Research,* Vol. 5, No. 1, Spring 1967.

Brief, Richard, P. and Owen, Joel, "Depreciation and Capital Gains: A New Approach", *The Accounting Review,* Vol. XLIII, No. 2, April 1968.

Brigham, Eugene F., "The Effects of Alternative Depreciation Policies on Reported Profits", *The Accounting Review,* Vol. XLIII. No. 1, January 1968.

Brockington, Raymond, "An Alternative Concept of Depreciation: Charge or Appropriation", *The Accountant,* Vol. 177, No. 5356 September 8th 1977.

Brown, D.J., "Time to Abandon the Reducing balance Method?"

*Accountancy,* Vol. LXXXII, No. 938, October 1971.

Buckley, Elizabeth, "Depreciation—A Conceptual Problem", *Accountancy,* Vol. 109, No. 1185, May 1992.

Burt, Oscar R., "A Unified Theory of Depreciation", *Journal of Accounting Research,* Vol. 10, No. 1, Spring 1972.

Caplin, Mortimer M. and Klayman, Robert A., "Depreciation—1965 Model", *The Journal of Accountancy,* Vol. 119, No. 4, April 1965.

Chowdhury, P.R., and Sarker, J.B., "Accounting Standards and Indian Accounting" *Unpublished Paper presented at the Seminar of Indian Accounting Association, Calcutta Branch,* Held in Department of Commerce, University of Burdwan, 1984.

Comiskey, Eugene E., "Market Response to Changes in Depreciation Accouning", *The Accounting Review,* Vol. XLVI, No. 2, April 1971.

Council of the Institute of Chartered Accountants in England and Wales", The disclosure of Depreciation in Accountants' Reports in Prospective and Similar Documents", *The Accountant,* Vol. CLIII, No. 4739, October 16th 1965.

Cramer, Joe J. Jr. and Schrader, William J., "Depreciation Accounting and Anomalous Self-Insurance Cost", *The Accounting Review,* Vol. XLV, No. 4, October 1970.

Davidson, Sidney and Drake, David F., "The Best Tax Depreciation Method—1964", *Journal of Business,* Vol. XXXVII, No. 3, July 1964.

Davidson, Sidney and Drake, David, "Capital Budgeting and the Best Tax Depreciation Method", *Journal of Business,* Vol. XXXIV, No. 4, October 1961.

Dean, Joel and Harriss, C. Lowell, "Railroad Accounting under the New Depreciation Guidelines and Investment Tax Credit", *The Accounting Review,* Vol. XXXVIII, No. 2, April 1963.

Desai, V.V., "Depreciation Policy", *The Management Accountant,* Vol. 10, No. 11, November 1975.

Dhameja, Nand, "Revaluation of Fixed Assets", *The Chartered Accountant,* Vol. XLV No. 7, January 1997.

Drebin, Allan R., "A Fallacy of Depreciation Translation", *Journal of Accounting Research,* Vol. 7, No. 2, Autumn 1969.

Durai, Lakshmi, "Some Other Aspects of Depreciation", *The Management Accountant,* Vol. 22, No. 8, August 1987.

Edwards, John Richard, "Depreciation and Fixed Asset Valuation in Railway

Company Accounts to 1911", *Accounting and Business Research*, Vol. 16, No. 63, Summer 1986.

Egginton, Don, "Depreciation methods and asset lives", *Accountancy*, Vol. 95, No. 1096, December 1984.

Egginton, Don, "Fixed assets: Costs, Lives and Depreciation", *Accountancy*, Vol. 95, No. 1095, November 1984.

Feinschreiber, Robert, "Accelerated Depreciation: A Proposal New Method", *Journal of Accounting Research*, Vol. 7, No. 1, Spring 1969.

Friberg, Ronald A., "Probabilistic Depreciation with a varying salvage value", *The Accounting Review*, Vol. XLVIII, NO 1, January 1973.

Ghosh, P.K., "Depreciation—A study", *The Management Accountant*, Vol. 22, No. 3, March 1987.

Goch, Desmond, "Depreciation—All Things to All Men", *The Accountant*, Vol. CL, No. 4670, June 20th 1964.

Goggans, Travis P., "Liberalized Depreciation and Investment Decisions", *The Journal of Accountancy*, Vol. 117, No. 5, May 1964.

Goyale, R.M., "Depreciation Cost Vs Valuation Concept", The Chartered Accountant, Vol. 19, Part II, May 1971.

Goyale, R.N., "A Comparative Study of Depreciation Tax-Laws in India, USA & UK", *The Chartered Accountant*, Vol. 21, Part-I, July 1972.

Goyale, R.N., "Accelerated Depreciation", *The Chartered Accountant*, Vol. XXVII, N0. 5, November 1978.

Greenball, M.N., "Appraising Alternative Methods of Accounting for Accelerated Tax Depreciation: A Relative Accuracy Approach", *Journal of Accounting Research*, Vol. 7, No. 2, Autumn 1969.

Greene, Edward D., "Changing from Declining Balance to Straight Line Depreciation", *The Accounting Review*, Vol. XXXVIII, No. 2, April 1963.

Gupta, Vinod, "Claim of Depreciation—Whether Optional", *The Chartered Accountant*, Vol. XXXIX No. 2, August 1990.

Gyol, S.K., "Depreciation Cost Under Changing Price Levels", *The Chartered Accountant*, Vol. XVII, Part X, April, 1969.

Heath, John Jr., "Property Valuation Problems and the Accountant", *The Journal of Accountancy*, Vol. 117, No. 1, January 1964.

Horwitz, Bertrand, "Depreciation and Cost Stability in Soviet Accounting", *The Accounting Review*, Vol. XXXVIII NO. 4, October 1963.

Hotelling, Harold, "A General Mathematical Theory of Depreciation", *Journal of the American Statistical Association*, Vol. 20, September 1925.

Ijiri, Yuji and Kaplan, Rabert S., "Probabilistic Depreciation and Its

Implications", *The Accounting Review*, Vol. XLIV, No. 4, October 1969.

Ijiri, Yuri and Kaplan, Robert S., "Sequential Models in Probabilistic Depreciation", *Journal of Accounting Research*, Vol. 8, No. 1, Spring 1970.

Iyer, S. Neelakanthan, "Depreciation—A New Concept", *The Management Accountant*, Vol. 15, No. 12, December 1980.

Jain, Nand Kishore, "Adoption for SLM of Depreciation", *The Chartered Accountant*, Vol. XV, Part II, August 1966.

Jen, Frank C. and Huefner, Ronald J., "Depreciation by Probability Life", *The Accounting Review*, Vol. XLV, No. 2, April, 1970.

Kachelmcier, Steven J. and Granof, Michael H., "Depreciation and Capital Investment Decisions: Experimental Evidence in a Governmental Setting", *Journal of Accounting and Public Policy*, Vol. 12, No. 4, Winter 1993.

Khandelwal, N.M., "Accounting Concept of Depreciation—why controversies", *The Management Accountant*, Vol. 13, No. 4, March 1978.

Kim, Moshe and Moore, Giora, "Economic vs Accounting Depreciation", *Journal of Accounting and Economics*, Vol. 10, No. 2, April 1988.

Kitchen, J., "Fixed Asset Values: Ideas on Depreciation 1892-1914", *Accounting and Business Research*, Vol. 9, No. 36, Autumn 1979.

Krishna Murti, K.G., "Depreciation and Capitalisation of Interest Under The Companies Act, 1956", *The Chartered Accountant*, Vol. XIX, Part X, December 1970.

Krishnaswamy, N., "Concept of Depreciation—An Analysis", *The Chartered Accountant*, Vol. XVIII Part VI, December 1969.

Lamden, Charles W., "Depreciation—A Reliability Gap", Reprinted in *The Journal of Accountancy*, Vol. 133, No. 4, April 1972.

Lev, Baruchand Theil, Henri, "A Maximum Entropy Approach to the Choice of Asset Depreciation", *Journal of Accounting Research*, Vol. 16, No. 2, Autumn 1978.

Lindhe, Richard, "Accelerated Depreciation for Income Tax Purpose—A Study of the Decision and Some Firms Who Made It", *Journal of Accounting Research*, Vol. 1, No. 2, Autumn 1963.

Livingstone, John Leslie, "Accelerated Depreciation, Cyclical Asset Expenditures and Deferred Taxes", *Journal of Accounting Research*, Vol. 5, No. 1, Spring 1967.

Livingstone, John Leslie, "Accelerated Depreciation, Tax Allocation and

Cyclical Asset Expenditure of Large Manufacturing Companies", *Journal of Accounting Research,* Vol. 7, No. 2, Autumn 1969.

Lopsley, Irvine, "A case for Depreciation Accounting in UK Health Authorities", *Accounting and Business Research,* Vol. 12, No. 45, Winter 1981.

Lowe, Howard D., "The Essentials of a General Theory of Depreciation", *The Accounting Review,* Vol. XXXVIII, No. 2, April 1963.

Ma, Ronald, "Accounting for Depreciation", *Accountancy,* Vol. LXXV, No. 855, November 1964.

Maher, Michael W. and Nantell, Timothy J., "The Tax Effects of Inflation: Depreciation, Debt and Miller's Equilibrium Tax Rates", *Journal of Accounting Research,* Vol. 21, No. 1, Spring 1983.

Mani, E.V., "Depreciation—A critical look at the concepts", *The Management Accountant,* Vol. 14, No. 7, July 1979.

Mathew, J. and Prasad, B., "Accounting Standard Setting Process in India—A Evaluation", *Journal of Accounting and Finance,* Vol. IX, No. 1, Spring, 1995.

Matthews, John W., "The Depreciation Device", *The Accountant,* Vol. CLI, No. 4679, August 22nd, 1964.

Matthews, John, "Yield Value Depreciation", *The Accountant,* Vol. 162, No. 4975, April 23rd, 1970.

McIntyre, Edward V., "Present value Depreciation and the Disaggregation Problem", *The Accounting Review,* Vol. LII, No. 1, January 1977.

Mehta, N.C., "Benefits in Surtax under the SLM of Depreciation", *The Chartered Accountant,* Vol. XIV Part X, April 1966.

Meyers, Stephen L., "An Examination of the Relationship Between Interperiod Tax Allocation and Present—value Depreciation", *The Accounting Review,* Vol. XLVIII, No. 1, January 1973.

Most, Kenneth S., "Depreciation Expenses and the effect of Inflation", *Journal of Accounting Research,* Vol. 22, No. 2, Autumn 1984.

Most, Kenneth S., "Scientific Estimation of Depreciation", *The Accountant,* Vol. CXXXVII, No. 4312, 10th August 1957.

Mukherjee, A. and Hanif, Md., "Accounting Concept of Depreciation", *The Management Accountant,* Vol. 31. No. 7, July 1996.

Mukherji, K., "Depreciation Expenditure and Taxable Income", *The Management Accountant,* Vol. 10, No. 10, October 1975.

Mycraft, "Depreciation: Two Fallacies Reexposed", *Accountancy,* Vol. LXXII, No. 924, August 1970

Myers, John H., "Depreciation Disclosure", *The Journal of Accountancy,* Vol. 120, No. 5, November 1965.

Nagaranjan, V., "Unabsorbed Loss and Depreciation Carry Forward and Set off", *The Chartered Accountant,* Vol. XXXVIII, No. 5, November 1989.

Nobes, Chris, "Depreciation: Can a new standard clear the way?", Accountancy, Vol. 96, No. 1099, March 1985.

Noke, Christopher, "Property depreciation: new let's be realistic", *Accountancy,* Vol. 90 No. 1036, December 1979.

Noke, Christopher, "The reality of property depreciation", *Accountancy,* Vol. 90, No. 1035, November 1979.

Nurnberg, Hugo, "A Note on the Financial Reporting of Depreciation and Income Taxes", *Journal of Accounting Research,* Vol. 7, No. 2, Autumn 1969.

Nurnbery, Hugo, "Present Value Depreciation and Income Tax Allocation", *The Accounting Review,* Vol. XLIII, No. 4, October 1968.

Panda, J. and Saha, P.K., "Standardisation of Depreciation Accounting", *The Indian Journal of Commerce,* Volume, XXXII, Part IV, No. 121, December 1979.

Patient, Matthew, "Depreciation on revalued fixed assets", *Accountancy,* Vol. 95, No. 1090, June 1984.

Pothuval, D.K., "Depreciation: Replacement Cost Method—A Critical Appraisal", *The Management Accountant,* Vol. 8, No. 8 August 1973.

Prabhakara Babu, C. and Sharma, Aradhana, "Interest and Depreciation: Capital Budgeting Analysis", *The Chartered Accountant,* Vol. XLIII, No. 9, March 1995.

Pye, Malcolm L., "Footnote on Declining–Balance Depreciation", *The Accounting Review,* Vol. XL, No. 2, April 1965.

Rai, R.C. "Depreciation Accounting in the Changing Techno-economic Scenario", *The Management Accountant,* 31, No. 6, June 1996.

Ramnath, S., "Depreciation on Block of Assets", *The Chartered Accountant,* Vol. XXXVI, No. 2, July 1987.

Ramnath, S., "Depreciation on Block of Assets", *The Management Accountant,* Vol. 23, No. 2, February 1988.

Rao, K. Venkata, "Depreciation Methods", *The Chartered Accountant,* Vol. XIV, Part XI, May 1966.

Rao, N. Sitarama, "Depreciation Accounting and Applied Problems", *The Management Accountant*, Vol. 5, No. 2, February 1970.

Rieks, R. Bruce, "Year to switch to Straight Line Depreciation", *The Accounting Review*, Vol. XXXIX, No. 3, July 1964.

Rodgers, Paul, "Tangible but tricky", *Accountancy*, Vol. 128, no. 1299, November 2001.

Roy, G.D., "Choice of Assets for Providing for Depreciation per Replacement Cost," *The Management Accountant*, Vol. 11, No. 3, March 1976.

Roy, G.D., "Limitations of Investment of Depreciation Provision in Fixed Assets", *The Management Accountant*, Vol. 11, No. 12, December 1976.

Sarma, M. Subrahamanya and Charyulu, M. Venugopala, "Accounting for Fixed Assets—A disclosure and transparency model", *The Management Accountant*, Vol. 30, No. 11, November 1995.

Schwab, Bernhard and Nicol, Robert E. G, "From Double Declining Balance to Sum-of-Years'—Digits Depreciation: An Optimum Switching Rule", *The Accounting Review*, Vol. XLIV, No. 2, April 1969.

Sen Gupta, S.N., "Depreciation—A Hurdle in Management Profile", *The Management Accountant*, Vol. 8, No. 1, January 1973.

Sen, Dilip Kumar, "Depreciation: Its Impact on Cash Flow—A case study", *The Management Accountant*, Vol. 21, No. 2, February 1986.

Shah, P.N., "Scheme for Simplification of Depreciation Allowance", *The Chartered Accountant*, Vol. XXVII, No. 1, July 1978.

Shah, Pravin P., "Current Controversies regarding Depreciation", *The Chartered Accountant*, Vol. XVII, Part IX, March, 1969.

Shah, V.R. and Shah, P.R., "Depreciation under Companies (Amendment) Act, 1988—A Critical Study", *The Chartered Accountant*, Vol. XXXVII, No. 2, August 1988

Sharma, Lajpathai, "Depreciation as a Fact" *The Chartered Accountant*, Vol. XIII, Part VI, December 1964.

Sherwood, Ken, "Depreciation, residual values and revaluations", *Accountancy*, Vol. 94, No. 1074, February 1983.

Sinha, G., "Anatomy of Accounting Standards", *Business Studies*, Vol. XIX, Nos. 1 and 2, January and July, 1996.

Skinner, R.C., "Fixed Asset Lives and Replacement Cost Accounting", *Journal of Accounting Research*, Vol. 20, No. 1, Spring 1982.

Stickney, Clyde P., "A Note on Optimal Tax Depreciation Research", *The Accounting Review*, Vol. LVI, No. 3, July 1981.

Subramaniam, R. Harihara, "Depreciation a Debatable Issue", *The Management Accountant,* Vol. 30, No. 6, June 1995.

Sunley, Emil M. Jr., "An Optimum Switch from Double Declining balance to Sum-of-the-years' Digits Depreciation", *The Accounting Review,* Vol. XLVI, No. 3, July 1971.

Surrey, Staniey S., "A Computer study of Tax Depreciation Policy", *The Journal of Accountancy,* Vol. 126, No. 2, August 1968.

Thomas, Arthur L., "The Amortization Problem: A simplified and Some Unanswered Question", *Journal of Accounting Research,* Vol. 3, No. 1, Spring 1965.

Thomsen, C. Torben, "Continuous and Consistent Depreciation Formulas", *The Accounting Review,* Vol. XLV, No. 1, January 1970.

Trumbull, Wendell P., "Difference Between Financial and Tax Depreciation", *The Accounting Review,* Vol. XLIII, No. 3, July 1968.

Vatter, William J., "Time-Adjusted Depreciation", *Journal of Accounting Research,* Vol. 7, No. 1, Spring 1969.

Venkataraman, V. "Development Rebate and Initial Depreciation", *The Management Accountant,* Vol. 11 No. 8, August 1976.

Venue, S., "Depreciation Accounting Conventions and Reported Costs—A Critique", *The Chartered Accountant,* Vol. 20, Part XI, May 1972.

Verma, Chandra Shekhar, "Is Depreciation a Source of Fund", *The Management Accountant,* Vol. 18, No. 3, March 1983.

Wakeman, Lee Macdonald, "Optimal Tax Depreciation", *Journal of Accounting and Economics,* Vol. 2, No. 3, December 1980.

Watson, Peter L., "Accounting foı Deferred Tax on Depreciable Assets", *Accounting and Business Research,* Vol. 9, No. 36, Autumn 1979.

Wells, M.C., "A Note on the Amortization of Fixed Assets", *The Accounting Review,* Vol. XLIII, No. 2, April 1968.

Whittington Smith, C.A., "Depreciation and the Integration of views on Accounting for Inflation", *The Accountant,* Vol. CXXXVII, No. 4330, December 14th 1957.

Wolk, Harry I., "Current value Depreciation: A Conceptual Clarification", *The Accounting Review,* Vol. XLV, No. 3, July 1970.

Wright, F.K., "An Evaluation of Ladelle's Theory of Depreciation", *Journal of Accounting Research,* Vol. 5, No. 2, Autumn 1967.

Wright, F.K., "Depreciation and Obsolescence in Current Value Accounting", *Journal of Accounting Research,* Vol. 3, No. 2, Autumn 1965.

Wright, F.K., "Towards a General Theory of Depreciation", *Journal of Accounting Research,* Vol. 2, No. 1, Spring 1964.

Wright, F. Kenneth, "Depreciation Theory and the Cost of Funds", The *Accounting Review,* Vol. XXXVIII, No. 1, January 1963.

## Encyclopaedias, Dictionaries and Others

*Encyclopaedia Americana*, New York, American Corporation International, Lexington Avenue, Vol. 8.

*Encyclopaedia Britannia*, London, Encyclopaedia Britannica Inc., Vo. 7.

*New Columbia Encyclopaedia*, London, Columbia University Press, 1975.

*Industrial Accountant's Encyclopaedia Dictionary,* Prentice-Hall Inc., Prepared by Editorial Staff of Prentice—Hall.

*Oxford Dictionary of Business English for Learners of English*, Edited by Allene Truck, Calcutta, Oxford University Press, 1994.

*Webster's New Twentieth Century Dictionary*, Second Edition, 1977.

Eric L. Kohler, *Dictionary for Accountants*, New Jersey, Prentice-Hall Inc., 1957.

Males, P. and Terry, N., *The Hand Book of International Financial Terms*, Oxford, Oxford University Press, 1999.

Indian Companies Act 1956.

Indian Income Tax Act 1961.

Canada—CICA Handbook Section 3061 and 3063.

Capitaline Corporate Databases.

## Websites

www.iasplus.com/country/canada.htm

www.iasplus.com/au/0509differences.pdf

www.iasplus.com/recource/gaap2001.pdf

www.iasplus.com/dttpubs/2005ifrsus.pdf

www.camagazine.com

www.iasplus.com/dttpubs/uk_ger.pdf

www.iasplus.com/dttpubs/pubs.htm#ce

www.kpmg.co.uk/pubs/ias_comp_ukusgaap.pdf

www.kpmg.co.uk/pubs/ias_gaap_german.pdf

www.iasplus.com/dttpubs/uk_fra.pdf

www.kpmg.co.uk/pubs/ias_dutch_gaap.pdf
www.iasplus.com/dttpubs/iasnlus.pdf
www.gwcglobal.com/gx/eng/about/sves/corporatereporting/Dutch SandD04.pdf
www.pwcglobal.com/gx/eng/about/svcs/corporatereporting/ BrazilSandD.pdf.
www.werksmans.co.za
www.asb.co.za/template.asp?MenuID=11
www.saiga.co.za
www.ey.com/global
www.asb.co.za/backoffice/contentdocs/grap_17_ppe.pdf
www.kpmg.co.uk/pubs/Extract_IFRS_Australia_GAAP.pdf
www.aasb.com.au
www.treasury.act.gov.au/accounting
www2g.biglobe.ne.jp/~ykawamer/gaap010.htm
www.asb.or.jp
www.asb.or.jp/e_asbj/begriff/ConceptualFramework.pdf
www.net-ir.ne.jp
www2g.biglobe.ne.jp/~ykawamer/gaap050htm
www.mof.go.jp/english/tax/taxes2004e_c.pdf
www.kpmg.co.uk/pubs/Extract_IFRS_Japanese.pdf
www.iasplus.com/china/asbe.pdf
www.icaew.co.uk/librarylinks/index.cfm?AUB=TB21_27450-41K
www.saica.co.za
www.suez.com/documents/english/SUE2_Transition_to_IFRS_042005.pdf
www.dtf.wa.gov.au/cms
wwwfp.mccneb.edu/intercultural/Documents/2003/International Accounting.doc
www.kpmg.co.uk/pubs/ias_comp_frusgaap.pdf

# Index